THE GROLIER LIBRARY
OF
SCIENCE BIOGRAPHIES

VOLUME 7

Marius–Parsons

Grolier Educational
Sherman Turnpike, Danbury, Connecticut 06816

Published 1997 by
Grolier Educational
Danbury Connecticut 06816

Copyright © 1996 by Market House Books Ltd.
Published for the School and Library market exclusively
by Grolier Educational, 1997

Compiled and Typeset by Market House Books Ltd, Aylesbury, UK.

General Editors
    John Daintith BSc, PhD
    Derek Gjertsen BA

Market House Editors
    Elizabeth Martin MA
    Anne Stibbs BA
    Fran Alexander BA
    Jonathan Law BA
    Peter Lewis BA, DPhil
    Mark Salad

Picture Research
    Linda Wells

Contributors
    Eve Daintith BSc
    Rosalind Dunning BA
    Garry Hammond BSc
    Robert Hine BSc, MSc
    Valerie Illingworth BSc, MPhil
    Sarah Mitchell BA
    Susan O'Neill BSc
    W. J. Palmer MSc
    Roger F. Picken BSc, PhD
    Carol Russell BSc
    W. J. Sherratt BSc, MSc, PhD
    Jackie Smith BA
    B. D. Sorsby BSc, PhD
    Elizabeth Tootill BSc, MSc
    P. Welch DPhil
    Anthony Wootton

Published by arrangement with
The Institute of Physics Publishing
Bristol BS1 6NX
UK

ISBN   Volume 7   0-7172-7633-3
           Ten-Volume Set   0-7172-7626-0
Library of Congress Catalog Number: 96-31474
Cataloging Information to be obtained directly from Grolier Educational.
First Edition
Printed in the United States of America

CONTENTS

PREFACE

ABOUT THE GROLIER LIBRARY OF SCIENCE BIOGRAPHIES

The 19th-century poet and essayist Oliver Wendell Holmes wrote:

> Science is a first-rate piece of furniture for a man's upper chamber, if he has common sense on the ground floor.

The Poet at the Breakfast-Table (1872)

While it has been fashionable in this century to assume that science is capable of solving all human problems, we should, perhaps, pause to reflect on Holmes's comment. Scientific knowledge can only be of value to the human race if it is made use of wisely by the men and women who have control of our lives.

If this is true, all thinking people need a solid piece of scientific furniture in their upper chambers. For this reason the editors and publishers of this series of books have set out to say as much about science itself as about the scientists who have created it.

All the entries contain basic biographical data – place and date of birth, posts held, etc. – but do not give exhaustive personal details about the subject's family, prizes, honorary degrees, etc. Most of the space has been devoted to their main scientific achievements and the nature and importance of these achievements. This has not always been easy; in particular, it has not always been possible to explain in relatively simple terms work in the higher reaches of abstract mathematics or modern theoretical physics.

Perhaps the most difficult problem was compiling the entry list. We have attempted to include people who have produced major advances in theory or have made influential or well-known discoveries. A particular difficulty has been the selection of contemporary scientists, in view of the fact that of all scientists who have ever lived, the vast majority are still alive. In this we have been guided by lists of prizes and awards made by scientific societies. We realize that there are dangers in this – the method would not, for instance, catch an unknown physicist working out a revolutionary new system of mechanics in the seclusion of the Bern patent office. It does, however, have the advantage that it is based on the judgments of other scientists. We have to a great extent concentrated on what might be called the "traditional" pure sciences – physics, chemistry, biology, astronomy, and the earth sciences. We also give a more limited coverage of medicine and mathematics and have included a selection of people who have made important contributions to engineering and technology. A few of the entries cover workers in such fields as anthropology and psychology, and a small number of philosophers are represented.

A version of this book was published in 1993 by the Institute of Physics, to whom we are grateful for permission to reuse the material in this set. Apart from adding a number of new biographies to the Institute of Physics text, we have enhanced the work with some 1,500 photographs and a large number of quotations by or about the scientists themselves. We have also added a simple pronunciation guide (the key to which will be found on the back of this page) to provide readers with a way of knowing how to pronounce the more difficult and unfamiliar names.

Each volume in this set has a large biographical section. The scientists are arranged in strict alphabetical order according to surname. The entry for a scientist is given under the name by which he or she is most commonly known. Thus the American astrophysicist James Van Allen is generally known as Van Allen (not Allen) and is entered under V. The German chemist Justus von Liebig is commonly referred to as Liebig and is entered under L. In addition, each volume contains a section on "Sources and Further Reading" for important entries, a glossary of useful definitions of technical words, and an index of the whole set. The index lists all the scientists who have entries, indicating the volume number and the page on which the entry will be found. In addition scientists are grouped together in the index by country (naturalized nationality if it is not their country of origin) and by scientific discipline. Volume 10 contains a chronological list of scientific discoveries and publications arranged under year and subject. It is intended to be used for tracing the development of a subject or for relating advances in one branch of science to those in another branch. Additional information can be obtained by referring to the biographical section of the book.

JD
DG 1996

PRONUNCIATION GUIDE

A guide to pronunciation is given for foreign names and names of foreign origin; it appears in brackets after the first mention of the name in the main text of the article. Names of two or more syllables are broken up into small units, each of one syllable, separated by hyphens. The stressed syllable in a word of two or more syllables is shown in **bold** type.

We have used a simple pronunciation system based on the phonetic respelling of names, which avoids the use of unfamiliar symbols. The sounds represented are as follows (the phonetic respelling is given in brackets after the example word, if this is not pronounced as it is spelled):

a *as in* bat
ah *as in* palm (pahm)
air *as in* dare (dair), pear (pair)
ar *as in* tar
aw *as in* jaw, ball (bawl)
ay *as in* gray, ale (ayl)
ch *as in* chin
e *as in* red
ee *as in* see, me (mee)
eer *as in* ear (eer)
er *as in* fern, layer
f *as in* fat, phase (fayz)
g *as in* gag
i *as in* pit
I *as in* mile (mIl), by (bI)
j *as in* jaw, age (ayj), gem (jem)
k *as in* keep, cactus (**kak**-tus), quite (kwIt)
ks *as in* ox (oks)
ng *as in* hang, rank (rangk)
o *as in* pot

oh *as in* home (hohm), post (pohst)
oi *as in* boil, toy (toi)
oo *as in* food, fluke (flook)
or *as in* organ, quarter (**kwor**-ter)
ow *as in* powder, loud (lowd)
s *as in* skin, cell (sel)
sh *as in* shall
th *as in* bath
th as in feather (**feth**-er)
ts *as in* quartz (kworts)
u *as in* buck (buk), blood (blud), one (wun)
u(r) *as in* urn (but without sounding the "r")
uu *as in* book (buuk)
v *as in* van, of (ov)
y *as in* yet, menu (**men**-yoo), onion (**un**-yon)
z *as in* zoo, lose (looz)
zh *as in* treasure (**tre**-zher)

The consonants b, d, h, l, m, n, p, r, t, and w have their normal sounds and are not listed in the table.

In our pronunciation guide a consonant is occasionally doubled to avoid confusing the syllable with a familiar word, for example, -iss rather than -is (which is normally pronounced -iz); -off rather than -of (which is normally pronounced -ov).

Ma

Marius, Simon

(1570–1624)

GERMAN ASTRONOMER

Born at Guntzenhausen in Germany, Marius (**mah**-ree-uus) was a pupil of Tycho Brahe. He gained notoriety in his clash with Galileo in 1614 when he claimed priority in the discovery of the Medicean planets – Jupiter's satellites. A four-year delay in making such a claim gives it little credibility but Marius had one final triumph over Galileo, who had named the new planets after the children of his patron Cosimo, the Grand Duke of Tuscany. Marius suggested the names Io, Europa, Ganymede, and Callisto, names we still use today. He was the first astronomer to observe telescopically the great spiral nebula in Andromeda.

Markov, Andrey Andreyevich

(1856–1922)

RUSSIAN MATHEMATICIAN

Born at Ryazan in Russia, Markov (**mar**-kof) studied at the University of St. Petersburg and later held a variety of teaching posts at the same university, eventually becoming a professor in 1893. He was an extremely enthusiastic and effective teacher. His mathematical interests were very wide, ranging over number theory, the theory of continued fractions, and differential equations. It was, however, his work in probability theory that constituted his most profound and enduring contribution to mathematics.

Among Markov's teachers was the eminent Russian mathematician Pafnuti Chebyshev, whose central interest was in probability. One of Markov's first pieces of important research centered on a key theorem of Chebyshev's – "the central limit theorem." He was able to show that Chebyshev's supposed proof of this result was erroneous, and to provide his own, correct, proof of a version of the theorem of much greater generality than that attempted by Chebyshev. In 1900 Markov published his important and influential textbook *Probability Calculus*, and by 1906 he had arrived at the fundamentally new concept of a *Markov chain*. A sequence of random variables is a Markov chain if the two probabilities conditioned on different amounts of information about the early part of the sequence are the same. This aspect of Markov's work gave a major impetus to the subject of stochastic processes.

The great importance of Markov's work was that it enabled probability theory to be applied to a very much wider range of physical phenomena than had previously been possible. As a result of his work a whole range of subjects, among them genetics and such statistical phenomena as the behavior of molecules, became amenable to mathematical probabilistic treatment.

Marsh, James

(1794–1846)

BRITISH CHEMIST

Marsh was employed for many years at the Royal Arsenal, Woolwich. In 1829 he became Michael Faraday's assistant at the Royal Military Academy on a salary of 30 shillings a week, on which he remained until his death. Apart from the invention of electromagnetic apparatus, for which he received the Society of Arts silver medal (1823), he is today best remembered for the test for the detection of arsenic (1836) named for him. Although Marsh was honored by numerous learned bodies for his discovery, he seems not to have gained financially by his work and on his death his wife and children were left in poverty.

Marsh, Othniel Charles

(1831–1899)

AMERICAN PALEONTOLOGIST

Born in Lockport, New York, Marsh studied at Yale and New Haven, as well as in Germany. He worked at Yale, from 1866 until his death, as professor of vertebrate paleontology, the first to hold such a post in America.

From 1870 onward Marsh organized and led a number of paleontological expeditions to parts of North America, during which were unearthed a large number of fossils of considerable importance in enlarging the knowledge of extinct North American vertebrates. He was accompanied on such expeditions by William (Buffalo Bill) Cody, who acted as a scout. In 1871 Marsh discovered the first American pterodactyl, as well as remains of Cretaceous toothed birds and ancestors of the horse.

These finds were described in a number of monographs, published by the U.S. Government. Marsh's other publications include *Fossil Horses of America* (1874) and *The Dinosaurs of North America* (1896).

Marsh's appointment as head of the U.S. Geological Survey's vertebrate paleontology section in 1882 contributed toward bitter rivalry with his fellow paleontologist Edward Cope.

Martin, Archer John Porter

(1910–   )

BRITISH CHEMIST

Martin, a Londoner by birth, was educated at Cambridge University, obtaining his PhD in 1936. He worked as a research chemist with the Wool Industries Research Association in Leeds from 1938 to 1946 and with Boots Research Department in Nottingham until 1948, when he joined the Medical Research Council. From 1959 until 1970 Martin was director of Abbotbury Laboratories Ltd.

In 1944 Martin and his colleague Richard Synge developed a chromatographic technique that proved indispensable to later workers investigating protein structures. Without this technique the explosive growth of knowledge in biochemistry and molecular biology would have been dampened by prolonged and tedious analyses of complex molecules.

Column chromatography was first invented by Mikhail Tsvett for the analysis of plant pigments in 1906. Martin was trying to isolate vitamin E and developed a new method of separation involving the distribution and separation of molecules between two immiscible solvents flowing in different directions – countercurrent extraction. From this rather cumbersome apparatus evolved the idea of partition chromatography, in which one solvent is stationary and the other moves across it. Martin and Synge tried different substances, such as silica gel and cellulose, to hold the stationary solvent and hit on the idea of using paper. Thus paper chromatography was introduced.

In this process a drop of the mixture to be analyzed is placed at the corner of a piece of absorbent paper the edge of which is dipped into an organic solvent. This will soak into the paper by capillarity taking with it the components of the mixture to be analyzed to different distances depending on their solubility. In the case of a protein, the identity of the various amino acids can be discovered comparing positions of the spots with a reference chart. The basic technique is easy to operate, quick, cheap, works on small amounts, and can separate out closely related substances.

For their work Martin and Synge were awarded the 1952 Nobel Prize for chemistry. Martin tended to treat the value of their contribution somewhat dismissively, pointing out that "All the ideas are simple and had peoples' minds been directed that way the method would have flourished perhaps a century earlier."

Marvel, Carl Shipp

(1894–1990)

AMERICAN CHEMIST

Born in Waynesville, Illinois, Marvel graduated from the Wesleyan University, Illinois, in 1915 and obtained his PhD from the University of Illinois, Urbana, in 1920. Immediately afterward he joined the faculty at Urbana and later served as professor of organic chemistry from 1930 until 1961.

Marvel devoted himself mainly to polymer research, publishing a survey of the subject in his *Introduction to the Organic Chemistry of High Polymers* (1959). He contributed largely to the understanding of vinyl polymers and, with the beginnings of the space program in the mid 1950s, produced many polymers resistant to high temperatures. One of the most successful of these high-temperature polymers was one based on repeating benzimadazole units.

During the war Marvel headed the research program into the development of synthetic rubbers. He also worked on the synthesis of organic molecules and in 1930 succeeded in synthesizing the amino acid methionine.

Maskelyne, Nevil

(1732–1811)

BRITISH ASTRONOMER

Maskelyne, who was born in London, was educated at Westminster School and Cambridge University. He became the fifth Astronomer Royal in 1765 and, from 1782, rector of North Runcton in Norfolk.

Maskelyne spent considerable time trying to solve the problem of determining longitude at sea. His preferred method was by means of lunar observation, since, on a trip to St. Helena in 1761, he had successfully used such a method. To popularize his technique he published his *British Mariner's Guide* in 1763 and started publishing in 1767 the *Nautical Almanac* to provide the necessary information. He was a member of the Board of Longitude, which had been set up in 1714 to decide on the award of the £20,000 prize for a solution to the problem. Perhaps his commitment to his lunar method made him blind to the value of the chronometer invented by John Harrison, which he was asked to judge. He refused to recommend it for the award.

Mather, Kenneth

(1911–1990)

BRITISH GENETICIST

Born at Nantwich in Cheshire, England, Mather graduated from the University of Manchester in 1931. He then joined the John Innes Horticultural Institution at Merton, Surrey, where the chromosome theory of heredity was then being developed. Here Mather investigated chromosome behavior, especially crossing over, his research being influenced by his association with Cyril Darlington.

Mather gained his PhD in 1933 and then spent a year at the plant breeding institute, Svalöf, Sweden. Experience at Svalöf convinced him that characters that vary continuously through a population are extremely important in breeding work. On his return to England he took up a lectureship at University College, London, under Ronald Fisher, who was developing statistical techniques that could be used to analyze such quantitative variation.

In 1938, after a year with T. H. Morgan in America, Mather returned to John Innes as head of the genetics department. It was already appreciated that quantitative variation is governed by many genes, each of small effect, and Mather termed such complexes "polygenic systems." He demonstrated that by applying selection to continuously varying characters one could greatly increase the range of variation beyond that found in the normal population. Continuous variation cannot be analyzed satisfactorily by conventional segregation ratios and Mather thus applied statistics to his results, terming this combination "biometrical genetics."

In 1948 Mather became professor of genetics at Birmingham University, where he remained until his appointment as vice-chancellor at Southampton University in 1965. As founder of biometrical genetics he wrote a number of books on the subject, which he greatly developed during his time at Birmingham in collaboration with J. L. Jinks. Mather returned to Birmingham in 1971 as honorary professor of genetics.

Matthews, Drummond Hoyle

(1931–   )

BRITISH GEOLOGIST

Matthews was educated at Cambridge University, where he obtained his PhD in 1962. After a short period working as a geologist in the Falkland Islands he returned to Cambridge, where he was appointed reader in marine geology from 1971 until 1982 and senior research associate from 1982 until 1990.

In collaboration with Frederick Vine he produced, in 1963, a fundamental paper on magnetic anomalies, *Magnetic Anomalies over Ocean Ridges*, which modified the sea-floor spreading hypothesis of Harry H. Hess.

Matthias, Bernd Teo

(1918–1980)

GERMAN–AMERICAN PHYSICIST

> If you see a formula in the *Physical Review*
> that extends over a quarter of a page, forget it.
> It's wrong. Nature isn't that complicated.
> —Quoted by A. L. Mackay in *A Dictionary
> of Scientific Quotations* (1991)

Matthias was born in Frankfurt, Germany, and educated at Rome University and at the Federal Institute of Technology, Zurich, where he obtained his PhD in 1943. He moved to the United States in 1947, became naturalized in 1951, and, after a brief period at the University of Chicago, joined the staff of the Bell Telephone Laboratories. In 1961 he returned to academic life when he was appointed professor of physics at the University of California, San Diego.

Matthias carried out extensive work on superconducting materials. In the early 1950s no existing theory of superconductivity allowed deductions as to which metals were superconductors and at what temperature – their transition point – they became so. Consequently Matthias set out to find such materials by experiment, testing thousands of alloys in the hope that some kind of pattern would emerge. He found that superconductivity depended on the number of outer electrons in the atom; substances with five or seven valence electrons most readily became superconductors and that they had transition points furthest above absolute zero. The crystal structure of the solid was another important factor. As a result of these empirical observations, Matthias and his collaborators were able to make new superconducting materials, including a niobium–germanium alloy with a transition temperature of 23 K. Matthias also worked on ferroelectric materials.

Matuyama, Motonori

(1884–1958)

JAPANESE GEOLOGIST

Matuyama (ma-too-yah-ma), who was born at Uyeda (now Usa) in Japan, was the son of a Zen abbot. He was educated at the University of Hiroshima and the Imperial University in Kyoto, where he was appointed to a lectureship in 1913. After spending the period 1919–21 at the University of Chicago working with Thomas Chamberlin he was made professor of theoretical geology at the Imperial University.

He conducted a gravity survey of Japan during the period 1927–32, extending this to also cover Korea and Manchuria, and studied marine gravity using the Vening–Meinesz pendulum apparatus in a submarine.

Matuyama made a significant discovery of the Earth's magnetic field and announced this in his paper *On the Direction of Magnetization of Basalt* (1929). From studying the remnant magnetization of some rocks he observed that it had appeared that the Earth's magnetic field had changed, even reversing itself in comparatively short times. The period between the late Pliocene and the mid-Pleistocene during which the field appeared to be opposite to present conditions became known as the

Matuyama reversed epoch. This reversed polarity, particularly as shown by the rocks of the ocean floor, was to prove crucial evidence for the seafloor spreading hypothesis of Harry H. Hess.

Mauchly, John William

(1907–1980)

AMERICAN COMPUTER
ENGINEER

The son of a physicist, Mauchly was born in Cincinnati, Ohio, and educated at Johns Hopkins University, Pennsylvania, where he obtained his PhD in 1932. After teaching physics at Ursinus College, Pennsylvania, from 1933 until 1941, Mauchly joined the staff of the Moore School of Electrical Engineering at Johns Hopkins.

In 1936 Mauchly had become interested in possible connections between sunspots and the weather. Appalled by the amount of statistical data available, Mauchly began to consider whether it could be analyzed automatically. The great breakthrough in Mauchly's ideas came with a visit in 1941 to Atanasoff, from whom he seems to have learned about arithmetic units made from vacuum tubes operating upon binary numbers. The jump from mechanical devices to electronics was a fundamental step.

At the same time the Ballistic Research Laboratory (BRL) was urgently seeking help to calculate the thousands of trajectories needed for their artillery. They were therefore willing to invest $500,000 in Mauchly's 1942 proposal to build what later became known as ENIAC (Electronic Numerator Integrator and Calculator). It was completed in late 1945 and was used by the BRL until 1955. ENIAC contained over 17,000 vacuum tubes, 70,000 resistors, weighed 30 tons, and consumed 174,000 watts. Fans were needed to dissipate the heat generated. But it was fast and, although the process was lengthy, it was also programmable.

Mauchly had collaborated on the project with Eckert. On its completion in 1945, they were already thinking of the next major advance, namely, the stored program. Their proposal to build EDVAC (Electronic Digital Variable Computer), a computer with a stored program, was financed by the Ordnance Department. They soon ran into problems with the Moore School and with John van Neumann, who competed with them for the patent rights to the stored program. Mauchly and Eckert resigned from the Moore School, which immediately lost its dominant role in American computer science. The EDVAC was finally completed in 1952, although by then the first stored-program computer had already been built by Maurice Wilkes in England.

After leaving the Moore School, Mauchly and Eckert set up their own business, the Electronic Control Company, and proposed to build a new computer, UNIVAC (Universal Automatic Computer). They were originally financed by the U.S. Census for which they rashly contracted to build the first UNIVAC for the fixed sum of $300,000. For a while things went well; another five orders were gained. But the constraints of a fixed-price contract led them to the verge of bankruptcy.

They were rescued by Henry Strauss, Chairman of the American Tote, who had dreams of controlling the totalizators of the racetracks of America through a linked net of UNIVACs. He invested $500,000 in the ailing company. It was insufficient, and when Strauss died in a plane crash in 1949 the Tote withdrew its backing. Another problem emerged when Army Intelligence denied Mauchly security clearance on the grounds that he had been connected with various supposedly Communist "front" organizations. As a result the company lost valuable military orders. Consequently Mauchly and Eckert sold out to Remington Rand in 1950. Long after the damage had been done, Mauchly's security clearance was restored in 1958.

Mauchly and Eckert remained with Remington and managed the production and sale of 46 UNIVACs. It was indeed a UNIVAC that publicly and successfully predicted in 1952 on television the outcome of the U.S. presidential election. But before long, against competition from IBM's 700 range, UNIVAC would become obsolete.

In 1964 Mauchly's patent was finally awarded to him, 17 years after the case had begun. The victory, however, was only temporary. Remington Rand had bought the patent with the company and consequently tried to collect on their new asset. The Honeywell company challenged this and in a case decided in 1972 it was judged that the rights to the invention of the stored program lay with Atanasoff.

Maudslay, Henry

(1771–1831)

BRITISH ENGINEER AND INVENTOR

Maudslay was the son of a workman from Woolwich, London. He was apprenticed to the locksmith Joseph Bramah, from whom he learned about precision metalwork. His skills soon became recognized and he was made Bramah's foreman.

Maudslay later set up his own business and over a period of 30 years he invented many pieces of machinery that were fundamentally important to the Industrial Revolution, including a screw-cutting lathe. Other inventions included machines for printing cloth, desalinating seawater, and making measurements accurate to one ten-thousandth of an inch. He was the first person to realize the importance of accurate plane surfaces for guiding tools.

Maunder, Edward Walter

(1851–1928)

BRITISH ASTRONOMER

Maunder, who was born in London, took some courses at King's College there but did not obtain a degree. After working briefly in a bank he became photographic and spectroscopic assistant at the Royal Observatory, Greenwich, in 1873. Maunder's appointment allowed Greenwich to branch out from purely positional work, for Maunder began a careful study of the Sun, mainly of sunspots and related phenomena.

After 1891 he was assisted by Annie Russell, a Cambridge-trained mathematician, who must have been one of the first women to be so employed. She became his wife in 1895.

It had been known since 1843 that the intensity of sunspot activity went through an 11-year cycle. In 1893 Maunder, while checking the cycle in the past, came across the surprising fact that between 1645 and 1715 there was virtually no sunspot activity at all. For 32 years not a single sunspot was seen on the Sun and in the whole period fewer sunspots were observed than have occurred in an average year since. He wrote papers on his discovery in 1894 and 1922 but they aroused no interest.

More sophisticated techniques developed in recent years have established that Maunder was undoubtedly correct in the detection of the so-called *Maunder minimum*. Also, the realization that the period of the minimum corresponds to a prolonged cold spell suggests that Maunder's discovery is no mere statistical freak. It may throw light on the Sun's part in long-term climatic change and on possible variations in the processes within the Sun that produce the sunspots.

Maupertuis, Pierre-Louis Moreau de

(1698–1759)

FRENCH MATHEMATICIAN, PHYSICIST, AND ASTRONOMER

These laws [of movement], so beautiful and so simple, are perhaps the only ones which the Creator and Organizer of things has established in matter in order to effect all the phenomena of the visible world.

—*Works*, Vol. I (1756)

Maupertuis (moh-pair-**twee**), who was born at Saint-Malo in northwest France, joined the army as a youth, leaving in 1723 to teach mathematics at the French Academy of Sciences in Paris. He traveled to England in 1728 where he became an admirer of Isaac Newton's work and was made a member of the Royal Society of London. He was responsible for introducing Newton's theories on gravitation into France on his return.

In 1736 Maupertuis led an expedition to Lapland to verify Newton's hypothesis that the Earth is not perfectly spherical by measuring the length of a degree of longitude. This was successful and as a result Maupertuis was invited by Frederick the Great to join his Academy of Sciences in Berlin.

Maupertius is best known as being, in 1744, one of the first to formulate the principle of least action, which was published in his *Essai de cosmologie* (1750; Essay on Cosmology). A similar principle had previously been formulated by Leonhard Euler as a result of his mathematical work on the calculus of variations, whereas Maupertuis had been led to formulate his version of the principle through his work in optics. In particular Maupertuis's attention was drawn to the need for such a principle by his interest in the work of Willebrord Snell and Pierre de Fermat. Fermat had shown how to explain Snell's law of refraction, which describes the behavior of a ray of light at the boundary of two media of different densities on the assumption that a ray of light takes the least time possible in traveling from the first medium to the second. However, Fermat's explanation implied that light travels more slowly in a denser medium and Maupertuis set out to devise an explanation of Snell's law that did not have this, to him, objectionable consequence. Maupertuis thought of his principle as the fundamental principle of mechanics, and expected that all other mechanical laws ought to be derivable from it. He attempted to derive from his principle a proof of the existence of God.

Maupertuis was not a mathematician of Euler's stature and his version of the principle was not as precisely formulated mathematically. However, his attempts to apply it to a much wider range of problems made it an influential formative principle in 18th- and 19th-century physical thinking. Joseph Lagrange, in his work on the calculus of variations, dispensed with the teleological and theological trimmings Maupertuis had given the principle and found wide application for it in mechanics. Subsequently the principle became less influential until it was revived and refined by William Hamilton.

Maupertuis, who had a quarrelsome character, became involved in violent controversy over the principle. Samuel König, another scientist at Frederick's court, claimed that it had been formulated earlier by Gottfried Liebniz. Maupertuis found himself on the receiving end of some of Voltaire's most biting satires, and eventually he was hounded out of Berlin.

Maury, Antonia Caetana de Paiva Pereira

(1866–1952)

AMERICAN ASTRONOMER

> In my opinion the separation by Antonia C. Maury of the c- and ac- stars is the most important advancement in stellar classification since the trials by [Herman Karl] Vogel and Pietro Angelo [Secchi].
> —Ejnar Hertzsprung, letter to William Henry Pickering, 22 July 1908

Maury, who was born at Cold Spring-on-Hudson, New York, came from a family with a distinguished scientific background. She was a cousin of Matthew Maury, the oceanographer, a niece of Henry Draper, the physician and astronomer after whom the Harvard star catalog was named, her sister became a paleontologist, while her father, a clergyman, was also a well-known naturalist. She herself was educated at Vassar, graduating in 1887, and in 1889 became an assistant to Edward Pickering at Harvard College Observatory. There she worked alongside an unusually large collection of women astronomers of whom the most eminent were Annie Cannon and Henrietta Leavitt. Apart from the years 1899–1908, when she lectured at various eastern colleges, she retained her position at Harvard until her retirement in 1935.

Much of her work was on the classification of stellar spectra for the Harvard catalog. At about the same time that Cannon was revising the system of spectral classification of stars, Maury proposed an additional modification that turned out to be of permanent significance. It was important to notice, she argued, not just the absence or presence of a particular spectral line but also its appearance. Stars with normal lines she marked "a," those with hazy lines "b," and those that were sharp she marked "c"; intermediate cases were marked "ab" or "ac." This has been described as the first step in using spectroscopic criteria for the luminosities of stars. Maury's spectral classifications, including those of 681 bright northern stars, were published in 1896 in the Harvard *Annals*. Ejnar Hertzsprung was quick to see the significance of her classification system and in 1905 pointed out that c-type and ac-type stars were brighter than a- or b-type stars and were in fact giants.

Maury spent many years studying and detecting spectroscopic binary stars and as early as 1889 had determined the period of Mizar, in Ursa Major. This was the first spectroscopic binary to be discovered, identified by Pickering earlier in the year. The two stars in a spectroscopic binary cannot be resolved visually but as they revolve they will each alternately approach and recede from an observer on the Earth. This causes an alternate lengthening and shortening of the emitted light waves and will produce a periodic doubling of the spectral lines. Maury's particular interest was the binary Beta Lyrae, the investigation of which she continued long after her retirement.

Maury, Matthew Fontaine

(1806–1873)

AMERICAN OCEANOGRAPHER

Maury, who was born in Fredericksburg, Virginia, graduated from Harpeth Academy in 1825 and joined the U.S. Navy as a midshipman. A leg injury in 1839 ended his sea career but, having made his reputation by his publication in 1836 of his *Treatise on Navigation*, he was chosen in 1842 to be superintendent of the Depot of Charts and Instruments in Washington. This post carried with it the directorship of the U.S. Naval Observatory and Hydrographic Office. Maury largely ignored astronomical work, emphasizing instead the study of oceanography and meteorology, and consequently aroused the opposition of the scientific establishment centered upon Joseph Henry and Alexander Bache.

He resigned his position with the outbreak of the American Civil War (1861) to become a commander in the Confederate Navy. After the war he took on, in 1865, the post of Imperial Commissioner for Immigration to the doomed Emperor Maximilian of Mexico to establish a confederate colony. Following the collapse of the Mexican Empire he spent some time in England writing textbooks before he was permitted to return to America where he became, in 1868, professor of meteorology at the Virginia Military Institute, remaining there until his death.

Maury has often been described as the father of oceanography. He wrote one of the earliest works on the topic, *The Physical Geography of the Sea* (1855), and he demonstrated the rewards to be gained from an increased knowledge of the oceans. From 1847 he began to publish his *Wind and Current* pilot charts of the North Atlantic, which could shorten sailing times dramatically. Claims were made that as much as a month could be saved on the sailing time for the New York–California voyage. This knowledge was acquired by the study of especially prepared logbooks and the collection of data in a systematic way from a growing number of organized observers.

After 1849 Maury had the use of two research vessels and began a study of ocean temperature and a collection of samples of the ocean floor. He was thus able to publish his *Bathymetrical Map of the North Atlantic Basin* (1854) showing a profile of the Atlantic floor between Yucatan and Cape Verde.

Maxwell, James Clerk

(1831–1879)

BRITISH PHYSICIST

I am very busy with Saturn on top of my regular work. He is all remodelled and recast, but I have more to do to him yet for I wish to redeem the character of mathematicians and make it intelligible.
—Letter to J. R. Droop (1857). Quoted by L. Campbell and W. Garnett in *The Life of James Clerk Maxwell* (1882)

Maxwell was born in Edinburgh and studied at the university there (1847–50) and at Cambridge (1850–54), becoming a fellow in 1855. He was professor of natural philosophy at Marishal College, Aberdeen, from 1856 until 1860, when he became professor of natural philosophy and astronomy at King's College, London. He resigned in 1865 and worked on his estate in Scotland researching and writing. From 1871 he was professor of experimental physics at Cambridge.

Maxwell is regarded as one of the great physicists of the 19th century. At the age of 15 he produced a paper on methods of drawing oval curves. In 1857 he published a paper on the rings of Saturn, in which he analyzed the dynamics of the rings and proved that they could not be wholly solid or liquid. His own theory was that they were made up of many particles, and he showed that such a system would be stable.

Maxwell is regarded as one of the founders of the kinetic theory of gases – the calculation of the properties of a gas by assuming that it is composed of a large number of atoms (or molecules) in random motion. Maxwell, around 1860, put forward a statistical treatment of gases in *Illustrations of Dynamical Theory of Gases*. Maxwell and Ludwig Boltzmann obtained a formula for the way in which the speeds of molecules were distributed over the number of molecules – the *Maxwell–Boltzmann distribution law*. The kinetic theory of gases disposed of the idea of heat as a fluid ("caloric").

One interesting notion coming out of his work on the kinetic theory was the statistical interpretation of thermodynamics. A particular point was the idea of *Maxwell's demon* (1871) – a small hypothetical creature that could open or close a shutter between two compartments in a vessel, separating the fast molecules from the slow ones, and thus causing one part of the gas to become hotter and the other colder. The system would appear to violate the second law of thermodynamics. (In fact it does not; the gas decreases in entropy but there is an increase in entropy in the demon, using the idea that entropy is connected with "information").

Maxwell's greatest work was his series of papers on the mathematical treatment of the lines of force introduced by Michael Faraday to visualize electromagnetic phenomena. He showed the connection between magnetism and electricity and demonstrated that oscillating electric charges would produce waves propagated through the electromagnetic field. He showed that the speed of such waves was similar to the experimentally determined speed of light, and concluded that light (and infrared and ultraviolet radiation) was in fact this electromagnetic wave. Maxwell went on to predict the existence of other forms of electromagnetic radiation with frequencies and wavelengths outside the infrared and ultraviolet regions. Heinrich Hertz first detected radio waves in 1888. Maxwell's theory was developed further by Hendrik Lorentz.

In *Dynamical Theory of the Electric Field* (1864) Maxwell put forward four famous differential equations (known simply as *Maxwell's equations*) describing the propagation of electromagnetic waves. These equations contain the speed of the waves, c, a value that is independent of the velocity of the source. This was one of the facts that led Einstein to his special theory of relativity. Maxwell also wrote *Treatise on Electricity and Magnetism* (1873).

May, Robert McCredie

(1936–   )

AUSTRALIAN–AMERICAN
THEORETICAL ECOLOGIST

Not only in research, but in the everyday world of politics and economics we would all be better off if more people realized that simple systems do not necessarily possess simple dynamical properties.

—*Nature* No. 261 (1976)

May was educated at the university in his native city of Sydney, obtaining his PhD in theoretical physics in 1960. He then taught applied mathematics at Harvard and physics at Sydney from 1962 until 1973, when he was appointed professor of zoology at Princeton. In 1988 he was appointed Royal Society research professor of zoology at Oxford University and Imperial College, London. Since 1995 he has also served as chief scientific adviser to the British government.

Whereas an earlier generation of theoretical physicists had become interested in biology through their desire to understand the molecules of life, May and his generation were more attracted to the problem of understanding the abundance and distribution of species. Greatly influenced by the pioneering work of Robert MacArthur, they could see tempting analogies between the flow of energy in a physical system and the structure and growth of an ecosystem.

May has worked on a number of detailed problems on the population dynamics of various species but is perhaps best known for his influential *Theoretical Ecology* (1976).

Mayer, Julius Robert von

(1814–1878)

GERMAN PHYSICIAN AND
PHYSICIST

Mayer (**mI**-er), the son of an apothecary from Heilbronn in Germany, studied medicine at the University of Tübingen, where he seems to have been a mediocre student. He continued his studies abroad in Vienna and Paris before accepting an appointment in 1840 as a ship's physician on a vessel bound for Java. On his return in 1841 he settled in Heilbronn working as a general practitioner.

When Mayer sailed to Java he was familiar with the views of Antoine Lavoisier that animal heat is produced by slow combustion in the body. Being forced to bleed some of the crew at Surabaya, he found that venous blood was surprisingly bright. Indeed, at first he thought that he had cut an artery by mistake. "This phenomenon riveted my earnest attention," he reported, drawing the correct conclusion that the blood was redder because in the tropics the body does not need to burn as much oxygen to maintain body temperature as it does in temperate regions. The observation led Mayer to speculate about the conversion of food to heat in the body, and also the fact that the body can do work. He came to the view that heat and work are interchangeable – that the same amount of food can be converted to different proportions of heat and work, but the total must be the same.

Moreover, Mayer appreciated that this equivalence should hold universally and tried to apply it to other systems and to make it quantitative. Unfortunately, at the time he was confused about such concepts as force and work and his ideas were presented in an obscure metaphysical style. His first paper on the subject was sent to *Annalen der Physik* (Annals of Physics); the editor, Johann Poggendorf, did not even acknowledge Mayer's letter. The paper was published in 1842 by Justus von Liebig in the journal *Annalen der Chemie und Pharmazie* (Annals of Chemistry and Pharmacy). The paper was almost totally ignored and Mayer published, in 1845, a pamphlet at his own expense – *Organic Motion Related to Digestion* – which fared no better than his paper.

In his arguments Mayer used the specific heat capacities of gases, i.e., the heat required to produce unit temperature rise in unit mass of gas. It was known that the specific heat capacity of a gas maintained at constant volume is slightly smaller than that at constant pressure. This difference in heat, for a given quantity of gas, Mayer interpreted as the work done by a gas expanding at constant pressure. He was able to find the amount of work required to produce unit amount of heat – thus obtaining what was later known as the mechanical equivalent of heat (J). He found a weight of 1 gram falling 365 meters corresponds to heating 1 gram of water 1°C. (This is equivalent to a value of J of 3.56 joules per calorie; the modern conversion factor is 4.18 joules per calorie.)

Mayer clearly anticipated James Joule and Hermann von Helmholtz in the discovery of the law of conservation of energy. The lack of recognition seems to have affected him strongly, for in the early 1850s he attempted suicide. His work was eventually recognized and he received many honors, including the Rumford medal of the Royal Society (1871).

Maynard Smith, John

(1920–   )

BRITISH BIOLOGIST

> The mixture of intellect and blasphemy was absolutely overwhelming and I've been attracted to that all the rest of my life.
> —On J. B. S. Haldane's *Possible Worlds*. Quoted by L. Wolpert and A. Richards in *A Passion for Science* (1988)

Maynard Smith was educated at Cambridge University, where he qualified as an engineer in 1941. He spent the next six years designing aircraft before deciding they were "noisy and old-fashioned" and moving to University College, London, to study zoology under J. B. S. Haldane. After obtaining his BSc in zoology in 1951 he remained as a lecturer in zoology until 1965 when he was appointed professor of biology at the University of Sussex. He became emeritus professor in 1985.

Maynard Smith, known to a wide public for his lucid *Theory of Evolution* (1958), has emerged as one of the leading theorists of the postwar years. Much influenced by W. D. Hamilton and Robert MacArthur, and using concepts taken from the theory of games formulated by John von Neumann in the 1940s, he introduced in the 1970s the idea of an evolutionary stable strategy (ESS).

Assuming that two animals are in conflict, then an ESS is one that, if adopted by the majority of the population, prevents the invasion of a mutant strategy. Stable strategies by definition thus tend to be mixed strategies.

Much of Maynard Smith's work on ESS was published in his *Mathematical Ideas in Biology* (1968). He also discussed why sexual modes of reproduction predominate over other means in *The Evolution of Sex* (1978). Maynard Smith has continued to write on evolutionary theory in such works as *Evolutionary Genetics* (1989) and *The Major Transitions of Evolution* (1995).

Mayow, John

(1640–1679)

ENGLISH PHYSIOLOGIST AND
CHEMIST

Some learned and knowing men speak very slightly of the *Tractatus quinque* [Fifth Treatise] of J. M. [John Mayow]…a particular friend of yours and mine told me yesterday, that as far as he had read him, he would shew to any impartial and considering man more errors than one on every page.
—Henry Oldenburg. Letter to Robert Boyle, July 1674.
Quoted in Robert Boyle, *Works*, Vol. VI (1772)

Mayow was born at Morvah in Cornwall, England, and educated at Oxford University. He became a doctor of law in 1670 but then turned to medicine.

In 1674 he published his *Tractatus quinque* (Fifth Treatise) in which he came close to discovering the composite nature of the atmosphere. He showed that if a mouse is kept in a closed container over water then the air in the container will diminish in quantity, its properties change, and the water will rise up into the container. The same effect, he realized, could be produced by burning a candle. He further pointed out that combustion and respiration stopped before all the air was used up. He preceded Joseph Priestley and Antoine Lavoisier by about a hundred years with his discoveries relating to respiration and combustion.

Mayr, Ernst Walter

(1904–   )

GERMAN–AMERICAN ZOOLOGIST

Born at Kempten in Germany, Mayr (mIr) was educated at the universities of Griefswald and Berlin, where he obtained his PhD in 1926. He then served as assistant curator of the museum there before moving to America in 1932. After spending many years at the Museum of Natural History, New York, he moved to Harvard in 1953 to serve as Agassiz Professor of Zoology, in which post he remained until his retirement in 1975.

As a field zoologist Mayr has worked extensively on the birds of the Pacific. Beginning with his *New Guinea Birds* (1941), he published a number of surveys and monographs on the ornithology of the area.

He is, however, better known for such works as *Systematics and the Origin of Species* (1942) and *Animal Species and Evolution* (1963) in which, at the same time as such other scholars as George Simpson and Theodosius Dobzhansky in America and Julian Huxley in Britain, he attempted to establish a neo-Darwinian synthesis. The enterprise has continued to hold together fairly well against the onslaughts of such critics as Motoo Kimura and has so far absorbed, without major upset, the massive inflow of data from the new discipline of molecular biology.

McAdam, John Loudon

(1756–1836)

BRITISH ENGINEER

In 1770 McAdam traveled from his native Ayrshire, in Scotland, to New York City, where he became a successful merchant and made his fortune. He then returned to Ayrshire (1783) and bought an estate there, using his own money to experiment with roadbuilding in the surrounding district.

In 1798 McAdam was given a government appointment in Falmouth, Cornwall. He recommended that roads should be raised, so that water could drain away, and should be built with large rocks covered over with smaller ones bound by slag. Bitumen is now used instead of slag, but the basic principle is the same in modern roads. He was appointed surveyor general of the Bristol roads in 1815 and there put his ideas on roadbuilding into practice.

McAdam published several papers and essays on roadbuilding, including *Remarks on the Present System of Road-Making*. In 1823, after a parliamentary enquiry, his recommendations were adopted by the public authorities. The methods spread and improved travel throughout the world. In 1827 he was appointed general surveyor of roads in Britain.

McCarthy, John

(1927–   )

AMERICAN COMPUTER SCIENTIST

Born in Boston, Massachusetts, McCarthy was educated at the California Institute of Technology and at Princeton, where he obtained his PhD in 1951. After holding junior posts successively at Princeton, Stanford, and Dartmouth, McCarthy joined the Massachusetts Institute of Technology in 1957 and immediately set up the Artificial Intelligence (AI) Laboratory. In 1962 he moved to Stanford, California, to the post of professor of computer science. In the following year he founded the Stanford AI Laboratory.

In many ways McCarthy is the founding father of AI. He coined the term in the mid 1950s, organized the 1956 Dartmouth conference, which largely defined the new discipline, and set up the first AI Laboratory in 1957. He was also the inventor (1956–58) of the computer language LISP (List Processing), in which much AI work is pursued. McCarthy was also responsible during the period between 1957 and 1962 for the development of time-sharing in computers.

McCarthy's position on AI has always remained radical and even extreme. Acts of intelligence, he has argued, can be reduced in all cases to propositions expressible in purely logicomathematical terms. Thus mistakes in AI arise not when logic is relied upon too much, but when the program is not rigorous enough. To avoid this it is necessary to formalize such concepts as causation, knowledge, and belief; these tasks have so far eluded McCarthy and his followers.

McCarty, Maclyn

(1911–   )

AMERICAN MICROBIOLOGIST

McCarty was born at South Bend, Indiana, and educated at Stanford and Johns Hopkins University, Pennsylvania, where he obtained his MD in 1937. After holding a junior appointment there he moved in 1940 to the Rockefeller Institute where he remained until his retirement in 1974, serving as physician-in-chief from 1961 and as vice-president from 1965.

In 1944 McCarty collaborated with Oswald Avery and Colin MacLeod in the experiment that first clearly revealed the transforming power of DNA. McCarty went on to work on streptococci and rheumatic fever.

McClintock, Barbara

(1902–1992)

AMERICAN GENETICIST

The daughter of a physician, McClintock was born in Hartford, Connecticut, and educated at Cornell's College of Agriculture, where she received her PhD in 1927 for work in botany. She remained at Cornell until 1936 supported by various grants from the National Research Council and the Guggenheim Foundation. But there was no future at Cornell for her as, until 1947, only the department of home economics appointed women professors. Fortunately a new genetics department was being set up in the University of Missouri by Craig Stadler, who knew and admired her work, and she was offered a post as assistant professor there, although it was made clear to her that any further advancement would be unlikely. She left in 1941, and in 1944 was elected to the National Academy of Sciences, becoming only the third woman to be so honored. McClintock then joined the Carnegie Institute's Cold Spring Harbor Laboratory, New York, where she remained until her death.

By the 1920s Morgan and other geneticists, working mainly with the *Drosophila* fruit fly, had established that gene action was connected with chromosomes and thereby established the new discipline of cytogenetics. *Drosophila* chromosomes, however, before the discovery of the giant salivary chromosomes by T. Painter in 1931, were too small to reveal much detail. McClintock chose to work with a variety of maize that possessed much more visible chromosomes. Further, the development of new staining techniques allowed McClintock to identify, distinguish, and number the ten maize chromosomes.

Morgan and his group had also demonstrated the existence of "linkage groups" in *Drosophila* – groups of genes, such as those for white eyes and maleness, linked together because the genes themselves were sited near each other on a chromosome. In a series of papers published between 1929 and 1931, McClintock established similar linkage groups in maize. Because maize chromosomes were more visible under the microscope than those of *Drosophila*, McClintock was able to identify the chromosomal changes responsible for a change in phenotype and thus confirmed Morgan's work.

McClintock's own Nobel Prize for physiology or medicine, awarded in 1983, was for later work done on the so-called "jumping genes." In the 1940s at Cold Spring Harbor, McClintock planted her maize and began to track a family of mutant genes responsible for changes in pigmentation. She was struck by the fact that mutation rates were variable. After several years' careful breeding, McClintock proposed that in addition to the normal genes responsible for pigmentation there were two other genes involved, which she called "controlling elements."

One controlling element was found fairly close to the pigmentation gene and operated as a switch, activating and turning off the gene. The second element appeared to be located further away on the same chromosome and was a "rate gene," controlling the rate at which the pigment gene was switched on and off. She further discovered that the controlling elements could move along the chromosome to a different site and could even move to different chromosomes where they would control different genes. McClintock gave a full description of the process of "transposition," as it became known, in 1951, in her paper *Chromosome Organization and Genic Expression.* McClintock's work was largely ignored until 1960, when controlling elements were identified in bacteria by Monod and Jacob.

McCollum, Elmer Verner

(1879–1967)

AMERICAN BIOCHEMIST

Born in Fort Scott, Kansas, McCollum was educated at the University of Kansas and at Yale, where he obtained his PhD in 1906. He taught at the University of Wisconsin from 1907 until 1917, when he was appointed to the chair of biochemistry at Johns Hopkins University, a post he retained until his retirement in 1944.

McCollum made a number of advances in the study of vitamins. He was the first, in collaboration with M. Davis in 1913, to demonstrate clearly their multiplicity. They found that rats fed with a diet lacking butterfat failed to develop. They assumed, therefore, the existence of a special factor present in butterfat without which the normal growth process could not take place. As it was clearly fat-soluble, it must be distinct from the antiberiberi factor proposed by Casimir Funk in 1912, which was water-soluble. McCollum named them fat-soluble–A and water-soluble–B, which later became vitamins A and B. In 1920 McCollum was able to extend the alphabet further by naming the antirachitic factor found in cod-liver oil vitamin D (C had already been appropriated to describe the antiscorbutic factor).

McCollum wrote widely on the subject of nutrition, his books including a standard text of the subject, *Newer Knowledge of Nutrition* (1918), which went through many editions, and *A History of Nutrition* (1957).

McConnell, Harden Marsden

(1927–   )

AMERICAN THEORETICAL CHEMIST AND BIOCHEMIST

McConnell, who was born in Richmond, Virginia, graduated from George Washington University in 1947 and received his doctorate from the California Institute of Technology in 1951. He served as professor of chemistry there from 1959 until 1964, when he was appointed to a similar chair at Stanford University.

McConnell's early work was on the movement of electrons in unsaturated hydrocarbons. He found a way of measuring the electron density on carbon atoms in these molecules. He has done extensive work on the theory of nuclear magnetic resonance spectroscopy in organic compounds, and also on electron spin resonance (in which absorption is by unpaired electrons rather than nuclei). Studies of the methyl radical (CH_3) by McConnell and his group have demonstrated that it is almost planar.

His work on magnetic resonance spectroscopy led to the introduction of spin labeling, a method in which biological compounds are labeled by adding a stable organic free radical. This converts normally nonparamagnetic systems to paramagnetic systems, which display resonance. Important facts about the structure of compounds can be obtained by examining this resonance. Thus spin labeling helped McConnell demonstrate that the phospholipids found in biological membranes have the properties of a liquid and so allow rapid transfer of molecules. Work on the double lipid layers of membranes has shown that its physical properties play a large part in the immune response. Such work has since become part of a major research effort based on several research centers.

McKusick, Victor Almon

(1921–)

AMERICAN PHYSICIAN AND GENETICIST

The son of a dairy farmer, McKusick was born in Parkman, Maine, and educated at Tufts University, Medford, Massachusetts. He went on to Johns Hopkins University, Baltimore, where he qualified as an MD in 1946 and where he trained as a cardiologist. McKusick has remained at Johns Hopkins and has served as professor of medicine from 1960 and, from 1985, as professor of medical genetics.

The name of McKusick has become identified with a book, an encyclopedic listing of human gene loci, titled *Mendelian Inheritance in Man*, but more commonly referred to as MIM. In 1911 E. B. Wilson identified the first gene locus – the gene for color blindness on the X-chromosome. Over the years other genes were identified and located. By 1966, when the first edition of MIM appeared, 68 genes had been mapped on the X-chromosome. McKusick went on to describe a total number of 1,487 human genes. By the eighth edition of MIM, published in 1988, improved techniques in cytogenetics allowed the identification of 4,344 gene loci. Two further editions of MIM, in 1990 and 1992, have continued to add to the total.

McLennan, Sir John Cunningham

(1867–1935)

CANADIAN PHYSICIST

Born the son of a miller and grain dealer from Ingersoll in Ontario, Canada, McLennan was educated at the University of Toronto. After graduating in 1892 he immediately joined the staff and later served as professor of physics from 1907 until his retirement in 1932. He then moved to England where he began, shortly before his death, to work on the use of radium in the treatment of cancer.

He had earlier collaborated with Ernest Rutherford during World War I on work in combating submarines. He is, however, best remembered for his work on the auroral spectrum. The existence of a green line with a wavelength of 5,377 angstroms without any apparent source had long puzzled scientists. In 1924, in collaboration with A. Shrumm, McLennan succeeded in obtaining similar lines in the laboratory from atomic oxygen, thus indicating their source.

It was also under McLennan that Toronto became a leading center for research into low-temperature physics. Helium was first liquefied there in 1923 when they reported the curious behavior of helium as its temperature dropped below 2.2 K. Without being aware of it they had observed the onset of superfluidity at the so-called lambda point where, as was to be reported in 1930 by W. Keesom, the heat conduction of helium suddenly increases enormously.

McMillan, Edwin Mattison

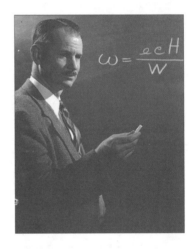

(1907–1991)

AMERICAN PHYSICIST

Born in Redonda Beach, California, McMillan was educated at the California Institute of Technology and at Princeton, where he obtained his PhD in 1932. He took up an appointment at the University of California at Berkeley in 1935, being made professor of physics in 1946 and director of the Lawrence Radiation Laboratory in 1958, posts he held until his retirement in 1973.

In 1940 McMillan and Philip Abelson announced the discovery of the first element heavier than uranium. The new element had a mass number 93 and a relative atomic mass of 239. It was named neptunium after the planet Neptune, just as 150 years earlier Martin Klaproth had named uranium after the planet Uranus. McMillan also suspected the existence of element 94 and in the same year was proved right by the discovery of the new element (plutonium) by Glenn Seaborg with whom he was to share the 1951 Nobel Prize for chemistry. The new elements were produced when uranium was bombarded with neutrons and were detected by virtue of their characteristic half-life.

McMillan also made a major advance in the development of Ernest Lawrence's cyclotron, which, in the early 1940s, had run up against a theoretical limit. Lawrence found that as his particles accelerated beyond a certain point their increase in mass, as predicted by Einstein's theory of relativity, was putting them out of phase with the electric impulse they were supposed to receive inside the cyclotron.

In 1945 McMillan proposed a neat solution in the synchrocyclotron (also independently suggested by Vladimir Veksler) in which the fixed frequency of the cyclotron was abandoned. The variable frequency of the synchrocyclotron could thus be adjusted to correspond to the relativistic mass gain of the accelerating particles and once more get into phase with them. In this way accelerators could be built that were forty times more powerful than Lawrence's most advanced cyclotron.

Medawar, Sir Peter Brian

(1915–1987)

BRITISH IMMUNOLOGIST

> Scientific discovery is a private event, and the delight that accompanies it, or the despair of finding it illusory does not travel.
> —*Hypothesis and Imagination*

The son of an Englishwoman and a Lebanese businessman trading in Brazil, Medawar was born in Rio de Janeiro and brought to Britain at the end of World War I. He was educated at Oxford, graduating in zoology in 1937, and remained there to work under Howard Florey. His first researches concerned factors affecting tissue-culture growth but during World War II he turned his attention to medical biology. He subsequently developed a concentrated solution of the blood-clotting protein fibrinogen, which could be used clinically as a biological glue to fix together damaged nerves and keep nerve grafts in position.

The terrible burns of many war casualties led Medawar to study the reasons why skin grafts from donors are rejected. He realized that each individual develops his own immunological system and that the length of time a graft lasts depends on how closely related the recipient and donor are. He found that grafting was successful not only between identical twins but also between nonidentical, or fraternal, twins. It had already been shown in cattle that tissues, notably the red-cell precursors, are exchanged between twin fetuses. This led to the suggestion by Macfarlane Burnet that the immunological system is not developed at conception but is gradually acquired. Thus if an embryo is injected with the tissues of a future donor, the animal after birth should be tolerant to any grafts from that donor.

Medawar tested this hypothesis by injecting mouse embryos, verifying that they do not have the ability to form antibodies against foreign tissue but do acquire immunologic tolerance to it. For this discovery Medawar and Burnet were awarded the 1960 Nobel Prize for physiology or medicine.

Medawar moved from Oxford in 1947 to the chair of zoology at Birmingham, a post he held until 1951 when he was appointed professor of zoology at University College, London. In 1962 he accepted the important post of director of the National Institute for Medical Research. For some years he tried to combine his research work with a heavy administrative load. But in 1969 Medawar suffered his first stroke. Although he continued as director until 1971, the stroke had seriously restricted his mobility and dexterity. Despite this he continued his research work on cancer at the Clinical Research Centre, London. A second stroke in 1980, and a third in 1984, brought Medawar's research career to an end.

He continued to write, however, and in 1986 published his autobiography, *Memoirs of a Thinking Radish*, and collected most of his early essays in *Pluto's Republic* (1982). It was in one of these essays, first published in 1964, that Medawar characterized science in a much quoted phrase as "the art of the soluble."

Mees, Charles Edward Kenneth

(1882–1960)

ANGLO-AMERICAN
PHOTOCHEMIST

The best person to decide what research shall be done is the man who is doing the research. The next best is the head of the department. After that you leave the field of best persons and meet increasingly worse groups. The first of these is the research director, who is probably wrong more than half the time. Then comes a committee which is wrong most of the time. Finally there is a committee of company vice-presidents, which is wrong all the time.
— On his experiences as research director at Eastman-Kodak in the 1930s.
Quoted in *Biographical Memoirs of Fellows of the Royal Society*,
Vol. VII (1961)

Mees, the son of a Wesleyan minister at Wellingborough in Northamptonshire, England, was educated at the University of London where he obtained his doctorate in 1906. After working for a company manufacturing photographic plates he emigrated to America in 1912, to become director of the research laboratory of Eastman-Kodak at Rochester, Minnesota, a post he held until his retirement in 1946.

In England Mees had worked on the development of plates of high sensitivity. This had attracted the attention of astronomers and in 1912 he was invited to join the staff of the Mount Wilson Observatory. Although he joined Eastman instead, he maintained his contacts with Mount Wilson, sending them, in the early 1930s, some of the fastest plates he had ever produced. In 1935 he organized the large-scale production of Kodachrome, the first color film made for the mass market. He also published *The Theory of the Photographic Process* (1942), a comprehensive and authoritative survey of the state of photographic science.

Meissner, Fritz Walther

(1882–1974)

GERMAN PHYSICIST

In 1933 Meissner (**mĪs**-ner), in collaboration with R. Oschenfeld, discovered what has since been known as the *Meissner effect*. He was examining the magnetic properties of materials as they became superconductive, a condition met with as the temperature of the element or compound falls below a critical point, i.e., critical temperature (T_c). It was found, quite unexpectedly, that if a solid lead sphere is placed in a magnetic field and the temperature allowed to fall below the T_c of lead, the magnetic field is expelled from the lead sphere, which becomes perfectly diamagnetic. The presence of the Meissner effect is now used as a routine test for superconductivity.

Meitner, Lise

(1878–1968)

AUSTRIAN–SWEDISH PHYSICIST

Meitner (**mĪt**-ner), the daughter of a lawyer, was born in Vienna and entered the university there in 1901. She studied science under Ludwig Boltzmann and obtained her doctorate in 1906. From Vienna she went to Berlin to attend lectures by Max Planck on theoretical physics. Here she began to study the new phenomenon of radioactivity in collaboration with Otto Hahn, beginning a partnership that was to last thirty years.

At Berlin she met with remarkable difficulties caused by prejudice against women in academic life. She was forced to work in an old carpentry shop and forbidden, by Emil Fischer, to enter laboratories in which males were working. In 1914, at the outbreak of World War I, she became a nurse in the Austrian army, continuing work with Hahn during their periods of leave. In 1918 they announced the discovery of the radioactive element protactinium.

After the war Meitner returned to Berlin as head of the department of radiation physics at the Kaiser Wilhelm Institute. Here she investigated the relationship between the gamma and beta rays emitted by radioactive material. In 1935 she began, with Hahn, work on the transformation of uranium nuclei under neutron bombardment. Confusing results had been obtained earlier by Enrico Fermi.

But by this time she was beginning to fear a different sort of prejudice. Following Hitler's annexation of Austria in 1938 she was no longer safe from persecution and, like many Jewish scientists, left Germany. With the help of Dutch colleagues she found refuge in Sweden, obtaining a post at the Nobel Institute in Stockholm. Hahn, with Fritz Strassman, continued the uranium work and published, in 1939, results showing that nuclei were present that were much lighter than uranium. Shortly afterward Lise Meitner, with Otto Frisch (her nephew), published an explanation interpreting these results as fission of the uranium nuclei. The nucleus of uranium absorbs a neutron, and the resulting unstable nucleus then breaks into two fragments of roughly equal size. In this induced fission, two or three neutrons are ejected. For this she received a share in the 1966 Enrico Fermi Prize of the Atomic Energy Commission.

Lise Meitner became a Swedish citizen in 1949 and continued work on nuclear physics. In 1960 she retired to Cambridge, England.

Mela, Pomponius

(about 44 AD)

IBERIAN GEOGRAPHER

> There is no definite decision whether this is the action of the universe through its own heaving breath...whether there exist some cavernous depressions for the ebb-tides to sink into,...whether the moon is responsible for currents so extensive.
> —On the action of the tides. *De chorographia*
> (43 AD; Concerning Chorography)

Mela (**mee**-la) probably came from southern Spain. He was the author of *De situ orbis* (A Description of the World), also known as *De chorographia* (Concerning Chorography), which is the first extant Latin geographical work.

The book borrowed largely from earlier Greek works and was simply a descriptive account of the lands surrounding the Mediterranean, with a brief description of the rest of the known world added. Mela retained the surrounding Oceanus of earlier maps and saw the continents of Africa, Asia, and Europe indented by the Caspian, Arabian, Persian, and Mediterranean seas. The Earth was divided into five zones – two arctic, one tropical, and two temperate – only the temperate zones being capable of supporting life. He seems to have been the first to realize that Spain juts out into the Atlantic. According to Strabo its coastline continued down from France in a straight line.

Mellanby, Sir Edward

(1884–1955)

BRITISH PHYSIOLOGIST

Mellanby, the son of a shipyard manager from West Hartlepool in northeast England, was educated at Cambridge University and at St. Thomas's Hospital, London, where he completed his medical studies. In

1913 he was appointed to the chair of physiology at King's College for Women (now Queen Elizabeth College), London. He remained there until 1920, when he moved to the chair of pharmacology at Sheffield University. However, he resigned this post in 1933 to take up the influential position of secretary to the Medical Research Council (MRC), which he held until his retirement in 1949.

In 1918 Mellanby fed puppies a variety of diets containing all the vitamins then known but found that they developed rickets. If, however, cod-liver oil or butter were added to the diet no symptoms appeared. This led him to suggest that the fat-soluble vitamin A in cod-liver oil and the antirachitic factor were identical.

However in 1922 Elmer McCollum showed that it was not the vitamin A in cod-liver oil that prevented rickets developing: when the oil was heated it would continue to cure xerophthalmia, an eye complaint due to vitamin A deficiency, but lost all antirachitic properties. He therefore proposed the existence of a fourth vitamin, D, later shown to be calciferol.

In fact the etiology of rickets turned out to be more complicated, since vitamin D can be made in the skin from its precursor, 7-hydrocholesterol, in the presence of sunlight. Thus rickets can be cured either by exposure to sunlight or by administration of calciferol in cod-liver oil.

While at the MRC Mellanby's most significant work was his support of Howard Florey in the work of isolating penicillin. It was largely owing to Mellanby that Florey was appointed to the Oxford professorship of pathology in 1935. Once there, the research that led to the isolation and extraction of penicillin was partly financed by the MRC on the recommendation of Mellanby.

Melloni, Macedonio

(1798–1854)

ITALIAN PHYSICIST

> Light and radiant heat are effects directly produced by two different causes.
> —*Annales de chimie* (1835;
> Annals of Chemistry)

Melloni (may-**loh**-nee) was professor of physics at the university in his native city of Parma from 1824 to 1831. However, his political activities in the unsuccessful revolutions of 1830 forced him to flee to France. He was later allowed to return to Italy and in 1839 appointed director of a conservatory of physics in Naples. He also directed, until 1848, the Vesuvius Observatory.

Melloni is especially noted for investigations into radiant heat. In 1831, together with Leopoldo Nobili, he published a description of a sensitive thermopile; further development of this instrument was due almost entirely to him. Melloni emphasized that just as there was variety in light rays so there were different kinds of radiant heat. He made numerous experiments on its absorption by solids and liquids, and introduced the word "diathermancy" (the ability to transmit heat radiations). By 1850 he had shown that infrared rays could be reflected, refracted, polarized, and cause interference effects as could ordinary light. In 1850 he published *La Thermochrôse*, a treatise that embodied his researches on radiant energy and gave details of his childhood love of science.

Melville, Sir Harry Work

(1908–)

BRITISH CHEMIST

Melville was educated at the university in his native city of Edinburgh, where he obtained his PhD. After a period (1933–40) at Cambridge University, Melville served as professor of chemistry at the University of Aberdeen (1940–48) and at Birmingham University (1948–56).

At this point in his career Melville moved mainly into science administration. He advised such bodies as the Ministry of Power and the Electricity Authority and from 1956 to 1965 served as secretary of the Department of Scientific and Industrial Research. He finally held the post of head of Queen Mary College, London, from 1967 until his retirement in 1976.

As a chemist, Melville is noted for his work on chain reactions involving free radicals, in which he followed up the ideas of Cyril

Hinshelwood and Nikolay Semenov and showed experimentally that they were correct. Later he studied the kinetics of polymerization chain reactions. He wrote *Experimental Methods in Gas Reactions* (1938) with Adalbert Farkas.

Melzack, Ronald

(1929–)

CANADIAN PSYCHOLOGIST

Melzack was born at Montreal in Quebec, Canada, and educated at McGill University there, completing his PhD in 1954. He spent the period from 1954 until 1957 as a research fellow at Oregon University Medical School. Soon after, following brief periods at University College, London, and the University of Pisa, Melzack joined the Massachusetts Institute of Technology (1959). He returned to McGill in 1963 as professor of psychology and as director of research at the Pain Clinic at Montreal General Hospital.

Much of Melzack's career has been devoted to the study of the psychology and physiology of pain. He has published a general account of the subject in his *The Puzzle of Pain* (Harmondsworth, 1973) and a massive comprehensive survey, *Textbook of Pain* (London, 1984).

In 1965, in collaboration with Patrick Wall, Melzack proposed the "gate theory" of pain. They saw the central nervous system (CNS) as something more than a channel along which signals passed; the channel contained gates which could be opened or closed to allow or bar the passage of stimuli. Where were the gates located and what controlled them? They were located, Melzack argued, in the dorsal horns of the spinal cord.

The control mechanism was a function of the different types of nerve fiber along which stimuli passed to the spinal cord. The thicker A fibers conduct sensory stimuli both to and from (afferent and efferent) the CNS at a speed of 120 meters per second; in contrast, the afferent fibers for pain are thinner and transmit impulses at no more than 2 meters per second. Melzack proposed that activity in large fibers tends to inhibit transmission (close the gate) while small-fiber activity tends to facilitate transmission (open the gate).

Melzack also noted that the spinal gating mechanism was influenced by nerve impulses descending from the brain. That is, brain activities "subserving attention, emotion, and memories of prior experience" can control sensory input. In this manner, for instance, soldiers wounded in battle may feel no immediate pain.

Melzack has used gate theory to explain such anomalous states as referred pain and phantom-limb pain. He has also sought ways to use his theoretical understanding in the control of pain.

Mendel, Gregor Johann

(1822–1884)

AUSTRIAN PLANT GENETICIST

The information technology of the gene is digital. This fact was discovered by Gregor Mendel in the last century, although he wouldn't have put it like that. Mendel showed that we don't blend our inheritance from our parents...we receive [it] in discrete particles.
—Richard Dawkins, *The Blind Watchmaker* (1986)

Born in Heinzendorf (now Hynčice in the Czech Republic), Mendel studied at Olmütz University before entering the Augustinian monastery at Brünn (now Brno in the Czech Republic) in 1843. His childhood experience of horticultural work as the son of a peasant farmer had given him an interest in the role of hybrids in evolution, and in 1856 he began plant-breeding experiments. He studied seven characters in pea plants and obtained important results after much laborious recording of character ratios in the progeny of crosses. From his experiments Mendel concluded that each of the characters he studied was determined by two factors of inheritance (one from each parent) and that each gamete (egg or sperm cell) of the organism contained only one factor of each pair. Furthermore he deduced that assortment into gametes of the factors for one character occurred independently of that for the factors of any other pair. Mendel's results are summarized today in his law of segregation and law of independent assortment (*Mendel's laws*).

Mendel's work is now recognized as providing the first mathematical basis to genetics but in its day it stimulated little interest. He read a brief account of his research to the Brünn Natural History Society in 1865 and asked members to extend his methods to other species, but none did. In

Characters of parents	First generation	Numbers in second generation	Ratio in second generation
Stem length			
tall	100%	787	2.84
short	—	277	1
Flower position			
axial	100%	651	3.14
terminal	—	207	1
Pod color (unripe)			
green	100%	428	2.82
yellow	—	152	1
Pod form (ripe)			
smooth	100%	332	2.95
wrinkled	—	299	1
Flower seed coat color			
purple/gray	100%	705	3.15
white/white	—	224	1
Seed form			
round	100%	5474	2.96
wrinkled	—	1850	1
Cotyledon color			
yellow	100%	6022	3.01
green	—	2001	1

MENDEL'S EXPERIMENTS The results of Mendel's pea-crossing experiments, showing the characteristic 3:1 ratio in the second generation.

1866 he published his work in the society's *Verhandlungen* (Proceedings), a journal distributed to 134 scientific institutions, and sent reprints of the paper to hybridization "experts" of the time. Karl Naegeli, the Swiss botanist, was skeptical of his results and suggested that he continue work on the hawkweeds (*Hieracium*), a genus now known to show reproductive irregularities and with which Mendel was bound to fail.

Mendel's work with peas, and later with *Matthiola*, *Zea*, and *Mirabilis*, had shown that characters do not blend on crossing but retain their identity, thus providing an answer to the weakness in Charles Darwin's theory of natural selection. Mendel read a copy of Darwin's *Origin of Species*, but unfortunately, Darwin never heard of Mendel's work.

Mendel became abbot of the monastery in 1868 and thereafter found less time to devote to his research. It was not until 1900, when Hugo de Vries, Karl Correns, and Erich von Tschermak came across his work, that its true value was realized.

Mendeleev, Dmitri Ivanovich

(1834–1907)

RUSSIAN CHEMIST

> There will come a time, when the world will be filled with one science, one truth, one industry, one brotherhood, one friendship with nature...This is my belief, it progresses, it grows stronger, this is worth living for, this is worth waiting for.
>
> —Quoted by Yu A. Urmanster in *The Symmetry of Nature and the Nature of Symmetry* (1974)

Mendeleev (men-de-**lay**-ef) was the youngest child of a large family living in Tobolsk, Siberia. His father was a local school teacher whose career was ended by blindness and to support the family his mother ran a glass factory. Mendeleev learned some science from a political refugee who had married one of his sisters. His father died in 1847, and soon after his mother's factory was destroyed by fire. She left Tobolsk with Mendeleev, determined that her last son should receive a good education, and placed him at the Pedagogic Institute of St. Petersburg only ten weeks before her death. He later studied in France under Henri Regnault and in Heidelberg with Robert Bunsen and Gustav Kirchhoff.

While abroad Mendeleev attended the famous conference at Karlsruhe in 1860 which did so much to settle the question of atomic weights. He returned to Russia shortly after and in a short time had completed his doctorate, written a textbook, and married. In 1866 he was elected to the chair of chemistry at St. Petersburg University where he remained until his retirement in 1890. His textbook *The Principles of Chemistry* was published between 1868 and 1870.

In 1869 Mendeleev published his classic paper *On the Relation of the Properties to the Atomic Weights of Elements*, which brought order and understanding to this confused subject. His first major proposal was his claim that the only way of classifying the elements is by their atomic weights. Optical, magnetic, and electrical properties vary with the state

I	II	III	IV	V	VI	VII	VIII		
H									
Li	Be	B	C	N	O	F			
Na	Mg	Al	Si	P	S	Cl			
K	Ca	□	□	As	S	Br			
Cu	Zn	□	Ti	V	Cr	Mn	Fe	Co	Ni
Rb	Sr	In	Sn	Sb	Te	I			
Ag	Cd	Y	Zr	Nb	Mo	□	Ru	Rh	Pd

PERIODIC TABLE   The table proposed by Mendeleev is shown above. Vertical columns are groups of elements with similar chemical properties. Horizontal rows in the table are called "periods" — across a period there is a gradual change of properties; for example, the period Li to F involves a change from metallic behavior (Li) to nonmetallic behavior (F). In order to group chemically similar elements, Mendeleev left gaps in the table for undiscovered elements.

the body is in at any particular moment; other properties, such as valence, yield conflicting results. When the elements are arranged in order of increasing atomic weight, Mendeleev found that they show a distinct periodicity of their properties. Arranging them in rows of increasing atomc weights produced columns of similar elements.

The table did not at first receive universal acceptance, but its value became apparent during the following 20 years. Through it Mendeleev was able to spot those elements that had been assigned incorrect atomic weights. Thus he suggested that the atomic weights of gold and tellurium must be wrong. There were three missing elements in his table, and he was able to predict their existence, valences, and certain physical properties. The three were eventually discovered – "eka-aluminum" (gallium, Paul Lecoq de Boisbaudran, 1875), "eka-boron" (scandium, Per Cleve, 1879), and "eka-silicon" (germanium, Clemens Winkler, 1885).

Mendeleev became the most famous Russian scientist of his day and received numerous medals and prizes although not, surprisingly, the Nobel Prize (in 1906 it was awarded to Ferdinand Moissan by one vote). Element 101 was named *mendelevium* in his honor.

Mengoli, Pietro

(1625–1686)

ITALIAN MATHEMATICIAN

Mengoli (men-**goh**-lee) was born in Bologna and studied there with Francesco Cavalieri. He was ordained a priest and held a chair in mathematics at Bologna. The mathematical work was chiefly on the calculus and infinite series and his most important work was with convergence and with integration. He was one of the first to establish results about the conditions under which infinite series converge. His work constitutes an important stage in the development of the fully fledged calculus of Isaac Newton and Gottfried Leibniz from such ideas as Cavalieri's method of indivisibles. Mengoli gave a definition of a definite integral, similar to that given by Augustin Cauchy.

Menzel, Donald Howard

(1901–1976)

AMERICAN ASTROPHYSICIST

Born in Florence, Colorado, Menzel graduated from the University of Denver in 1920 and obtained his PhD from Princeton in 1924. In 1926 he was appointed to the staff of the Lick Observatory in California. He became assistant professor of astronomy at Harvard in 1932, then served as professor of astrophysics (1938–71), and from 1954 to 1966 was director of the Harvard College Observatory.

Menzel worked mainly on the solar system, investigating planetary atmospheres and the constitution of the Sun. He improved on the work of Henry Russell in 1929 on the abundance of the elements in the Sun: he estimated that the Sun contained 81.76% hydrogen and 18.17% helium by volume, leaving 0.07% for the rest of the elements.

Menzel also used spectrographic methods to work out, with J. H. Moore, the rotational period of Neptune, finding it to be 15.8 hours.

Mercator, Gerardus

(1512–1594)

DUTCH CARTOGRAPHER AND GEOGRAPHER

Mercator (mer-**kay**-ter), originally named Kremer, was born at Rupelmonde, now in Belgium. At the University of Louvain (1530–32) he was a pupil of Gemma Frisius. After learning the basic skills of an instrument maker and engraver, he founded his own studio in Louvain in 1534. Despite accusations of heresy and imprisonment in 1544, he remained in Louvain until 1552, when he moved to Duisburg and opened a cartographic workshop.

Mercator first made his international reputation as a cartographer in 1554 with his map of Europe in which he reduced the size of the Mediterranean from the 62° of Ptolemy to a more realistic, but still excessive, 52°. He produced his world map in 1569 and his edition of Ptolemy in 1578, while his *Atlas*, begun in 1569, was only published by his son after his death. It was intended to be a whole series of publications describing both the creation of the world and its subsequent history. Mercator was the first to use the term "atlas" for such works, the book having as its frontispiece an illustration of Atlas supporting the world.

The value of Mercator's work lies not just in his skills as an engraver, but also in the introduction of his famous projection in his 1569 map of the world. Navigators wished to be able to sail on what was called a rhumb-line course, or a loxodrome, i.e., to sail between two points on a constant bearing, charting their course with a straight line. On the surface of a globe such lines are curves; to project them onto a plane chart Mercator made the meridians (the lines of longitude) parallel instead of converging at the Poles. This made it straightforward for a navigator to plot his course but it also produced the familiar distortion of the *Mercator projection* – exaggeration of east–west distances and areas in the high latitudes.

The big difference, apart from projection, between Mercator's and classical maps was in the representation of the Americas. He was not the first to use the name America on a map, that distinction belonging to Martin Waldseemüller in 1507, but he was the first to divide the continent into two named parts – *Americae pars septentrionalis* (northern part of America) and *Americae pars meridionalis* (southern part of America).

Mercer, John

(1791–1866)

BRITISH CHEMIST

Mercer was the son of a cotton spinner from Dean in England and worked in the industry as a boy until, in 1807, he started a small dyeing business. He spent the rest of his life introducing new dyes and techniques into the industry. He seems to have been largely self-educated, learning his chemistry from one of the available mechanics manuals, Parkinson's *Chemical Pocket Book* (1791).

In 1814 Mercer introduced his first new dye, an orange one produced from sulfide of antimony, followed by a yellow dye from lead chromate and a bronze dye from manganese. He worked mainly in the calico-print side of the industry. His major innovation, the process of *mercerizing*, was patented in 1850. He found that cloth soaked in caustic soda would become stronger, take up dye more readily, and acquire a lustrous silken sheen. Another contribution of his was a method of printing fabric by a photographic process.

Apart from his industrial chemistry Mercer became interested in more theoretical problems through his friendship with Lyon Playfair formed in the early 1840s. He suggested an early theory of catalytic action and also contributed papers on the chemical activity of light and on atomic weights.

Merrifield, Robert Bruce

(1921–   )

AMERICAN BIOCHEMIST

Born in Fort Worth, Texas, Merrifield was educated at the University of California, Los Angeles, where he received his PhD in 1949. He began work immediately at Rockefeller University, New York, and was appointed to the chair of biochemistry in 1966, a post he held until his retirement in 1992.

In the 1950s Merrifield began work on solid-phase peptide synthesis (SPPS). Peptides, like proteins, are composed of chains of amino acids, but have shorter and less complicated chains. Naturally occurring ones possess important physiological properties. The ability to synthesize peptides cheaply and quickly would lead to numerous commercial and medical gains. Yet the synthesis of a polypeptide using traditional methods could take many months.

In peptides the amine end ($-NH_2$) of one amino acid reacts with the carboxyl end ($-COOH$) of another. To prepare a pure product of known structure, amino acids have to be coupled in a specific sequence. To achieve this the amine group on one amino acid and carboxyl group on the other must be blocked, so that the other two ends are the ones reacting. And this must be done as each further amino acid is added. In addition, at each stage the product must be isolated and purified. This will involve crystallizing the products. The synthesis of a hundred-unit peptide would involve ninety-nine such procedures. The need for improvement in the technique was painfully clear to peptide chemists.

Merrifield's innovation was to apply an ion-exchange technique by bonding the amino acids, one at a time, to an insoluble solid support. A polystyrene resin was the original choice. As the solid support was insoluble in the various solvents used, all the intermediate products and impurities could be simply washed away by using the appropriate reagent. Much initial work was required in setting up the right kinds of activating agents, blocking agents, and solvents. In 1964 in eight days Merrifield single-handedly synthesized bradykinin, a nine-amino-acid peptide that dilates blood vessels.

One further aspect of Merrifield's process is that it can be fully automated. To demonstrate the power and potential of his method Merrifield undertook in 1965 the automatic synthesis of insulin. With 51 amino acids and two peptide chains held together by two disulfide bridges, the molecule was a formidable challenge. Although more than 5,000 operations were involved in assembling the chains, most of these were carried out automatically in a few days. The linking of the two chains, however, was achieved by more traditional methods. The resulting insulin was active in the standard biological assay.

For his development of the technique Merrifield was awarded the 1984 Nobel Prize for chemistry.

Merrill, Paul Willard

(1887–1961)

AMERICAN ASTRONOMER

Merrill was born in Minneapolis, Minnesota, and graduated from Stanford University in 1908. He obtained his PhD in 1913 from the University of California. After teaching at the University of Michigan from 1913 to 1916 and serving briefly with the U.S. Bureau of Standards in Washington, he was appointed to the staff of the Mount Wilson Observatory in 1919, remaining there until his retirement in 1952.

It was in his retirement year that he detected the lines of technetium in the spectra of S-type stars, a class of cool red giant stars. This was surprising for the most stable isotope of technetium has a half-life of about 2.6 million years, which is much shorter than the lifetime of a star. Merrill thought it unlikely that there was an unknown stable isotope of technetium found only on S-type stars and argued rather that it was being produced within the stars by some form of nuclear reaction. The technetium lines are now accepted as strong evidence for one of the nuclear processes by which the heavy elements are thought to be created in the interiors of stars.

Mersenne, Marin

(1588–1648)

FRENCH MATHEMATICIAN, PHILOSOPHER, AND THEOLOGIAN

> Most men are glad to find work done, but few want to apply themselves to it, and many think that this search is useless or ridiculous.
> —*Les préludes de l'harmonie universelle* (1634; Prelude to Universal Harmony)

> [Mercene was] a man of simple, innocent, pure heart, without guile...a man than whom none was more painstaking, inquiring, experienced.
> —Pierre Gassendi, letter to Louis de Valois, 4 September 1648

Mersenne (mair-**sen** or mer-**sen**), who was born at Oize in France, was educated at the famous Jesuit college at La Flèche. After this he studied theology at the Sorbonne in Paris and became a Catholic priest in the Order of Minims in 1611. He spent most of the rest of his life teaching at their convent near Place Royale but he also traveled extensively in Europe.

Despite his commitment to the Catholic faith, Mersenne took a very lively interest in the rapidly developing world of the physical sciences, seeing his task as one of using the new discoveries as a means to defend Catholic orthodoxy. Probably his most important contribution to science was his role as a communication link between scientists. He kept in contact with as many eminent scientists of the day as possible, as his enormous correspondence testifies, and there were few 17th-century men of science of any importance who did not correspond with Father Mersenne. His convent at Place Royale became a regular meeting place for what were in effect conferences of leading scientists and philosophers. Among those who gathered here were Blaise Pascal, René Descartes, Pierre de Fermat, and the philosopher Thomas Hobbes.

Mersenne himself was particularly interested in problems of scientific methodology. He doubted the range and usefulness of the Euclidean axiomatic method advocated for the sciences, especially by Descartes. Mersenne was a vigorous opponent of the various forms of skepticism that were popular at the time, and was much interested in the viability of the new mechanistic world picture which the new science seemed to bring with it. Mersenne's interests extended to nonscientific aspects of philosophy and he was one of the first to try to popularize the idea of an invented universal language. His interest in science was by no means purely theoretical and he did important practical work in optics and acoustics.

Mersenne proposed, in 1644, his *Mersenne numbers*. These are numbers generated from the formula $2^p - 1$, in which p is a prime. This formula does not represent all primes but it contributed to developments in the theory of numbers.

Merton, Robert

(1910–)

AMERICAN SOCIOLOGIST

> Most institutions demand unqualified faith; but the institution of science makes skepticism a virtue.
>
> —*Social Theory and Social Structure* (1962)

Merton was educated at Temple University, in his native city of Philadelphia, and then at Harvard, where he obtained his PhD in 1935. He served as tutor at Harvard until 1939, and taught briefly at Tulane, New Orleans, before he moved to Columbia, New York, in 1941. Here he held the post of professor of sociology from 1963 until his retirement in 1979.

Merton's doctoral thesis, *Science, Technology, and Society in Seventeenth-Century England* (1938; 1970 reissue, New York), has been the subject of much discussion ever since its publication. Merton's bold thesis, since known as the *Merton hypothesis*, claimed that there were significant links during the period between puritanism and science. He also argued that much of the motivation of early science was practical and linked to such activities as navigation, mining, artillery, and metallurgy. Merton's claims were based upon a careful study of, among other things, the subject matter of articles in the Philosophical Transactions of the Royal Society (1665–1702) and an analysis of the religious leanings of members of the Society.

Merton has also undertaken a study of multiple discoveries in science. A number of discoveries in science appear to have been made independently by two or more people at almost the same time. A notable example is the theory of evolution proposed by Darwin and by Wallace in 1859. Merton has argued that these are not simple coincidences – they are not uncommon and may even be the norm. By 1961 he had analyzed some 264 cases of which 179 involved two independent discoverers and 8 involved six independent workers.

A further issue illuminated by Merton has been the social dynamics of science. It was Merton's work that demonstrated the crucial role that priority of discovery and publication played in science. He also identi-fied, as integral features, communalism, universalism, disinterestedness, and skepticism. Merton's papers in this field, written with wit, learning, and insight, have been collected in his *The Sociology of Science* (Chicago, 1979).

Merton, Sir Thomas Ralph

(1888–1969)

BRITISH PHYSICIST AND INVENTOR

Merton had an unusual scientific career. He was born in Wimbledon, near London, into a family of considerable wealth that derived from their metal-trading business. After leaving Oxford University in 1910 he moved to London and engaged in spectroscopic research in his private laboratory. He appears to have spent World War I in the Secret Service working on the development of secret inks. He returned to Oxford in 1919 and, although he later held the professorship of spectroscopy from 1923 to 1935, he obviously preferred his private laboratory, for most of his work was performed at his country residence, Winforton House, Herefordshire. From this address he produced a number of important publications on atomic spectra, which appeared until 1927. Thereafter he published nothing for a further twenty years until, in 1947, he pro-duced the first of a number of papers on his newly developed interfer-ence microscope.

Some of this time was clearly devoted to perfecting a number of in-ventions, some of which were of great value in World War II. The most important of these was his two-layer long-persistence screen for cathode-ray tubes used in radar, based on work done in 1905.

Merton built up one of the most important collections of Renais-sance paintings in private hands. Many of the important pieces from his collection now grace the National Gallery, London. He was knighted in 1944.

Meselson, Matthew Stanley

(1930–   )

AMERICAN MOLECULAR BIOLOGIST

Meselson, who was born in Denver, Colorado, studied liberal arts at the University of Chicago and physical chemistry at the California Institute of Technology, Pasadena. After he obtained his PhD in 1957 he remained at the Institute until 1960 when he moved to Harvard, where he served from 1964 as professor of biology and from 1976 as Thomas Dudley Cabot professor of natural sciences.

In 1957 Meselson, in collaboration with Franklin Stahl, conducted one of the classic experiments of molecular biology, which clearly revealed the semiconservative nature of DNA replication. It seemed likely that when the double helix of DNA duplicated, each new helix, and hence each daughter cell, would contain one DNA strand from the original helix; in the jargon of the time, replication would be semiconservative. The other possibility was that one daughter molecule would contain both the old strands and the other daughter molecule both the new strands – conservative replication.

Meselson and Stahl grew many generations of the bacterium *Escherichia coli* on a simple culture medium containing ammonium chloride (NH_4Cl), labeled with the heavy isotope of nitrogen, ^{15}N, as the only nitrogen source. They then added normal ^{14}N nitrogen to the medium and removed bacterial cells at intervals, extracting their DNA by ultracentrifugation. The density of the DNA in successive samples could be determined by the method of equilibrium density gradient centrifugation, in which samples of differing density diffuse into discrete bands corresponding to their own effective density. Ultraviolet absorption photographs of these bands allowed the concentration of DNA in each band to be determined. The results showed that (following the introduction of ^{14}N) after one doubling of the *E. coli* bacteria all the DNA molecules contained equal amounts of ^{15}N and ^{14}N, i.e., they were all half labeled. After two generations there were equal amounts of half-labeled

DNA molecules and wholly ^{14}N molecules. This effectively demonstrated that replication is semiconservative. The results were published in the Proceedings of the National Academy of Sciences U.S., as *The Replication of DNA in Escherichia coli* (1958).

Meselson has also worked with Sidney Brenner and François Jacob on the mechanism of viral infection. In 1961, working with the virus T4, they showed that on invasion of a host bacterial cell the viral DNA releases messenger RNA, which, when it arrives at the host ribosomes, instructs these to make viral protein rather than bacterial proteins.

Mesmer, Franz Anton

(1734–1815)

AUSTRIAN PHYSICIAN

Mesmer (**mez**-mer or **mes**-mer) was born at Iznang (now in Germany). He studied medicine at the University of Vienna, graduating in 1766 with a thesis, clearly indicative of his later work, on *The Influence of the Planets on the Human Body*.

Mesmer's ideas developed from Newtonian physics. The idea that bodies like the Moon and the Sun could influence such terrestrial phenomena as that of the tides was a very powerful one. For, if matter could act over seemingly empty space, then, Mesmer extrapolated, virtually any object could be used to explain the behavior of any other. The clearest statement of Mesmer's theory is contained in his account, in 1779, of the discovery of "animal magnetism." He believed that heavenly bodies, the Earth, and living things affected each other through a universally distributed fluid that could "receive, propagate, and communicate all motion."

He applied his ideas to medical treatment and, using magnets, obtained his first cure in 1774 with a distant relative who appeared to be suffering from such hysterical symptoms as vomiting, convulsions, and paralysis. Later, Mesmer dispensed with applying magnets, replacing them by a variety of devices more likely to increase the patient's amenability to suggestion. However his methods met with hostility in Vienna so he moved in 1778 to Paris, where he won the support of Marie Antoinette. Nevertheless in 1784 a royal commission was set up to investigate his procedures, which included Antoine Lavoisier, the American minister to France, Benjamin Franklin, and a certain Dr. Guillotin, whose name is now associated with the execution device whose use he advocated during the French Revolution. The report concluded dismissively that "the imagination without magnetism produces convulsions, and that magnetism without imagination produces nothing."

Consequently Mesmer, disappointed by the reception of the French savants, moved on once more. However, in 1843 "mesmerism" received the first sign of scientific recognition when James Braid wrote that he had separated "animal magnetism" from what he termed "hypnotism," a term he had deliberately introduced to replace "mesmerism."

Messel, Rudolph

(1848–1920)

GERMAN CHEMICAL INDUSTRIALIST

Messel (**mes**-el) was the son of a barber from Darmstadt in Germany. He was apprenticed to a chemical manufacturer before studying chemistry at the universities of Zurich, Heidelberg, and Tübingen. In 1870 he traveled to England, where he served initially as assistant to Henry Roscoe in Manchester.

In 1875 Messel took out a patent for a new process for the production of sulfuric acid. In the contact process developed by Peregrine Philips in the 1830s the use of a catalyst was essential, but one of the drawbacks of the process was that the expensive platinum catalyst soon became contaminated and useless. Messel showed that the contamination of the catalyst could be avoided if the sulfur dioxide used was first carefully purified. With the help of W. S. Squire, he was able to develop a satisfactory industrial version of the process at their Silvertown plant in 1876. The fuming sulfuric acid produced was in great demand by the early years of the 20th century and this demand escalated enormously in World War I.

Messier, Charles

(1730–1817)

FRENCH ASTRONOMER

The systematic listing by Messier in 1784 marked an epoch in the recording of observations.

—Harlow Shapley, *Star Clusters* (1930)

Messier (mes-**yay**), who was born in Badonviller in France, arrived in Paris in 1751 and was taken on as a clerical assistant by J. Delisle at the Naval Observatory sited in the Collège de Cluny. He quickly learned how to use the Observatory instruments and began a lifetime's obsessive search for comets. Dubbed the "comet ferret" by Louis XV, Messier is credited with the discovery of 13 comets between 1759 and 1798. The computation of the cometary orbits, however, was left to his more mathematically sophisticated colleagues.

In 1758 he observed what appeared to be a faint comet in Taurus. Further examination revealed it to be a nebula, an immense cloud of gas. Messier thought it sensible to provide a list of such objects "so that astronomers would not confuse these same nebulae with comets just beginning to shine." He published his first list of 45 nebulae in 1774 under the title *Catalogue des nebeleuses et des amas étoiles* (Catalog of Nebulae and Star Clusters). Two supplements published in 1783 and 1784 increased the number of nebulae to 103.

The nebulae listed in the catalogs were given the identifying letter M and a number; for example, the Andromeda nebula is commonly referred to as M31.

Metchnikoff, Elie

(1845–1916)

RUSSIAN–FRENCH ZOOLOGIST AND CYTOLOGIST

Thus it was in Messina that the great event of my scientific life took place. A zoologist until then, I suddenly became a pathologist.
—On his observation of phagocytes in starfish larvae

Metchnikoff (mech-ni-**kof** or **myech**-nyi-kof) was born at Ivanovka near Kharkov (now in Ukraine) and educated at Kharkov University. After holding posts under Rudolf Leuckart at Göttingen and Giessen, and under Karl Siebold at Munich, he taught zoology at Odessa and St. Petersburg. From 1873 to 1882 he was professor of zoology and comparative anatomy at Odessa.

He spent the years 1882–86 at Messina in Italy where, working on starfish larvae, he first noticed that certain nondigestive cells enclose and engulf foreign particles introduced into the body. These cells he called phagocytes and, extending his studies, he demonstrated that they also occur in man – they are the white blood corpuscles. He realized that they are important in the body's defenses against disease, in engulfing bacteria and other foreign bodies in the blood. These advances were outlined in such publications as *Intra-Cellular Digestion* (1882), *The Comparative Pathology of Inflammation* (1892), and *Immunity in Infectious Diseases* (1905). For his work on phagocytosis, Metchnikoff was awarded, in 1908, the Nobel Prize for physiology or medicine jointly with Paul Ehrlich.

In 1886 Metchnikoff was appointed director of the new bacteriological institute at Odessa; two years later he went to the Pasteur Institute in Paris, which he directed from 1895 to 1916, succeeding Pasteur himself.

In 1903 Metchnikoff, working with Emile Roux, showed that syphilis could be transferred to apes. He also did research on cholera. His later years were largely concerned with a study of the aging factors in man and means of inducing longevity, discussed in *The Nature of Man* (1904) and *The Prolongation of Human Life* (1910).

Metius, Jacobus

(1580–1628)

DUTCH INSTRUMENT MAKER

Metius (**may**-tee-u(r)s) was born at Alkmaar in the Netherlands; together with Hans Lippershey and Zacharias Janssen, he is credited with the invention of the telescope. His father was a cartographer while his brother, Adriaen, was an astronomer and mathematician who had worked with Tycho Brahe at Hven and had taught the famous mathematician and philosopher René Descartes.

Metius put in a claim for a patent for his "perspicilla" (telescope) in October 1608, but he was beaten to it by Lippershey who had put in a similar claim just two weeks earlier.

Meton

(about 432 BC)

GREEK ASTRONOMER

> Meton the son of Pausanius, who has a reputation in astronomy, set out the so-called nineteen-year period, taking the beginning from the thirteenth of Skirophorion [month in the Athenian civil calendar] at Athens.
> —Diodorus (5th century BC)

Nothing is known about the life and personality of Meton (**mee**-ton). His proposed cycle, called the *Metonic cycle*, which was not accepted by the citizens of Athens, was designed to bring the lunar month and the solar year into some form of acceptable agreement. As the lunar month is about 29½ days and the solar year is 365¼ days there is no way a whole number of months can make up a year. An early solution to the problem was the *octaeteris*, in which three intercalary (inserted) months are added to each eight-year cycle. This would lead to an error of alignment of a day and a half each eight years. Meton's suggestion was an improvement on this. He realized that 235 lunar months and 19 solar years are both 6,939 days. To bring the two cycles into phase would need 7 intercalary months spread over the 19 years of the full cycle. This would produce a solar year only 30 minutes too long. The Metonic cycle was eventually adopted by the Greeks and was used until the introduction of the Julian calendar in 46 BC. The Jewish calendar still uses it.

Meyer, Julius Lothar

(1830–1895)

GERMAN CHEMIST

Meyer (**mI**-er) was the son of a doctor from Varel in Germany. He qualified in medicine himself in 1854 after studying at Zurich and Würzburg and gained his PhD from the University of Breslau in 1858. At first his interests were physiological but he slowly moved into chemistry. He became professor of chemistry at Karlsruhe in 1868 where he stayed until he moved to the chair at Tübingen (1876–95).

Meyer is best remembered for his early work on the periodic table. He was much impressed by Stanislao Cannizzaro, expounding his work in his book *Die modernen Theorien der Chemie* (1864; Modern Chemical

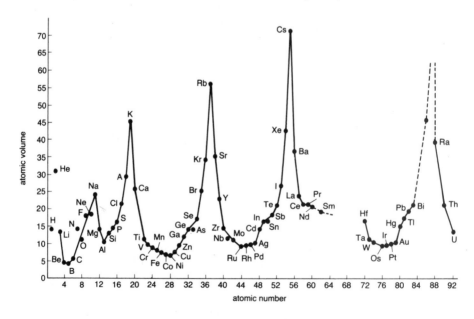

LOTHAR MEYER'S CURVES   *Curves showing the periodicity of the chemical elements.*

Theory). In writing his textbook it had occurred to him that the properties of an element seem to depend on its atomic weight. Meyer plotted the values of a certain physical property, atomic volume, against atomic weight. He found clear signs of periodicity, the graph consisting of a series of four sharp peaks. He noticed that elements with similar chemical properties occur at comparable points on the different peaks; e.g., the alkali metals all occur at the tops of the peaks.

Meyer did not publish his table until 1870 so he was preempted by Dmitri Mendeleev, who had published his periodic table in 1869. Meyer never disputed Mendeleev's priority and later stated that he lacked sufficient courage to have gone on to predict the existence of undiscovered elements.

Meyer, Karl

(1899–1990)

AMERICAN BIOCHEMIST

Meyer gained his MD from the university in his native city of Cologne in 1924 and his PhD from Berlin University in 1928. He moved to the University of California, Berkeley, in 1930, and in 1933 transferred to the College of Physicians and Surgeons at Columbia, where he has spent the rest of his career. He served as professor of biochemistry from 1954 until his retirement in 1967.

Meyer studied the acidic mucopolysaccharides found in connective tissue and isolated two of these, hyaluronic acid and chondroitin sulfate. He also discovered that various bacteria have enzymes – hyaluronidases – that can break down hyaluronic acid. It was later shown that these enzymes are the same as the "spreading factors" isolated from various sources, such as snake venom and leeches. Meyer and his colleagues found that there are three different types of chondroitin sulfate, and in 1953 he isolated a third mucopolysaccharide, keratosulfate, found in the cornea. This was later also found in cartilage. Meyer also investigated the production and distribution of mucopolysaccharides and was able to show that Marfan's syndrome, an inherited disease of connective tissue, is associated with large amounts of keratosulfate in cartilage.

Meyer, Viktor

(1848–1897)

GERMAN CHEMIST

Meyer's father was a wealthy Berlin merchant in the textile trade. He studied at the universities of Heidelberg and Berlin, receiving his PhD in 1867. He held chemistry chairs at Stuttgart (1871), Zurich (1872–85), and Göttingen (1885–89) and succeeded Robert Bunsen at Heidelberg (1889–97).

Meyer synthesized a number of organic compounds. In 1882 he discovered the compound thiophene through the failure of a color test for benzene in one of his lecture demonstrations. He had used a sample of benzene obtained from benzoic acid instead of from petroleum. He also introduced apparatus for the determination of the vapor density of organic substances. It was Meyer who prepared the way for Jacobus Van't Hoff by pointing out that isomeric methylene chlorides do not occur, i.e., two different forms of CH_2Cl_2 are never found, and he introduced the term stereoisomerism into chemistry.

Meyerhof, Otto Fritz

(1884–1951)

GERMAN–AMERICAN BIOCHEMIST

Meyerhof (**mI**-er-hof), who was born at Hannover in Germany, devoted the greater part of his academic life to the study of the biochemistry and metabolism of muscle; he shared the Nobel Prize for physiology or medicine with Archibald Hill in 1922. He held professorships at Kiel and Heidelberg universities, was director of physiology at the Kaiser Wilhelm Institute for Biology, Berlin, and was director of research at the Paris Institute of Biology. In 1940 he emigrated to America, where he joined the medical faculty of the University of Pennsylvania.

Meyerhof demonstrated that the production of lactic acid in muscle tissue, formed as a result of glycogen breakdown, was effected without the consumption of oxygen (i.e., anaerobically). The lactic acid was reconverted to glycogen through oxidation by molecular oxygen, during muscle rest. This line of research was continued by Gustav Embden and Carl and Gerty Cori who worked out in greater detail the steps by which glycogen is converted to lactic acid – the *Embden–Meyerhof pathway*.

Michaelis, Leonor

(1875–1949)

GERMAN–AMERICAN CHEMIST

Michaelis (mi-kah-**ay**-lis) was educated at the university in his native city of Berlin and at Freiburg. He worked in the laboratory of the Berlin Municipal Hospital from 1906 to 1922, when he took up the post of professor of biochemistry at the Nagoya Medical School, Japan. In 1926 Michaelis emigrated to America and after spending four years at Johns

Hopkins moved to the Rockefeller Institute of Medical Research, where he remained until his retirement in 1940.

In 1913 Michaelis, in collaboration with L. M. Menten, formulated one of the earliest precise and quantitative laws applying to biochemical systems. They were trying to picture the relation between an enzyme and its substrate (the substance it catalyzes) and, in particular, how to predict and understand the reaction rate, that is, how much substrate is acted upon by an enzyme per unit time, and the basic factors that stimulate or inhibit this rate. The kind of graph obtained when reaction rate is plotted against substrate concentration showed that additional substrate concentration sharply increases the reaction rate until a certain point is reached when the rate appears to become completely indifferent to the addition of any further amounts of substrate.

Michaelis saw this as indicating that the reaction between enzyme and substrate is a very specific one. In the early phase of the curve there was enzyme lacking substrate; as this was increased more and more enzyme came into play, increasing the reaction rate. Eventually, however, there will come a point when all the enzyme is being used and from that point the addition of any amount of substrate can have no effect on the reaction rate. This variation in rate was subsequently described by the *Michaelis–Menten equation.*

Michaelis's insight into the working of the enzyme–substrate complex was quite remarkable as no hard evidence for its existence was to emerge for a good many years, not in fact until Britton Chance was able to produce spectroscopic evidence in 1949.

Michel, Hartmut

(1948–   )

GERMAN CHEMIST

Michel (mik-el) was born at Lüdwigsburg in Germany and educated at the University of Warburg, where he obtained his PhD in 1977. He moved to the Max Planck Institute for Biochemistry at Martinsried, near Munich, and remained there until 1987, when he moved to Frankfurt to head the biophysics division.

By 1970 chemists had succeeded in uncovering the basic chemistry of photosynthesis but little was known about the process at the molecular level. It was established that the process occurred in the photosynthetic reaction centers first identified by Roderick Clayton in the late 1960s. These are to be found embedded in the membranes of the photosynthetic vesicles. Within the reaction centers was a complex protein structure. Before further progress could be made, the structure of the proteins would have to be worked out, but first it would be necessary to crystallize the proteins.

Michel first tackled the problem in 1978. While it was relatively easy to crystallize water-soluble proteins, membrane proteins, which react with both fats and water, were only partially soluble in water. Michel used a molecule in which one end was attracted to water (hydrophilic) while the opposite end was water repellent (hydrophobic). By binding the hydrophobic ends of the organic molecules to the hydrophobic ends of the protein membranes the hydrophilic ends alone would lie exposed. The complex structure could then be dissolved in water and crystallized. By 1982 Michel had succeeded in crystallizing the membrane proteins of the bacterium *Rhodopseudomonas viridis*.

For this work Michel shared the 1988 Nobel Prize for chemistry with Johann Diesenhofer and Robert Huber.

Michell, John

(1724–1793)

ENGLISH GEOLOGIST AND ASTRONOMER

Michell studied at Cambridge University and became a fellow. In 1762 he was appointed Woodward Professor of Geology but left academic life to take up a post as rector at Thornhill, Yorkshire, in 1764.

Before his departure from Cambridge he published, in 1760, a fundamental paper, *Conjectures Concerning the Cause, and Observations upon the Phenomena of Earthquakes*. After the great Lisbon earthquake (1755) this was a fashionable subject. Michell assigned the cause of earthquakes to the force generated by high-pressure steam, produced when water suddenly met subterranean fires. He appreciated that such a force would generate waves in the Earth's crust and tried to estimate the velocity of these, giving a not unreasonable figure of 1,200 miles per hour. Finally, Michell showed various means to determine the point of origin of the earthquake.

In 1790 he constructed a torsion balance to measure gravitational attraction and thus the mean density of the Earth. Michell was unable to use this before his death, but Henry Cavendish carried on his work, deriving a value for the density of the Earth in 1798.

Michell also made contributions to astronomy. In 1767 he published a paper on double stars, pointing out with originality and insight that there are far too many of them to result from a random scattering and therefore they must in many cases constitute a genuine binary system. He also devised a method for calculating the distance of the stars.

Michelson, Albert Abraham

(1852–1931)

AMERICAN PHYSICIST

Physical discoveries in the future are a matter of the sixth decimal place.
— Quoted by A. L. Mackay in *A Dictionary of Scientific Quotations* (1991)

Michelson, who was born at Strelno (now Strzelno in Poland), came to America with his parents when he was two years old. He graduated from the U.S. Naval Academy in 1873 and remained there to teach physics and chemistry. Some five years later he began his work on measuring the speed of light and to this end he traveled to Europe to study optics at the Collège de France, Heidelberg, and Berlin. When he returned to America he left the navy to become professor of physics at the Case School, Cleveland. In 1882 he estimated the speed of light as 186,320 miles per second. This was the most accurate value then available and remained so for another ten years, when Michelson made an even more accurate measurement.

In the course of this work Michelson developed an interferometer, an instrument that can divide a beam of light in two, send the beams in different directions, and then unite them again. If the two beams traveled the same distance at different speeds (or different distances at the same speed) then, on being brought together again, the waves would be out of step and produce interference fringes on a screen. Michelson used the interferometer to test whether light traveling in the same direction as the Earth moves more slowly than light traveling at right angles to this direction. This was effectively testing the presence of the "ether" – a substance that was supposed to exist in all space. Because the ether was thought to be motionless and the Earth moved through it, then it followed that light traveling in the same direction as the Earth would be impeded.

Michelson first conducted this experiment in 1881 in Berlin and got a negative result, that is, there were no interference fringes and thus no evidence that the two beams were traveling at different speeds. He repeated the procedure several times under increasingly elaborate conditions until, in 1887, with Edward Morley, the experiment was made under near perfect conditions at the Case School. Again the ether could not be detected. This result questioned much orthodox physical theory, and it remained for Einstein to develop the special theory of relativity to explain the constancy of the speed of light. Michelson was awarded the 1907 Nobel Prize in physics for this work.

Michelson also applied interference techniques to astronomical measurements and was able to measure the diameters of various heavenly bodies by contrasting the light emitted from both sides. He also continued to make increasingly more accurate estimates of the speed of light and he suggested that the wavelength of light waves should be used as the length standard rather than the platinum–iridium meter in Paris. This suggestion was taken up in 1960 when light waves from the inert gas krypton became the standard measure.

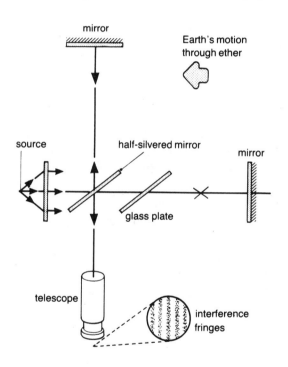

MICHELSON–MORLEY EXPERIMENT   The rays of light are split and recombined in the telescope to give fringes. The system was mounted on a large bed of stone, which could be rotated through 90°. It was shown that this rotation did not affect the position of the fringes. Michelson and Morley did this experiment a large number of times at different times of the day and night and at different times of the year. On no occasion could they detect any effect.

Midgley, Thomas Jr.

(1889–1944)

AMERICAN CHEMIST

Midgley's father was an inventor and held several patents in wire drawing and for various types of rubber tire. Midgley was born in Beaver Falls, Pennsylvania, and educated at Cornell, graduating in mechanical engineering in 1911. In 1916 he joined the research staff of the Dayton (Ohio) Engineering Laboratories Company.

The first problem Midgley tackled was the sometimes quite violent engine knock produced by the fuel of his day. He began work on this in 1917, shortly after the company had been taken over by General Motors. Midgley was able to show that engine knock was a property of the fuel used and realized that the solution lay in finding an additive to eliminate the knock. Midgley's first breakthrough came when he argued (wrongly) that a dye added to the fuel would allow it to absorb more radiant heat and vaporize sooner. As the only oil-soluble dye available was iodine he tried this and found that it worked. A few simple tests showed that it was the iodine and not the color that was crucial, and Midgley began a long struggle to find a cheaper additive. From his studies of chemistry Midgley was led to tetraethyl lead (1921), which continues to be unsurpassed as an antiknock fuel additive, although it is now banned in many places as an environmental hazard.

The second problem Midgley attempted to resolve for General Motors was to find a nonflammable, cheap, and nontoxic refrigerant gas (several customers having already been poisoned by sulfur dioxide used in refrigerators). Midgley experimented with the fluorides and discovered dichlorodifluoromethane, now commonly known as freon. Within a few years this became the almost universal refrigerant.

In 1940 Midgley contracted polio, from which he died.

Miescher, Johann Friedrich

(1844–1895)

SWISS BIOCHEMIST

Miescher (**mee**-sher) came from a distinguished scientific family from Basel in Switzerland: both his father, also called Johann Friedrich, and his uncle, Wilhelm His, held the chair of anatomy at the University of Basel. Miescher himself studied medicine at Basel but, feeling that his partial deafness (produced by a severe attack of typhus) would be a drawback for a physician, turned to physiological chemistry. He consequently spent the period from 1868 to 1870 learning organic chemistry under Felix Hoppe-Seyler at Tübingen and physiology at Leipzig in the laboratory of Carl Ludwig. In 1871 he was appointed professor of physiology at Basel.

It was while working on pus cells at Tübingen in 1869 that Miescher made his fundamental discovery. It was thought that such cells were made largely of protein, but Miescher noted the presence of something that "cannot belong among any of the protein substances known hitherto." In fact he was able to show that it was not protein at all, being unaffected by the protein-digesting enzyme pepsin. He also showed that the new substance was derived from the nucleus of the cell alone and consequently named it "nuclein." Miescher was soon able to show that nuclein could be obtained from many other cells and was unusual in containing phosphorus in addition to the usual ingredients of organic molecules – carbon, oxygen, nitrogen, and hydrogen. It was not until 1871 that Miescher's paper, delayed by Hoppe-Seyler (who wanted to confirm the results), was published. In it he announced the presence of a nonprotein phosphorus-containing molecule in the nuclei of a large number of cells.

Just what precise role the molecule played in the cell was not revealed until the structure of nucleic acid, as it was renamed by Richard Altmann in 1889, was announced by James Watson and Francis Crick in 1953. Miescher continued to work on the nuclein extracted from the sperm of the Rhine salmon for the rest of his short life. He spent much time puzzling on the chemistry of fertilization, even speculating in 1874 that "if one wants to assume that a single substance...is the specific cause of fertilization then one should undoubtedly first of all think of nuclein." Unfortunately Miescher failed to follow up his suggestion, preferring to explore physical models of fertilization. However, his work on nuclein was eagerly taken up by other organic chemists, and by 1893 Albrecht Kossel had succeeded in recognizing four nucleic acid bases.

Milankovich, Milutin

(1879–1958)

CROATIAN MATHEMATICIAN

Milankovich (mi-**lan**-ko-vich), who was born at Dalj in Croatia, was educated at the Institute of Technology in Vienna, where he obtained his PhD in 1904. He then moved to the University of Belgrade, remaining there for the rest of his career except for the period 1914–18, during which he was a prisoner of war, but was allowed to pursue his researches in the library of the Hungarian Academy of Science in Budapest.

Milankovich was the most talented of the scientists who worked in the tradition of James Croll in trying to explain the development of the Earth's climate by reference to astronomical events. From 1911 to 1941, when he published his *Canon of Insolation and the Ice Age Problem*, he tried obsessively, in numerous works, to reconstruct the past climate of the Earth and the planets.

Milankovich realized that the key to past climates was the amount of solar radiation received by the Earth, which varies at different latitudes and depends upon three basic factors. One is the degree of ellipticity of the Earth's orbit, which varies over 100,000 years from being nearly circular to a noticeable ellipticity and which could reduce the amount of insolation by 30%. Secondly, over about 21,000 years a precessional change occurs, which will determine whether the northern or the southern hemisphere receives the most radiation. Finally, the tilt of the Earth's axis to the plane of its orbit changes over about 40,000 years from 21.8° to 24.4°.

Over a period of 30 years Milankovich constructed radiation curves for the last 650,000 years for the summer northern hemisphere from 5°N to 75°N. At first his results looked most impressive for he identified nine climatic minima, which fitted closely the four ice ages identified by Albrecht Penck. However, with the advent of more precise and accurate dating techniques his results are now considered doubtful.

Miller, Dayton Clarence

(1866–1941)

AMERICAN PHYSICIST

Born in Strongsville, Ohio, Miller obtained his PhD from Princeton in 1890. He was later appointed to the chair of physics at the Case School of Applied Science, Cleveland, Ohio.

It was at the Case School that the famous experiment to detect the presence of the ether was performed in 1887 by Albert Michelson and Edward Morley. The existence of an ether would produce different values for the speed of light in different directions. Miller was dissatisfied with the negative result of the experiment and he repeated the experiment with Morley under varying conditions over the period 1897–1908 without coming up with anything conclusive. Morley lost interest but Miller was as determined as he was suspicious.

In 1925 he took his equipment to the 6,000-foot (1,830-m) peak of Mount Wilson in California. At last he thought he had detected a difference of 6 miles per second for light traveling at right angles to the Earth's orbit. Confident of his result he cabled Albert Einstein on Christmas Day 1925, announcing the discovery of ether drift. Einstein suspected, rightly as it turned out, that Miller's results were due to different temperature conditions.

Miller, Hugh

(1802–1856)

BRITISH GEOLOGIST

Almost every fragment of clay, every splinter of sandstone, every limestone nodule contained its organism – scales, spines, plates, bones, entire fish...were I to sum up all my happier hours, the hour would not be forgotten in which I sat down on a rounded boulder of granite by the edge of the sea and spread out on the beach before me the spoils of the morning.
—On his first discovery of fossil fishes in the Old Red Sandstone

Miller was born in Cromarty, northern Scotland, and during his early life apprenticed himself to a stonemason, becoming a journeyman in 1819. The pursuit of his trade led him to travel widely in Scotland and he acquired an unrivaled knowledge of its detailed geology. He also began to write poetry on the political issues of the day. After a period as a bank accountant he was offered the editorship of the newly formed influential Scottish paper, *The Witness*, and became a key figure in the political and theological disputes that led to the 1843 split in the Church of Scotland.

His main geological work was originally published in his newspaper and collected in book form as *The Old Red Sandstone* (1841), which went through 20 editions before 1900. In this he described the fossils he had found in Devonian strata and, as in his later work *Footsteps of the Creator* (1847), he opposed the view that the record of the rocks provided evidence for the evolution of species.

Miller succeeded in showing that the Old Red Sandstone was relatively rich in fossils, particularly fossil fish. He used the evidence provided by the fossil fish to pose a problem to those, such as Robert Chambers and later Charles Darwin, who wished to think in such terms as the progress, development, or evolution of species. He argued that "if fish could have risen into reptiles, and reptiles into mammalia, we would necessarily expect to find lower orders of fish passing into higher." Miller claimed that in the Old Red Sandstone it is the fish of the higher orders that appear first, thus there was no room for progression.

Miller, Jacques Francis Albert Pierre

(1931–   )

FRENCH–AUSTRALIAN IMMUNOLOGIST

Miller, who was born at Nice in the south of France, was educated at the University of Sydney, Australia, and at University College, London, where he obtained his PhD in 1960. He then held brief appointments at the Chester Beatty Research Institute in London and the National Cancer Institute in Bethesda, Maryland. Miller returned to Australia in 1966 to serve as head of the experimental pathology department at the Hall Institute of Medical Research, Melbourne.

In 1961 Miller succeeded in solving an ancient medical mystery. The thymus gland is a large organ placed in the chest beneath the breastbone. Surprisingly, until 1961 scientists lacked any clear idea of the role played by such a prominent body. The normal technique in such a situation is to watch for any changes in the behavior of the subject when the organ has been removed. In this case thymectomy seemed to make no discernible difference to the behavior of any experimental animal.

Working within this tradition Miller performed a surgical operation of great skill, the removal of the thymus from one-day-old mice. As the mice weigh no more than a gram and are no bigger than an inch it is not difficult to see why such an operation had been little attempted before. In this case, however, the excision did lead to dramatic and obvious changes. The mice failed to develop properly and usually died within two to three months of the operation. Just what was wrong with them became clear when Miller went on to test their ability to reject skin grafts, a sure sign of a healthy immune system. Miller's mice could tolerate grafts from unrelated mice and sometimes even from rats. This made it quite clear that the thymus was deeply involved in the body's immune system but just what precise role it played was to occupy immunologists for a decade or more.

Much of Miller's work was performed independently, also in 1961, by a team under the direction of Robert Good at Minnesota.

Miller, Stanley Lloyd

(1930–   )

AMERICAN CHEMIST

Born at Oakland in California, Miller was educated at the universities of California and Chicago where, in 1954, he was awarded his PhD. Since 1960 he has taught at the University of California, San Diego, being appointed to a professorship in chemistry in 1968.

In 1953 Miller published a famous paper, *A Production of Amino Acids under Possible Primitive Earth Conditions*, in which he reported the results of an experiment carried out while still a graduate student at Chicago under the direction of Harold Urey.

It was thought that the early atmosphere of the Earth could well have been something like that now existing on Jupiter and Saturn, namely one rich in methane (CH_4) and ammonia (NH_3). Miller mixed water vapor with ammonia, methane, and hydrogen in a closed flask and subjected it to a high-voltage electrical discharge. Sensitive analysis with paper chromatography produced a number of organic molecules. In addition to hydrocyanic acid, formic acid, acetic acid, lactic acid, and urea were two of the simpler amino acids, alanine and glycine.

As it is from the amino acids that the proteins are constructed many scholars saw this as clear evidence for the spontaneous origin of life. It has however been shown that such random processes could not yet have produced a single protein without the assumption of additional operating principles. Such principles have been suggested by Manfred Eigen and Sol Spiegelman.

Millikan, Robert Andrews

(1868–1953)

AMERICAN PHYSICIST

The son of a Congregational minister from Morrison, Illinois, Millikan was educated at Oberlin, where he studied classics, and Columbia University, where he obtained his PhD in 1895. After a year in Europe, studying under Max Planck and Walther Nernst, he took up an appointment in 1896 at the University of Chicago, being promoted to a full professorship in 1910. Millikan moved to the California Institute of Technology in 1921 as director of the Norman Bridge Laboratory, a position he held until his retirement in 1945.

In 1909 Millikan started on a project that was to win for him the 1923 Nobel Prize for physics – the determination of the electric charge of the electron. His apparatus consisted of two horizontal plates that could be made to take opposite charges. Between the plates he introduced a fine spray of oil drops whose mass could be determined by measuring their fall under the influence of gravity and against the resistance of the air. When the air was ionized by x-rays and the plates charged, then an oil drop that had collected a charge would be either repelled from or attracted to the plates depending on whether it had collected a positive or negative charge. By measuring the change in the rate of fall and knowing the intensity of the electric field Millikan was able to calculate the charges on the oil drops. After taking many careful measurements he was able to come to the important conclusion that the charge was always a simple multiple of the same basic unit, which he found to be $4.774 \pm 0.009 \times 10^{-10}$ electrostatic units, a figure whose accuracy was not improved until 1928. Millikan followed this with a prolonged attempt from 1912 to 1916 to demonstrate the validity of the formula introduced by Albert Einstein in 1905 to describe the photoelectric effect, work that was cited in Einstein's Nobel award.

In 1923 he began a major study of cosmic rays, first identified in 1912 by Victor Hess, which was to occupy him for the rest of his career.

His first aim was to show that they did not originate in our atmosphere. To do this, he devised an ingenious set of observations made at two lakes in the San Bernadino mountains of southern California. The lakes were many miles apart and differed by 6,700 feet (2,042 m) in altitude. The difference in altitude would have the same effect on intensity of cosmic rays as six feet of water. He found that the intensity of ionization produced by the incoming cosmic rays in the lower lake was the same as the intensity six feet deeper in the higher lake. This showed, he claimed, that the rays do come in definitely from above and that their origin is entirely outside the layer of atmosphere between the levels of the two lakes.

Millikan then went on to theorize about the nature of the cosmic rays. He argued that they were electromagnetic radiation photons, for if they were charged particles they would be influenced by the Earth's magnetic field and therefore more likely to arrive in higher rather than lower latitudes. Millikan had failed to detect any such effect with latitude. In fact Millikan's theories were soon disproved for Arthur Compton did detect a latitude effect.

Mills, Bernard Yarnton

(1920–   )

AUSTRALIAN PHYSICIST AND
RADIO ASTRONOMER

Mills was born at Manly in New South Wales, Australia. After graduating from the University of Sydney in 1940, he joined the staff of the Commonwealth Scientific and Industrial Research Organization, CSIRO, where he worked initially on the development of radio astronomy. In 1960 he joined the staff of the University of Sydney to form a radio-astronomy group; he subsequently served as professor of physics there from 1965 to 1985.

Mills is best known for his design of a radio interferometer, known as the *Mills cross* radio telescope. In 1954 he completed the construction of the first Mills cross at Fleurs, near Sydney. It consists of two fixed inter-secting arrays of dipole antennas running along the ground in an east–west and north–south direction for 1,500 feet (457.2 m). It was with this system that the first radio survey of the southern hemisphere, the MSH, was performed; some 2,000 sources at a wavelength of 11.43 feet (3.5 m) were examined and the results published from 1958 to 1961.

When plans to build an optical telescope at Sydney University fell through, Mills was offered the accumulated funds of 200,000 Australian dollars to construct a "super" cross. The instrument has arms 1 mile long along which cylindrical parabolic reflectors are fixed in position. It is sited at the Molonglo Radio Observatory near Hoskinstown, New South Wales, and was completed in 1960.

Mills, William Hobson

(1873–1959)

BRITISH CHEMIST

Mills, the son of a London architect, was educated at Cambridge University, England, and at Tübingen University in Germany. After serving as head of chemistry at the Northern Polytechnic, London (1902–12), Mills returned to Cambridge where he served as reader in stereochemistry from 1931 until his retirement in 1938.

In 1925 Mills, in collaboration with E. Warren, confirmed the hypothesis of Alfred Werner concerning the tetrahedral configuration of the ammonium ion. During World War I, he also worked on problems of photography. The then-existing emulsions were sensitive only to the blue and violet part of the spectrum; the military, however, were keen to photograph any changes in the German trench system in the red light of dawn. Working with William Pope, Mills succeeded in remedying the deficiency with the development of the cyanine dyes.

Milne, Edward Arthur

(1896–1950)

BRITISH MATHEMATICIAN AND
ASTROPHYSICIST

Milne, the son of a headmaster from Hull in eastern England, studied at Cambridge University (1914–16). He returned there in 1919 after working on ballistics during World War I and was appointed as assistant director of the Cambridge Solar Physics Observatory in 1920. He lectured in both mathematics and astrophysics. In 1924 he became professor of applied mathematics at the University of Manchester where he remained until 1928. In 1929 Milne was appointed professor of mathematics at Oxford, a post he held, apart from a period working for the Ordnance Board (1939–44), until his death in 1950.

Milne's wartime work had involved studies of the Earth's atmosphere. From 1920 he extended this to theoretical research on the atmospheres of stars, concentrating on the flow of radiation through these outermost layers of stars and on the ionization of the component atoms. In collaboration with Ralph Fowler, Milne used the ionization theory of Meghnad Saha to determine and fix the temperature scale for the known sequence of stellar spectra. Thus just by knowing that a star falls into spectral type G permitted its temperature (5,000–6,000 kelvin) to be inferred.

Following three years' research into stellar structure Milne turned in 1932 to the development of his theory of "kinematic relativity." This was an alternative to Einstein's theory of general relativity and contained a new cosmological model of the universe from which he evolved new systems of dynamics and electrodynamics. It was Milne who introduced the "cosmological principle" that simply states that the universe appears essentially the same from wherever it is observed. This is still the basis of much of modern cosmology and became for Milne one of the axioms of an axiomatic cosmology that he hoped to construct in a purely deductive way. "Starting from first principles (like Descartes)" his aim was to "pursue a single path towards the understanding of this unique entity the universe; and it will be a test of the correctness of our path that we should find at no point any bifurcation of possibility. Our path should nowhere provide any alternatives." However, Milne did find alternative universes littering his path and in each case he behaved as Descartes had done before him and selected that alternative he favored as being the only one compatible with the rationality of the Creator.

Milne's world model, which is now seen as a misguided curiosity, led nowhere. But for his early death he might well have developed it and brought it more into line with orthodox cosmology.

Milne, John

(1850–1913)

BRITISH SEISMOLOGIST

Milne, who was born at Liverpool in England, was educated at King's College, London, and at the Royal School of Mines. After fieldwork in Newfoundland and Labrador (1872–74) he was appointed, in 1875, professor of geology and mining at the Imperial College of Engineering, Tokyo.

Milne developed a passion for seismology and became known as "Earthquake Milne" in Tokyo. He was instrumental in forming the Seismological Society of Japan in 1880. His first priority was to organize the recording, collecting, and distribution of data. He asked the postal authority in each town throughout Japan to return to him a weekly record of the numbers of earthquakes experienced and he also set up over 900 stations for more detailed recording of seismic activity. Milne also invented, in 1880, a seismograph and he spent much time devising simple and hardy seismographs, which could be used by the relatively unskilled in a wide variety of conditions.

Milne returned to England in 1894 and made his home at Shide, on the Isle of Wight. This became the center of an international system for the collection and distribution of seismological data. His publications included *Earthquakes* (1883) and *Seismology* (1898).

Milstein, César

(1927–)

BRITISH MOLECULAR BIOLOGIST

Milstein was born at Bahia Blanca in Argentina and attended the University of Buenos Aires, receiving his degree in 1952 and his doctorate in 1957. Three years later he was granted a PhD by Cambridge University. Milstein returned to his native Argentina in 1961 to head the Molecular Biology Division of the Instituto Nacional de Microbiologiá in Buenos Aires. In 1963 he joined the staff of the Medical Research Council's Laboratory of Molecular Biology in Cambridge and in 1983 he was appointed head of the Division of Protein and Nucleic Acid Chemistry, a post in which he remained until his retirement in 1994.

Milstein is best known for producing the first monoclonal antibodies, using a technique developed at the MRC's Laboratory in collaboration with the German immunologist, George Köhler, and first reported by them in 1975. The pair went on to show how it was possible to manufacture quantities of antibody of any desired specificity employing cultures of so-called "hybridoma" cells. Monoclonal antibodies have found wide-ranging application in biology, medicine, and industry, especially for diagnostic tests and assays. For his part in developing this revolutionary technology, Milstein was awarded the 1984 Nobel Prize for physiology or medicine, which he shared with Köhler and Niels Jerne.

Minkowski, Hermann

(1864–1909)

RUSSIAN–GERMAN MATHEMATICIAN

> The views of space and time which I wish to lay before you have sprung from the soil of experimental physics, and therein lies their strength. They are radical. Henceforth space by itself, and time by itself, are doomed to fade away into mere shadows, and only a kind of union of the two will preserve an independent reality.
> —Quoted by L. D. Henderson in *The Fourth Dimension and Non-Euclidean Geometry in Modern Art* (1983)

Minkowski (ming-**kof**-skee) was born at Alexotas in Russia to parents of German origin. In 1872 the family returned to Germany, settling in Königsberg (now Kaliningrad). Minkowski studied alongside David Hilbert at the University of Königsberg, under Adolf Hurwitz, and gained his PhD in 1885. He taught at Bonn (1885–94) and Königsberg (1894–96) and then worked with Hurwitz at the Zurich Federal Institute of Technology (1896–1902). At Hilbert's instigation a new chair of mathematics was created for Minkowski at the University of Göttingen and he worked there (1902–09) until his death.

In 1883, when still 18, Minkowski was awarded the Grand Prix des Sciences Mathématiques of the Paris Academy of Sciences. The award was shared with Henry J. Smith for their work on the theory of quadratic forms. Minkowski remained occupied with the arithmetic of quadratic forms for the rest of his life. In 1896 he gave a detailed account of his "geometry of numbers" in which he developed geometrical methods for the treatment of certain problems in number theory.

During his short period at Göttingen Minkowski worked closely with David Hilbert and decisively influenced Hilbert's interest in mathematical physics. Minkowski's most celebrated work was in developing the mathematics that played a crucial role in Einstein's formulation of the theory of relativity. Einstein knew when he published the special theory of relativity in 1905 that the universe could not be adequately described using normal, or Euclidean, three-dimensional geometry. Minkowski's seminal idea was to view space and time as forming together a single four-dimensional continuum or manifold, known as "space–time," rather than two distinct entities. In normal three-dimensional geometry, any point in space can be identified by three coordinates. The analog of this point in three-dimensional space is an event localized both in space and time in four-dimensional space–time.

Minkowski put forward his concept of space–time, or *Minkowski space* as it is sometimes called, in 1907 in his book *Space and Time*. Einstein himself was very forthright about the extent to which the theory of relativity depended on Minkowski's innovatory work. Space–time was a useful and elegant format for special relativity, and was essential for general relativity, published in 1916, in which space–time is allowed to be curved. It is the curvature of space–time that accounts for the phenomenon of gravitation.

Minkowski, Rudolph Leo

(1895–1976)

GERMAN–AMERICAN ASTRONOMER

Minkowski was born at Strasbourg (now in France) and educated at the University of Breslau (now Wrocław in Poland), where he obtained his PhD in 1921. He taught at Hamburg University until 1935, when he emigrated to America and took up an appointment at the Mount Wilson Observatory. In 1960 he moved to the University of California at Berkeley where he remained until his retirement in 1965.

In 1951 Minkowski, in collaboration with Walter Baade, made the first identification of a discrete radio source, Cygnus A. It seemed to be one of the brightest objects in the radio sky and possessed a peculiar spectrum. It also turned out to be an extremely distant object, as determined from the red shift of its spectral lines. It must therefore have an immense output of radio energy. Minkowski allowed himself to be converted to Baade's view that Cygnus A was a pair of colliding galaxies. The fact that its radio map revealed two nuclei seemed to confirm this. Minkowski and Baade made many other optical identifications of radio sources, including 3C 295, which possesses the same distinctive shape and unusual emission lines of Cygnus A.

Failure to detect evidence of the appropriate relative galactic motion, which should be apparent if Cygnus A were two colliding galaxies, has led to the rejection of this idea.

Minot, George Richards

(1885–1950)

AMERICAN PHYSICIAN

The son of a physician from Boston, Massachusetts, Minot was educated at Harvard, where he obtained his MD in 1912. After working briefly at Johns Hopkins University he moved back to Harvard in 1915 and served as professor of medicine from 1928 until his retirement in 1948.

In 1926, with his assistant William Murphy, Minot discovered a cure for pernicious anemia. This was based on earlier work by George Whipple showing that red-cell production could be increased in dogs by adding liver to their diets. In 1924 Minot began feeding some of his patients with small amounts of liver. He was soon able to report that most of their symptoms disappeared within a week and that within 60 days their red cell counts were back to normal. As pernicious anemia was invariably fatal at that time the new therapy was life saving.

It was not until 1948 that the vital ingredient in liver, vitamin B_{12}, was actually isolated and purified. For their worl on liver therapy, Minot, Whipple, and Murphy shared the 1934 Nobel Prize for physiology or medicine.

Minsky, Marvin Lee

(1927–   )

AMERICAN COMPUTER SCIENTIST

> Logic doesn't apply to the real world.
> —Quoted by D. R. Hofstadter and D. C. Dennet in *The Mind's I*

The son of a surgeon, Minsky was born in New York and educated at Harvard and at Princeton, where he obtained his PhD in 1954. He taught at Harvard before moving to the Massachusetts Institute of Technology

(MIT) in 1957 as professor of mathematics, a post he occupied until 1962 when he became professor of electrical engineering. He also served as director of the Artificial Intelligence (AI) Laboratory (1964–73).

In the summer of 1956 Minsky attended a conference on AI at Dartmouth, New Hampshire. Here, it was generally agreed that powerful modern computers would soon be able to simulate all aspects of human learning and intelligence. Much of Minsky's later career has been spent testing this claim.

Under Minsky's direction a number of AI programs have been developed at MIT. One of the earliest, a program to solve problems in calculus, showed that most problems could be solved by a careful application of about 100 rules. The computer actually received a grade A in an MIT calculus exam. Other programs developed such topics as reasoning by analogy, handling information expressed in English, and how to catch a bouncing ball with a robotic arm.

But Minsky soon became aware that AI had a number of problems to overcome. For example, in one project a computer with a robotic arm and a TV camera was programmed to copy an assembly of bricks. Although it could quickly recognize the bricks and their relationships to each other, it found the stacking more difficult. It tried to stack the blocks from the top down, releasing brick after brick in midair. Computers simply do not have an innate knowledge of gravity or, he has pointed out, many other things we take for granted, such as that chairs painted a different color remain the same chair, or that boxes must be opened before things can be put inside.

He also noted problems with "perceptrons," designed by Frank Rosenblatt in 1960 with the supposed ability to respond to and recognize certain patterns with the aid of an array of 400 photocells. In collaboration with Seymour Papert, Minsky published a critical account of this work in *Perceptrons* (1968) showing, in purely formal terms, that the powers of perceptrons were strictly limited. They could not, for example, be relied upon to tell when a figure was connected. A cat's tail protruding from a chair would prevent the perceptron from identifying either the cat or the chair.

In 1974 Minsky introduced the notion of "frames." A frame is a package of knowledge stored in the mind, which allows us to understand many things about a certain topic. For example, the "dog frame" includes what dogs look like, the sorts of things they do, and many other aspects of their nature and behavior. Because we possess numerous such frames we are able to communicate about the world without too much confusion, and to distinguish routinely between the "bark" of a tree and the "bark" of a dog. Only when a computer could be stocked with an enormous number of "frames," some interlocking, others slotted hierarchically in other frames, could it begin to show signs of intelligence.

While speculating about developments in the 1990s Minsky has referred to "societies of the mind." A computer capable of recognizing shadows would be unable to process perspective or parallax. Yet, the untutored human mind can normally handle all three. The aim should therefore be to write a program "that allows each expert system to exploit the body of knowledge that lies buried in the others." It remains to be seen whether Minsky's "society" can be realized.

Misner, Charles William

(1932–)

AMERICAN ASTRONOMER

> Space acts on matter, telling it how to move. In turn, matter reacts back on space telling it how to curve.
>
> —*Gravitation* (1973)

Born in Jackson, Michigan, Misner was educated at Notre Dame University, Indiana, and at Princeton, where he obtained his PhD in 1957. He remained at Princeton until 1963 when he moved to the University of Maryland, College Park, becoming professor of physics in 1966.

In 1969 Misner posed what is known as the "horizon paradox." The universe on a large scale appears to be remarkably homogenous and isotropic, in particular with respect to the cosmic microwave background radiation discovered in 1965. How, given the initial conditions of the big bang, could such uniformity have arisen?

The problem is that no physical process can take place over distances at a speed faster than the speed of light. Consequently there must be, at any particular time, a distance (the "horizon distance") beyond which light or any other process could not have spread since the moment of the big bang itself. Calculations show that sources of the cosmic background radiation would have been separated by 90 times the horizon distance when emitted. How then, Misner asked, could the universe have reached a state of equilibrium and appear so uniform? The standard big-bang model merely assumed the uniformity of the universe as an initial condition.

For a time Misner sought to develop one of the so-called "mixmaster models" in which it was assumed that the universe began in an inhomogenous and anisotropic state and became uniform through the interplay of frictional forces as the universe expanded. This, however, merely trades one set of assumptions for another. A more favored response to the horizon paradox has been presented by the idea of an inflationary model of the big bang proposed in 1980 by Guth.

Misner is also well known as coauthor with Kip Thorne and John Wheeler of *Gravitation* (1973), one of the seminal textbooks of modern cosmology.

Mitchell, Maria

(1818–1889)

AMERICAN ASTRONOMER

Mitchell was born in Nantucket, Massachusetts, the daughter of William Mitchell, who started life as a cooper and became a school teacher and amateur astronomer of some distinction. Her brother, Henry Mitchell, became the leading American hydrographer. She herself was mainly educated by her father, whom she helped in the checking of chronometers for the local whaling fleet and in determining the longitude of Nantucket during the 1831 eclipse. From 1824 to 1842 she worked as librarian at the Nantucket Athenum and in 1849 she became the first woman to be employed full time by the U.S. Nautical Almanac, with whom she computed the ephemerides of Venus. Finally, in 1865 she was appointed professor of astronomy and director of the observatory at the newly founded Vassar College.

Maria Mitchell was clearly fortunate to come from a highly talented family. She was also helped by coming from Nantucket, an area where women were expected to demonstrate an unusual degree of independence while the local men were absent on their long whaling voyages. It was also an area where it was common for the average person to possess a familiarity with mathematics, astronomy, and navigation. She is mainly remembered today for her discovery, in 1847, of a new comet.

Mitchell, Peter Dennis

(1920–1992)

BRITISH BIOCHEMIST

Born at Mitcham in Surrey, England, Mitchell was educated at Cambridge University, where he obtained his PhD in 1950. He remained at Cambridge, teaching in the department of biochemistry, until 1955 when he moved to Edinburgh University as director of the Chemical Biology Unit. In 1964 Mitchell made the unusual decision to set up his own private research institution, the Glynn Research Laboratory, in Bodmin, Cornwall.

It was well known that the cell obtains its energy from the adenosine triphosphate (ATP) molecule; it was also clear that ATP was made by coupling adenosine diphosphate (ADP) to an inorganic phosphate group by the process known to biochemists as oxidative phosphorylation. What was less clear was just how this happened and it was widely assumed that it was controlled by a number of enzymes. Despite considerable effort the proposed enzymes remained surprisingly elusive.

Beginning in 1961 Mitchell proposed a completely different and totally original model, without any obvious precursors and judged to be unorthodox to the point of eccentricity. He suggested a physical mechanism by which an electrochemical gradient is created across the cellular membrane; this, in turn, creates a proton current capable of controlling the phosphorylation.

For his account of such processes Mitchell was awarded the 1978 Nobel Prize for chemistry.

Mitscherlich, Eilhardt

(1794–1863)

GERMAN CHEMIST

Mitscherlich (**mich**-er-lik), who was born at Neuende in Germany, studied oriental languages at Heidelberg and Berlin. He then turned to the study of medicine at Göttingen in 1817, where he became interested in crystallography. For two years he worked with Jöns Berzelius in Stockholm, returning to Berlin in 1821, where he was appointed to the chair of chemistry.

While working on arsenates and phosphates, Mitscherlich realized that substances of a similar composition often have the same crystalline form, and from this he formulated, in 1819, his law of isomorphism. This was in opposition to the orthodox view of René Haüy that each substance has a distinctive crystalline form. Despite Haüy's rejection of the law, Berzelius accepted it and was quick to spot its significance, for if the composition of a substance X is known, and it is also known that X has a similarity of crystalline form with Y, then Y's composition can be derived. Thus knowing the composition of sulfur trioxide as SO_3, and that it has a similar form to "chromic acid," Berzelius was able to give this compound the composition CrO_3. Using this technique Berzelius produced his revised table of atomic weights in 1826.

Mitscherlich also discovered selenic acid (1827), named benzene, and showed, in 1834, that if benzene reacts with nitric acid it forms nitrobenzene.

Möbius, August Ferdinand

(1790–1868)

GERMAN MATHEMATICIAN

Möbius (**mu(r)**-bee-uus) worked mainly on analytical geometry, topology, and theoretical astronomy. He was born at Schulpforta in Germany and held a chair in theoretical astronomy at Leipzig, making numerous contributions to the field with publications on planetary occultations ("eclipses") and celestial mechanics. His more purely mathematical work centers on geometry and topology.

Möbius is chiefly famed for his discovery of the *Möbius strip*, a one-sided surface formed by giving a rectangular strip a half-twist and then joining the ends together. He introduced the use of homogeneous coordinates into analytical geometry and did significant work in projective geometry, inventing the *Möbius net*, which became of central importance in the future development of the subject.

Mohl, Hugo von

(1805–1872)

GERMAN BOTANIST

Mohl (mohl) was born at Stuttgart in Germany and studied medicine at Tübingen, graduating in 1828. He became professor of physiology at Bern in 1832. Optics and botany were his main interests, however, and he followed both by pursuing a career in plant microscopy; in 1835 he accepted the chair of botany at Tübingen, where he remained until his death.

In 1846 Mohl gave the name "protoplasm" to the granular colloidal material around the cell nucleus and in 1851 proposed the now-confirmed view that the secondary cell walls of plants are fibrous in structure. He was the first to suggest that new cells arise through cell division, from observations on the alga *Conferva glomerata*, and also the first to investigate the activity of stomata (pores) in the epidermis.

Mohorovičić, Andrija

(1857–1936)

CROATIAN GEOLOGIST

Mohorovičić (moh-ho-**roh**-vi-chich) was born the son of a shipwright in Volosko, Croatia, and educated at the University of Prague. He worked initially as a teacher and at the meteorological station in Bakar before being appointed a professor at the Zagreb Technical School in 1891 and at Zagreb University in 1897.

In 1909 he made his fundamental discovery of the *Mohorovičić discontinuity* (or *Moho*). From data obtained while he was observing a Croatian earthquake in 1909, Mohorovičić noticed that waves penetrating deeper into the Earth arrived sooner than waves traveling along its surface. He deduced from this that the Earth has a layered structure, the crust overlaying a more dense mantle in which earthquake waves could travel more quickly. The abrupt separation between the crust and the mantle Mohorovičić calculated as being about 20 miles (32 km) below the surface of the Earth; this is now called the Mohorovičić discontinuity.

As the crust is much thinner under the ocean beds – in some places only 3 miles thick – a project was set up in the 1960s to drill through the crust to the mantle. Mohole, as it became known, failed, however, largely as a result of the great financial cost involved and the inadequate technological expertise available for such a project.

Mohs, Friedrich

(1773–1839)

GERMAN MINERALOGIST

Mohs (mohs or mohz) was born at Gernrode in Saxony and studied at Halle and at the Freiberg Mining Academy under Abraham Werner. In 1812 he became curator of the mineral collection at the Johanneum in Graz. He succeeded Werner at Freiberg in 1818 and in 1826 he was appointed professor of mineralogy at Vienna.

In 1812 Mohs introduced the scale of mineral hardness – *Mohs scale* – named for him. Ten minerals whose hardness is known are ordered on a scale ranging from 1 (talc) to 10 (diamond), the general rule being that a higher number will scratch all lower numbers. The hardness of a mineral is judged by the ease with which its surface is scratched by these minerals whose values are known, and it can be given a numerical value.

Moissan, Ferdinand Frédéric Henri

(1852–1907)

FRENCH CHEMIST

Moissan (mwah-**sahn**) came from a poor background in Paris, France. He was the son of a railroad worker and was apprenticed to a pharmacist before studying chemistry under Edmond Frémy at the Muséum

National d'Histoire Naturelle, Paris (1872). From 1880 he worked at the Ecole Supérieure de Pharmacie, being elected to the chair of toxicology in 1886 and the chair of inorganic chemistry in 1889. In the next year he became professor of chemistry at the University of Paris.

Moissan began studying fluorine compounds in 1884 and in 1886 succeeded in isolating fluorine gas by electrolyzing a solution of potassium fluoride in hydrofluoric acid, the whole process being contained in platinum. He received the Nobel Prize for chemistry for this work in 1906.

He also worked on synthetic diamonds. He was impressed by the discovery of tiny diamonds in some meteorites and concluded from this that if the conditions undergone by these in space could be reproduced in the laboratory it would be possible to convert carbon into diamond. He therefore put iron and carbon into a crucible, heated it in an electric furnace, and while white hot cooled it rapidly by plunging it into liquid. In theory, he felt that the cooling should exert sufficient pressure on the carbon to turn it into diamond. He claimed to have succeeded in producing artificial diamonds but there was a suggestion that one of his assistants had smuggled tiny diamonds into the mixture at the beginning of the experiment. Moissan did, however, use his electric furnace for important work in preparing metal nitrides, borides, and carbides, and in extracting a number of less common metallic elements, such as molybdenum, tantalum, and niobium.

Molina, Mario José

(1943–   )

MEXICAN PHYSICAL CHEMIST

Molina, the son of a diplomat, studied chemical engineering at the University of Mexico. After further study in Europe at the University of Freiburg and at the Sorbonne, Molina moved to the University of California, Berkeley, where he gained his PhD in 1972. He worked initially as a postdoctoral student at the Irvine campus of the University of California with F. S. Rowland. Following a spell at the Jet Propulsion Laboratory he moved to MIT in 1989 as professor of environmental sciences.

Rowland had become interested in the fate of the chlorofluorocarbons (CFCs) used as the propellant in most aerosol cans, and asked his new colleague if he would be interested in working out what happened to them as they rose into the stratosphere. It would be, Molina later confessed, "a nice, interesting, academic exercise."

He quickly worked out that as CFCs were stable they would eventually accumulate in the upper atmosphere. There, he argued, they would be broken up by ultraviolet light and chlorine atoms would be released. Rowland suggested that Molina should analyze how free chlorine atoms would behave. Molina suspected that a chain reaction would be produced, reducing the amount of ozone in the upper atmosphere. Despite this, Molina still thought the effect would be negligible. It was only when he discovered that the amount of CFCs released each year was about 1 million tonnes that he realized that much of the ozone layer could be destroyed. Molina published his results in a joint paper with Rowland in 1974. The National Academy of Sciences issued a report in 1976 confirming the work of Molina and Rowland and in 1978 CFCs used in aerosols were banned in the United States. In 1984 Joe Farman detected a 40% ozone loss over Antarctica.

For his work on CFCs and the ozone layer Molina shared the 1995 Nobel Prize for chemistry with Rowland and Paul Crutzen, thus becoming the first Mexican to receive a Nobel Prize for science.

Mond, Ludwig

(1839–1909)

GERMAN–BRITISH INDUSTRIAL CHEMIST

Mond (mond or mohnt) was the son of a prosperous merchant from Kassel, in Germany. After studying at the local polytechnic he continued his chemical education under Adolph Kolbe at Marburg and Robert

Bunsen at Heidelberg. He ran some small chemical businesses on the Continent before going to Britain in 1862, where he took out a patent for the recovery of sulfur from the waste left by the Leblanc alkali process. In 1867 he started a factory in Widnes in partnership with John Hutchinson. The process was not really satisfactory and was to be superseded by that of Alexander Chance announced in 1882.

The Leblanc process was expensive in waste products and in 1861 Ernest Solvay patented a new process that was continuous and theoretically cheaper and cleaner. In 1872 Mond purchased the option to use the new process in Britain. He went into partnership with John Brunner at Winnington, Cheshire, in 1873 and they founded the firm of Brunner, Mond, and Company. It was not until 1880 that they made a profit after having twice faced ruin. Mond started his own production plant to guarantee cheap and plentiful supplies of ammonia for the Solvay process. Coal was burnt in an airstream producing ammonia and producer gas, a cheap fuel. He set up a plant to produce and sell the gas to the industrial West Midlands.

The Leblanc process, while not as efficient as the Solvay process in the production of soda, did have the advantage of also producing commercial quantities of bleaching powder. In 1886 Mond invented a process to remedy this in the Solvay process. Ammonium chloride vapor was pumped over nickel oxide, producing nickel chloride. This, when heated, yielded chlorine to be used for the production of bleaching powder and the ammonia could be returned to the start of the operation. Nickel valves used in this process dissolved away in the gas produced and, on investigation, Mond found that when heated to 60°C nickel will combine with carbon monoxide to produce nickel carbonyl. When heated to higher temperatures this breaks down to give pure nickel and reusable carbon monoxide. This discovery led to the formation of the Mond Nickel Company.

Mond became an extremely wealthy man and was the first of a new generation of chemical industrialists. From his private fortune he left £100,000 to equip the Davy–Faraday laboratory at the Royal Institution in London. He was also a connoisseur in art and he left to the National Gallery, London, his superb collection of paintings. Brunner, Mond, and Company became in 1926 part of Imperial Chemical Industries (ICI) through amalgamation.

Mondino de Luzzi

(*c.* 1275–1326)

ITALIAN ANATOMIST

> Now the bones of the chest are many and are not
> continuous, in order that it may be expanded and
> contracted, since it has ever to be in motion.
> —*Anatomica* (1316; Anatomy)

Mondino (mon-**dee**-noh), the son of a Bolognese apothecary, studied medicine first with his father and then at the University of Bologna, where he graduated in 1300. Known as the "Restorer of Anatomy," he completed, in 1316, his *Anatomica* (Anatomy), the text that dominated anatomical teaching for two centuries. The work however made few advances and repeated many ancient errors. Thus many of the classical fictions such as the spherical stomach, the seven-chambered uterus, the five-lobed liver, and the perforations in the septum of the heart are once again carefully described and illustrated in the rather primitive diagrams of his text.

Although Mondino writes of "anatomizing" people it is by no means clear that he actually performed the dissection himself. He may rather have read from the text, as was the custom, while his assistant used the knife and a demonstrator indicated the appropriate parts. Such classes were not intended to be research investigations into human anatomy but rather illustrations of an authoritative text. If there was a disagreement between what the body contained and what the text stated ought to be in it, this would be explained by the state of the body, a diseased organ, normal human variability, or even the incompetence of the dissector.

Mondino's manual owes its success to a growing 14th-century need for such a work. Medical schools were just beginning to insist that students should witness at least one complete dissection and as Mondino's text was available it captured the market.

Monge, Gaspard

(1746–1818)

FRENCH MATHEMATICIAN

> Monge knew to an extraordinary degree how to conceive of the most complicated forms in space, to penetrate to their general relation and their most hidden properties with no other help than his hands.
> —Michel Chasles, *Aperçu historique sur l'origine et le développement des méthodes en géométrie* (1837; Historical Note on the Origin and Development of Geometrical Methods)

Monge (monzh), who was born at Beaune in France, was trained as a draftsman at Mézières, where he later became professor of mathematics (1768). During the French Revolution he served on the committee that formulated the metric system (1791), became minister of the navy and the colonies (1792–93), and played a vital part in organizing the defense of France against the counterrevolutionary armies. He contributed significantly to the founding of the Ecole Polytechnique in 1795. Monge met Napoleon in 1796 and saw active service in Napoleon's army during the Egyptian campaign (1798–1801).

Monge's major mathematical achievements were the invention of descriptive geometry and the application of the techniques of analysis to the theory of curvature. The latter ultimately led to the revolutionary work of Georg Riemann on geometry and curvature.

Following Napoleon's fall from power in 1815, Monge was expelled from the French Academy and deprived of all his honors.

Monod, Jacques Lucien

(1910–1976)

FRENCH BIOCHEMIST

Language may have created man, rather than man language.
> —Inaugural lecture at the Collège de France, 3 November 1967

In science, self-satisfaction is death. Personal self-satisfaction is the death of the scientist. Collective self-satisfaction is the death of the research. It is restlessness, anxiety, dissatisfaction, agony of mind that nourish science.
> —*New Scientist*, 17 June 1976

Monod (mo-**noh**) was born in Paris, France, and graduated from the university there in 1931; he became assistant professor of zoology in 1934, having spent the years immediately following his graduation investigating the origin of life. After World War II, in which he served in the Resistance, he joined the Pasteur Institute, becoming head of the cellular biochemistry department in 1953.

In 1958 Monod began working with François Jacob and Arthur Pardee on the regulation of enzyme synthesis in mutant bacteria. This work led to the formulation, by Monod and Jacob, of a theory explaining gene action and particularly how genes are switched on and off as necessary. In 1960 they introduced the term "operon" for a closely linked group of genes, each of which controls a different step in a given biochemical pathway. The following year they postulated the existence of a molecule, messenger RNA, that carries the genetic information necessary for protein synthesis from the operon to the ribosomes, where proteins are made. For this work Monod and Jacob were awarded the 1965 Nobel Prize for physiology or medicine, which they shared with André Lwoff, who was also working on bacterial genetics.

In 1971 Monod became director of the Pasteur Institute and in the same year published the best-selling book *Chance and Necessity*, in which he argued that life arose by chance and progressed to its present level as a necessary consequence of the pressures exerted by natural selection.

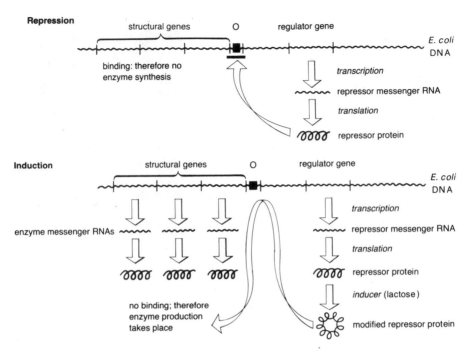

THE OPERON OF MONOD AND JACOB   This operon, which controls lactose mettabolism in the bacterium Escherichia coli, consists of stuctural genes and an operator gene (O). Close by is a regulatro gene. In the absence of lactose (top) repressor protein inhibits synthesis of the enzyme required for lactose metabolism by binding to the operoator. When lactose (the inducer) is present (bottom), it modifies the shape of the repressor protein so that it cannot bind to the operator.

Monro, Alexander (Primus)

(1697–1767)

SCOTTISH ANATOMIST

Monro's father, John, was a surgeon serving first in the army of William III before settling in Edinburgh into private practice. Alexander Monro, who was born in London, was educated at the University of

Edinburgh and then entered into an apprenticeship with his father. He later pursued his medical studies first in London under William Cheselden and then, in 1718, with Hermann Boerhaave in Leiden. He returned to Edinburgh in 1719 and in the following year was appointed to the first chair of anatomy, or indeed of any medical subject, at the university.

This was the beginning of the famous Edinburgh medical school. It was also the beginning of three generations of Monros in charge of the school. As they were all called Alexander they are normally distinguished by their order in the sequence with the founder known as "Primus." Under Monro the school flourished with the number of students admitted quadrupling before his retirement in 1764.

Monro published one original work, *Anatomy of Human Bones* (1726), but his career was mainly devoted to teaching and the establishment of the new medical school. In 1752 he produced one of the earliest figures for mortality arising from amputations. The figures are somewhat puzzling for he claimed a mortality of only 8% while Joseph Lister in the early days of antiseptic surgery had figures as high as 25%.

He was succeeded by his youngest son, Alexander, or "Secundus."

Monro, Alexander (Secundus)

(1733–1817)

SCOTTISH ANATOMIST

Monro, the son of Alexander Monro "Primus," entered the university in his native city of Edinburgh at the age of 12. He began the study of medicine in 1750 being made conjoint professor of anatomy with his father in 1754, a year before his graduation. He took over completely on his father's retirement in 1764, holding the chair himself until his own retirement in 1807.

Of the three Monros Secundus was the most significant. His most important work, although it involved him in a prolonged priority dispute with William Hunter, was his *De venis lymphaticis* (1757; On the Lymphatic Veins), which clearly distinguished between the lymphatic and circulatory systems. He also produced one of the earliest works of comparative anatomy in his *Structure and Physiology of Fishes* (1785). His name is preserved by his description in 1764 of the *foramen of Monro*, an opening connecting the lateral and third ventricles in the brain.

Monro continued the family tradition, being succeeded by his son, also called Alexander and referred to as "Tertius."

Montagnier, Luc

(1932–   )

FRENCH VIROLOGIST

Montagnier (mon-ta-**nyay**), who was born at Chabris in France, was educated at the universities of Poitiers and Paris. He joined the Viral Oncology Unit of the Pasteur Institute in 1972 and was appointed professor of virology in 1985.

Montagnier's team at the Institute were searching for, among other things, possible links between cancers and retroviruses. The retroviruses had been described in 1970 by Temin and Baltimore and were distinguished from other viruses by having RNA rather than DNA genes. In early 1983 they were presented with a blood sample from a patient showing early signs of AIDS. Reverse transcriptase, an enzyme characteristic of retroviruses, was found in the blood. Montagnier sought to identify the virus. It was not HTLV-1, a retrovirus recently discovered by Robert Gallo, as serum from the AIDS patient did not react with samples of HTLV-1 provided by Gallo. The virus was found in T-4 cells, specialized lymphocytes of the immune system, and was therefore named LAV as an acronym for "lymphadenopathy associated virus." Electron micrographs taken of LAV differed from those of HTLV-1.

Montagnier went on to develop a blood test for the presence of LAV. Antibodies to LAV were found in a number of patients with AIDS. As the sensitivity of the test increased, Montagnier was able to identify more and more AIDS patients and by October 1983 he was convinced that LAV was the cause of AIDS. By this time, however, Gallo had isolated a new retrovirus, HTLV-3, which he was equally convinced was the cause of AIDS. It was eventually agreed, despite some considerable initial controversy, that HTLV-3 and LAV were to all intents and purposes the same virus. In 1986 it was officially renamed HIV and the patent for HIV blood tests carried the names of both Gallo and Montagnier.

A further advance was made by Montagnier in late 1985 while examining blood samples from Guinea-Bissau in West Africa. He was puzzled by the fact that some of the samples came from apparently HIV-negative AIDS patients, even though they had been tested with a sensitive new probe. Montagnier resolved the issue by isolating a virus from the samples which differed from electronmicrographs of HIV-1. Montagnier named the virus HIV-2 and demonstrated that antibodies to the new virus were commonly found in blood samples from West African AIDS patients.

Montgolfier, Etienne Jacques de

(1745–1799)

FRENCH BALLOONIST

Montgolfier, Michel Joseph de

(1740–1810)

FRENCH BALLOONIST

Etienne and Michel Montgolfier (mon-gol-**fyay** or mont-**gol**-fee-er), the sons of a paper manufacturer from Vidalon-les-Annonay, Lyons, engaged themselves in various enterprises. Michel founded his own paper factory in 1771, while Etienne practiced as an architect until 1782 when called upon to run the family factory at Vidalon. In later life Michel abandoned business and was appointed in 1800 to the faculty of the Conservatoire des Arts et Métiers.

Like many before, the brothers had noticed how pieces of paper thrown into the fire would often rise aloft in a column of hot air. They were interested enough to see whether paper bags filled with hot smoke would rise. Satisfied with their small-scale experiments they became convinced that something much larger was viable. On 4 June 1783 they gave the first public demonstration of their work at Annonay. The balloon was made of linen and lined with paper, measured 36 feet across, and weighed 500 pounds. Once inflated over a fire burning chopped straw, the balloon ascended to a height of 6,000 feet before coming down ten minutes later, a mile and a half away. News quickly spread throughout France. Called to Versailles they demonstrated their balloon, this time carrying a sheep, a cock, and a duck, before Louis XVI and Marie Antoinette. The balloon landed two miles away in a wood with the animals none the worse for their journey.

The first manned flight was made by François de Rozier in Paris in October 1783. Of the brothers, only Michel flew in the balloon, making an ascent of 3,000 feet with seven other people in 1784.

Moore, Stanford

(1913–1982)

AMERICAN BIOCHEMIST

Moore, who was born in Chicago, Illinois, graduated in chemistry from Vanderbilt University in 1935 and received his PhD from the University of Wisconsin in 1938. He then joined the staff of the Rockefeller Institute, spending his entire career there and serving as professor of biochemistry from 1952 onward.

One of the major achievements of modern science has been the determination by Frederick Sanger in 1955 of the complete amino acid sequence of a protein. Sanger's success with the insulin molecule inspired Moore and his Rockefeller colleague, William Stein, to tackle the larger molecule of the enzyme ribonuclease. Although their work was lightened by the availability of techniques pioneered by Sanger the labor involved was still immense until eased by their development of the first automatic amino-acid analyzer.

They inserted a small amount of the amino-acid mixture into the top of a five-foot column containing resin. They then washed down the mixture using solutions of varying acidity. The individual amino acids travel down the column at different rates depending on their relative affinity for the solution and for the resin. It is possible to adjust the rates of travel so that the separate amino acids emerge from the bottom of the column at predetermined and well-spaced intervals. The colorless amino acids were then detected with ninhydrin, a reagent that forms a blue color on heating with proteins and amino acids. A continuous plot of the intensity of the blue color gives a series of peaks, each corresponding to a certain amino acid with the area under the peak indicating the amount of each.

By the end of the 1950s Moore and Stein had not only established the sequence of ribonuclease but they were also able to indicate the most likely active site on the single-chained molecule. For this work they shared the 1972 Nobel Prize for chemistry with Christian Anfinsen.

Mordell, Louis Joel

(1888–1972)

AMERICAN–BRITISH
MATHEMATICIAN

Mordell had his first mathematical education at school in his native city of Philadelphia. He decided to try for a scholarship to Cambridge University, England, and having scraped together enough money for a one-way ticket made the crossing, took the exam, and got the scholarship. Mordell taught at Birkbeck College, London, from 1913 to 1920. From 1920 to 1945 he held posts at the Manchester College of Technology and at Manchester University. While in Manchester he got to know Sydney Chapman, and the two remained life-long friends. From 1945 to 1953 he held the Sadleirian Chair in Mathematics at Cambridge.

Mordell's central interest was in the theory of numbers and, in particular, Diophantine equations. He worked on the theory of modular functions and their applications to the theory of numbers. In the 1920s he published his most important single result, the Mordell finite basis theorem. André Weil later generalized it, and the result, which plays a fundamental role in number theory, is now usually known as the *Mordell–Weil theorem*. Among his other works are results on the estimation of trigometric and character sums, cubic surfaces and hypersurfaces, and the geometry of numbers.

Morgagni, Giovanni Batista

(1682–1771)

ITALIAN PATHOLOGIST

Morgagni (mor-**gah**-nyee) was born at Forli in Italy and educated at the University of Bologna; after graduating in philosophy and medicine in 1701, he worked as a demonstrator in anatomy and served as assistant to his former teacher, Antonio Valsalva. In 1712 he moved to the University of Padua and served there as professor of anatomy from 1715 until his death.

In 1761 Morgagni published his classic work, *De sedibus et causis morborum per anatomen indagatis* (On the Seats and Causes of Diseases as Investigated by Anatomy) in which he used the reports of 640 autopsies, many carried out personally, to produce this pioneering text in morbid anatomy. There were earlier collections of autopsies, such as the work of Theophilus Bonet whose *Sepulchretum* (1679; Cemetery) reported over 3,000, but they tended to be uncritical compilations with an emphasis on the bizarre.

With a general decline in the plausibility of the humoral theory of disease, scientists began the long search for a viable alternative. Morgagni took one of the first steps by searching for the cause of disease in the lesions present in particular organs. He would begin by presenting a full clinical picture of the disease, which he would then try to link with the presence of some lesion observed during the autopsy. With experience he began to find that he could frequently predict the lesion from the case history alone.

Many were to follow him over the next century. Some, like Marie François Bichat and Rudolph Virchow, would propose alternative "seats" for disease in the tissues and cells respectively. To others, like Louis Pasteur, the crucial question raised by the new pathological anatomy of Morgagni was what caused the lesions, the answer to which would ultimately lead to the discovery of pathogens.

Morgan, Thomas Hunt

(1866–1945)

AMERICAN GENETICIST

The participation of a group of scientific men united in a common venture for the advancement of research fires my imagination to the kindling point.
—Letter to George Ellery Hale, 9 May 1927

Born in Lexington, Kentucky, Morgan studied zoology at the State College of Kentucky, graduating in 1886. He received his PhD from Johns Hopkins University in 1890 and from 1891 to 1904 was associate professor of zoology at Bryn Mawr College. He carried out his most important work between 1904 and 1928, while professor of experimental zoology at Columbia University. Here he became involved in the controversy that followed the rediscovery, in 1900, of Gregor Mendel's laws of inheritance.

Many scientists had noted that Mendel's segregation ratios fitted in well with the observed pattern of chromosome movement at meiosis.

Morgan, however, continued to regard Mendel's laws with skepticism, especially the law of independent assortment, and with good reason. It was known by then that many more characters are determined genetically than there are chromosomes and therefore each chromosome must control many traits. It was also known that chromosomes are inherited as complete units, so various characters must be linked together on a single chromosome and would be expected to be inherited together.

In 1908 Morgan began breeding experiments with the fruit fly *Drosophila melanogaster*, which has four pairs of chromosomes. Morgan's early results with mutant types substantiated Mendel's law of segregation, but he soon found evidence of linkage through his discovery that mutant white-eyed flies are also always male. He thus formulated the only necessary amendment to Mendel's laws – that the law of independent assortment only applies to genes located on different chromosomes.

Morgan found that linkages could be broken when homologous chromosomes paired at meiosis and exchanged material in a process known as "crossing over." Gene linkages are less likely to be broken when the genes are close together on the chromosome, and therefore by recording the frequency of broken linkages, the positions of genes along the chromosome can be mapped. Morgan and his colleagues produced the first chromosome maps in 1911.

For his contributions to genetics, Morgan received the Nobel Prize for physiology or medicine in 1933. A prolific writer, his most influential books – produced with colleagues at Columbia – are *The Mechanism of Mendelian Heredity* (1915) and *The Theory of the Gene* (1926).

Morgan, William Wilson

(1906–1994)

AMERICAN ASTRONOMER

Morgan, who was born in Bethesda, Tennessee, studied at the Washington and Lee University and then at the University of Chicago where he obtained his BSc in 1927 and his PhD in 1931. The following year he took up an appointment at the Yerkes Observatory, where he served as professor from 1947 to 1966 and Sunny Distinguished Professor of Astronomy from 1966 to 1974. He was Director of the Yerkes and McDonald observatories from 1960 to 1963.

The standard system of spectral classification of stars, the Henry Draper system, assigned the majority of stars to one of the classes, O, B, A, F, G, K, or M, which were each subdivided into ten categories numbered from 0 to 9. In this classification our Sun is assigned the number G2. Useful as the Draper system is, Morgan realized that it had its limitations. He pointed out that the system was based only on the surface temperature of stars and commonly produced cases where two stars, like Procyon in Canis Minor and Mirfak in Perseus, fell into the same spectral class, F5 in this case, yet differed in luminosity by a factor of several hundreds.

Consequently, in collaboration with Philip Childs Keenan and Edith Kellman, he introduced the *Yerkes system* or *MKK system* (also known as the Morgan–Keenan classification) in 1943 in *An Atlas of Stellar Spectra with an Outline of Spectral Classification*. The new system was two dimensional, containing in addition to the spectral typing a luminosity index. This was used to classify stars in terms of their intrinsic brightness by means of Roman numerals from I to VI, and ranged from supergiants (I), giants (II and III), subgiants (IV), main-sequence stars (V), to subdwarfs (VI). Procyon thus becomes a F5 IV star while Mirfak is a distinguishable F5 I supergiant.

In the 1940s Walter Baade had shown that hot O and B stars were characteristic members of the spiral arms of a galaxy. Morgan and his colleagues thus began to trace out the structure of our own Galaxy by searching for clouds of hydrogen ionized by O and B stars. By 1953 they claimed to have identified the Perseus, Orion, and Sagittarius arms of the Galaxy, thus providing good evidence for its spiral structure. Morgan also worked on star brightness and discovered so-called "flash" variables – stars that change their luminosity very quickly. He also worked on galaxy classification.

Morley, Edward Williams

(1838–1923)

AMERICAN CHEMIST AND PHYSICIST

Morley's father was a congregational minister from Newark, New Jersey. For reasons of health Morley was educated at home and appears to have been a precocious child, starting Latin at the age of 6 and being able to read Greek at 11. He taught himself chemistry by mastering the textbook of Benjamin Silliman when only 14. He received his higher education at Williams College (1857–60) and Andover Theological Seminary (1861–64). As he felt he was not fit enough to follow his father into the ministry he opted instead for a university career and in 1869 was appointed professor of natural history and chemistry at Western Reserve College, Hudson, Ohio.

Morley was a very careful and patient experimentalist. In 1878 he began a study of the variations in oxygen content of the atmosphere. This was followed in the period 1883–94 by a study of the relative weights of oxygen and hydrogen in pure water. After the weighings of literally thousands of samples he produced figures to five decimal places and accurate to one part in 300,000.

He is, however, best remembered for his collaboration with Albert Michelson in their famous experiment to detect the Earth's motion through the ether. Morley was not completely convinced by the negative result and did further experiments with Dayton Clarence Miller. Despite many refinements no conclusive effect was found.

Morse, Samuel

(1791–1872)

AMERICAN INVENTOR AND PAINTER

What God hath wrought.
—The first message sent on Morse's telegraph (1844)

Morse, the inventor of telegraphy, was born the son of a Calvinist minister and distinguished geographer in Charlestown, Massachusetts. Although not very keen on study at school, he was sent to Yale. Apart from painting, his main interest, he was stimulated to further study by lectures on electricity. In 1810 he graduated and took a job as a clerk in Boston. He visited England in 1811 to study painting, returning in 1815 to earn his living as a portrait painter. He was a founder and first president (1826–45) of the National Academy of Design at New York. Throughout his life Morse was politically conservative and religiously orthodox, at one point being involved in campaigning against "licentiousness" in the theater.

In 1832, after overhearing a conversation about electromagnets, he had the idea of a design for the electric telegraph. Although the idea itself was not entirely new, his was the first definite design. By 1835 he had built a working model and from 1837 onward he concentrated his attention on developing the telegraph system, helped out by several friends. A year later he devised the *Morse code*, a system of dots and dashes for sending messages as electrical signals. In 1843 Congress financed the first telegraph line, between Washington and Baltimore.

Morton, William Thomas Green

(1819–1868)

AMERICAN DENTIST

Morton, who was born the son of a small farmer and village shopkeeper in Charlton City, Massachusetts, is believed to have trained as a dentist at the Baltimore College of Dentistry. After a brief partnership with Horace Wells, Morton set up in practice in Boston.

To alleviate the pain of tooth extraction Morton experimented with such drugs as opium and alcohol, but only succeeded in making his patients violently sick. The chemist Charles Jackson advised Morton to try ether, an old student standby, as a local anesthetic. This was moderately effective and Morton decided to try ether inhalation to produce general anesthesia. He first used ether to extract a tooth on 30 September 1860. His initial successes left Morton confident enough to offer to demonstrate his technique at the Massachusetts General Hospital. He was successful in using it on a patient who was undergoing a tumor operation. His innovation was well received by the leading surgeon John Warren and the use of ether quickly gained acceptance in medical practice. The news soon spread to Europe and in December 1846 Robert Liston, the skilled British surgeon, used ether in a painless and successful leg amputation at University College Hospital, London.

Morton subsequently went to a lot of trouble trying to patent his anesthetic and fight off competitors, notably Jackson, who were claiming priority. His wrangling with Jackson, the government, and the law courts achieved little and Morton died virtually penniless while traveling to New York to answer yet another attack on him from Jackson.

Mosander, Carl Gustav

(1797–1858)

SWEDISH CHEMIST

Born at Kalmar in Sweden, Mosander (moo-**san**-der) started his career as a physician and became Jöns Berzelius's assistant after a time in the army. He became curator of minerals at the Royal Academy of Science in Stockholm before succeeding Berzelius as secretary. In 1832 he became professor of chemistry and mineralogy at the Karolinska Institute, Stockholm.

Mosander worked chiefly on the lanthanoid elements. These had been known since the discovery of yttrium by Johan Gadolin in 1794 and cerium by Martin Klaproth in 1803. He began by examining the earth from which cerium had been isolated, ceria. From this he derived in 1839 the oxide of a new element, which he called lanthanum, from the Greek meaning "to be hidden." In 1843 he announced the discovery of three new rare-earth elements – erbium, terbium, and didymium. As it happened, didymium was not elementary, being shown in 1885 by Karl Auer von Welsbach to consist of two elements – praseodymium and neodymium.

Moseley, Henry Gwyn Jeffreys

(1887–1915)

BRITISH PHYSICIST

Moseley came from an academic family in Weymouth, southwest England. He graduated in natural sciences from Oxford University in 1910 and then joined Ernest Rutherford at Manchester University to work on radioactivity, although he soon turned his attention to x-ray spectroscopy. He returned to Oxford in 1913 to continue his work under J. S. E. Townsend.

When x-rays are produced by an element a continuous spectrum is emitted together with a more powerful radiation of a few specific wavelengths characteristic of the element. To investigate the positive charge on atomic nuclei Moseley examined these characteristic spectral lines using crystal diffraction. For a number of elements, he discovered a regular shift in the lines with increasing atomic weight. From this he determined for each element an integer approximately proportional to the square root of the frequency of one of its spectral lines. This integer, now called the atomic number (or proton number), equaled the positive charge on the atomic nuclei. Moseley's work led

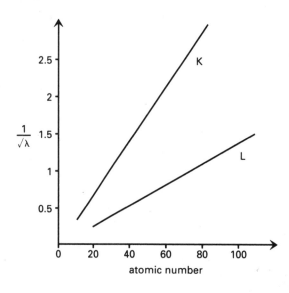

MOSELEY'S LAW   The relationship between characteristic x-rays and atomic number for the chemical elements.

to major improvements in Dmitri Mendeleev's periodic table and enabled elements to be classified in a new and more satisfactory manner.

At the outbreak of World War I Moseley enlisted in the army and was commissioned in the Royal Engineers. His death, from a sniper's bullet at Gallipoli, cut short what promised to be a most brilliant career in science.

Mössbauer, Rudolph Ludwig

(1929–)

GERMAN PHYSICIST

Born at Munich in Germany, Mössbauer (**mu(r)s**-bow-er or **mos**-bow-er) was educated in Munich-Pasing and, after a year in industrial laboratories, studied physics at the Munich Technical University. There he passed his intermediate degree in 1952, and completed his thesis in 1954. From 1955 to 1957 he did postgraduate research at the Max-Planck Institute for Medical Research in Heidelberg, gaining his doctorate from the Technical University in 1958.

From 1953 he had been studying the absorption of gamma rays in matter, in particular the phenomenon of nuclear resonance absorption. Normally, when an atomic nucleus emits a gamma ray, it will recoil, and this recoil action will influence the wavelength of the gamma ray emitted. Mössbauer discovered that, contrary to classical predictions, at a sufficiently low temperature the nucleus can be locked into position in the crystal lattice, and it is the lattice itself that recoils, with negligible effect on the wavelength. The result is that the wavelength can be defined with extremely high precision (about 1 part in 10^{12}). As with emission, so it is with absorption; a crystal of the same material under similar conditions absorbs gamma rays at the same highly specific wavelength – a resonance phenomenon akin to a well-tuned radio receiver and transmitter. If, however, the conditions are slightly different, the small changes in wavelength can be accurately compensated and thus measured using the Doppler effect (by moving the source relative to the receiver).

This phenomenon of recoilless nuclear resonance absorption, now known as the *Mössbauer effect*, has given physicists and chemists a very useful tool through the high precision of measurement it allows. In particular, it allowed the first laboratory testing (and verification in 1960) of the prediction of Einstein's general theory of relativity that the frequency of an electromagnetic radiation (in this case gamma rays) is influenced by gravity. The Mössbauer effect is now commonly employed as a spectroscopic method in chemical and solid-state physics because of its ability to detect differences in the electronic environments surrounding certain nuclei (*Mössbauer spectroscopy*).

In 1960, after finishing his studies at the Technical University, Mössbauer went on to continue his investigations of gamma absorption at the California Institute of Technology, Pasadena, where he was appointed professor of physics the next year. In 1961 he also received the Nobel Prize for physics, sharing the honor with Robert Hofstadter who had advanced knowledge of the nucleus by electron-scattering methods. Mössbauer is currently a professor at the Munich Technical University.

Mott, Sir Nevill Francis

(1905–1996)

BRITISH PHYSICIST

Born at Leeds in England, Mott studied at Cambridge University, gaining his bachelor's degree in 1927 and his master's in 1930. He never pursued a doctorate, but from 1930 until 1933 was a lecturer and fellow of Gonville and Caius College, Cambridge. Subsequently he moved to Bristol University as a professor of theoretical physics. In 1948 he became director of Bristol's physics laboratories, but returned later to Cambridge as Cavendish Professor of Experimental Physics, where he served from 1954 until his retirement in 1971.

Mott's work in the early 1930s was on the quantum theory of atomic collisions and scattering. With Harrie Massey he wrote the first of several classic texts, *The Theory of Atomic Collisions* (1934). Other influential texts that followed were on *The Theory of Properties of Metals and Alloys* with H. Jones (1936) and *Electronic Processes in Ionic Crystals* with R. W. Gurney (1940). Each marked a significant phase of active research. Mott began to explore also the defects and surface phenomena involved in the photographic process (explaining latent-image formation), and did significant work on dislocations, defects, and the strength of crystals.

By the mid 1950s, Mott was able to turn his attention to problems of disordered materials, liquid metals, impurity bands in semiconductors, and the glassy semiconductors. His models of the solid state became more and more complex, and included an analysis of electronic processes in metal–insulator transitions, often called *Mott transitions*.

In 1977 Mott shared the Nobel Prize for physics with Philip Anderson and John Van Vleck for their "fundamental theoretical investigations of the electronic structure of magnetic and disordered systems." Mott was knighted in 1962. His autobiography, *A Life in Science*, was published in 1986.

Mottelson, Benjamin Roy

(1926–   )

AMERICAN–DANISH PHYSICIST

Mottelson, who was born in Chicago, Illinois, graduated from Purdue University in 1947 and gained his PhD in theoretical physics at Harvard University in 1950.

From Harvard, Mottelson gained a traveling fellowship to the Institute of Theoretical Physics in Copenhagen (now the Neils Bohr Institute). There he worked with Neils Bohr's son, Aage Bohr, on problems of the atomic nucleus. In particular, they considered models of the nucleus and combined the two principal theories current at the time – one based on independent particles regarded as arranged in shells and the other treating the nucleus as a collective entity exhibiting liquid-drop-like behavior – and advanced a unified theory. They worked out the consequences of the interplay between the individual particles and the collective motions, specified the structure of the rotational and vibrational excitations and the coupling between them, and showed how the collective concepts could be applied to the nuclei of various elements. For their work on nuclear structure Mottelson, Bohr, and James Rainwater (Bohr's earlier collaborator at Columbia University) shared the 1975 Nobel Prize for physics.

Mottelson held a research position in CERN (the European Center for Nuclear Research) from 1953 until 1957, then returned to Copenhagen to take up a professorship at the Nordic Institute for Theoretical Atomic Physics (NORDITA) adjacent to the Neils Bohr Institute. He took Danish nationality in 1973.

Together with Aage Bohr, he has published *Nuclear Structure* (2 vols., 1969–75).

Moulton, Forest Ray

(1872–1952)

AMERICAN ASTRONOMER

Born in Osceola County, Michigan, Moulton was educated in frontier schools, Albion College, and the University of Chicago where he obtained his PhD in 1899. He taught there until 1926, being made full professor in 1912. From 1927 to 1936 he worked in business before returning to science as executive secretary of the American Association for the Advancement of Science from 1936 to 1948.

Moulton is still remembered for his formulation of the planetismal theory of the origin of the planets in collaboration with Thomas Chamberlin in 1904. They suggested that a star had passed close to the Sun and that this resulted in the ejection of filaments of matter from both stars. The filaments cooled into tiny solid fragments, "planetesimals." On collision the small particles stuck together (a process known as "accretion"). Thus over a very long period, grains became pebbles, then boulders, then even larger bodies. For larger bodies, the gravitational force of attraction would accelerate. In this way the protoplanets formed. This formation by accretion is still accepted although the stellar origin of the planetesimals has been largely dropped.

Mueller, Erwin Wilhelm

(1911–1977)

GERMAN–AMERICAN PHYSICIST

Mueller (**moo**-ler or **myoo**-ler) was born in Berlin and studied engineering at the university there, gaining his PhD in 1935. He worked in Berlin at Siemens and Halske (1935–37) and at Stabilovolt (1937–46). Subsequently he was at the Altenberg Engineering School (1946–47) and the Fritz Haber Institute (1948–52), from where he moved to the Pennsylvania State University. He became a naturalized American in 1962.

He is noted for his fundamental experimental work on solid surfaces. In 1936 he invented the field-emission microscope. In this device, a fine metal point is placed a distance away from a phosphorescent screen in a high vacuum with a very high negative voltage applied to the point. Electrons are emitted from the surface under the influence of the electric field (field emission) and these travel to the screen where they produce a magnified image of

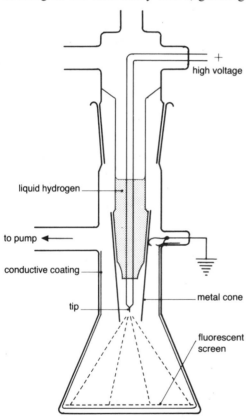

FIELD-ION MICROSCOPE The field-ion microscope invented by Erwin Mueller.

the surface of the tip. The instrument is used to study reactions at surfaces.

In 1951 he made a further advance using the principle of field ionization. In the field-ion microscope the tip is at a positive potential in a low pressure of inert gas. Atoms of gas adsorbing on the tip are ionized and the positive ions are repelled from the tip and produce the image. The resolution is much better than in the field-emission microscope; in 1956, by cooling the tip in liquid helium, Mueller was able to resolve individual surface atoms for the first time.

As a further refinement Mueller used a field-ion microscope with a mass spectrometer, so that individual atoms on the surface could be seen, desorbed, and identified (the atom-probe field-ion microscope).

Muller, Alex

(1927–   )

SWISS PHYSICIST

Born at Basel in Switzerland, Muller (**mool**-er) was educated at the Federal Institute of Technology, Zurich, where he obtained his PhD in 1958. After working for a few years at the Batelle Institute in Geneva, he returned to Zurich (1963) to take up a post at the IBM Research Laboratory at Rüschlikon, where he has remained ever since.

In 1911 Kammerlingh-Onnes discovered the phenomenon of superconductivity. He found that a current passing through mercury at 4 K, that is four degrees above absolute zero, met with no resistance. To utilize this discovery fully the temperature at which materials became superconductive, the critical temperature (T_c), would have to be raised to some more economically accessible level. Yet 75 years' intensive research had raised the critical temperature no higher than 23.3 K for a niobium–germanium alloy. And to cool the alloy to this point requires bathing it in either expensive liquid helium (bp 4.2 K) or the cheaper but flammable liquid hydrogen (bp 20.3 K).

Muller first began to work on the problem in 1983. He ignored the usual candidates for a high critical temperature and turned instead to look at ceramic metal oxides. This was partly because his laboratory had worked with oxides of this kind for many years and had built up a considerable expertise in them. Also, he suspected, their lattice structure was of the right kind to allow superconductivity. In January 1986 Muller, working with his IBM colleague Georg Bednorz, found that a mixed lanthanum, barium, and copper oxide showed a change to superconducting behavior below 35 K (−238° C). Once the initial advance had been made, other physicists were quick to follow and to confirm and extend Muller's work.

The significance of Muller's discovery was recognized with unusual speed by the Nobel authorities when, in the following year, they awarded the Nobel Prize for physics jointly to Muller and Bednorz.

Müller, Franz Joseph, Baron von Reichenstein

(1740–1825)

AUSTRIAN GEOLOGIST

Müller (**mool**-er), who was born at Nagyszeben (now in Romania), was the son of a treasury official. He studied law in Vienna and mining at Schemnitz in Hungary. After a period working in the state saltworks in Transylvania, he was appointed successively as director of the state mines of the Tyrol (1775–78), of Transylvania (1778–1802), and of Austria–Hungary (1802–18).

Officials had known for some time that the ores of Transylvania produced less gold and silver than elsewhere and it was assumed that they contained significant amounts of antimony. In 1782 Müller extracted from the local ores the substance responsible for the shortfall – a substance that he thought might be a new element. He sent some samples to Torbern Bergman, who confirmed that it was not antimony. Martin Klaproth later demonstrated that it was indeed a new element and named it tellurium, from the Latin *tellus* (earth).

Muller, Hermann Joseph

(1890–1967)

AMERICAN GENETICIST

> Death is an advantage to life...Its advantage lies chiefly in giving ampler opportunities for the genes of the new generation to have their merits tested out... by clearing the way for fresh starts.
>
> —*Science* No. 121 (1955)

Born in New York City, Muller (**mul**-er) was awarded a scholarship to Columbia University in 1907 and specialized in heredity during his undergraduate studies. On graduation he took up a teaching fellowship in physiology at Cornell Medical School, gaining his master's degree in 1912 for research on the transmission of nerve impulses. During this period he continued working at Columbia in his spare time, contributing to the genetic researches on *Drosophila* fruit flies. He was employed officially at Columbia in 1912 and received his PhD in 1916 for his now classic studies on the crossing over of chromosomes. He was also a coauthor of *The Mechanism of Mendelian Heredity* (1915), a fundamental contribution to classical genetics.

In 1915, at the request of Julian Huxley, Muller moved to the Rice Institute, Houston, Texas, where he began studying mutation. By 1918 he had found evidence that raising the temperature increases mutation rate. In 1920, after a brief spell back at Columbia, he joined the University of Texas as an associate professor, becoming a professor in 1925. In 1926 he found that x-rays induce mutations, a discovery for which he eventually received the 1946 Nobel Prize for physiology or medicine.

In 1933 Muller spent the first of eight years in Europe at the Institute for Brain Research, Berlin. Hitler's rise to power forced him to leave Germany and he moved to the Academy of Sciences, Leningrad, at the invitation of Nikolai Vavilov. Muller believed that in a communist state he would be able to develop his own socialist ideas and apply his research to improve the human condition. However the advent of Lysenkoism effectively hampered most genetic research in Russia and Muller left, volunteering to serve in the Spanish Civil War. He then worked at the Institute of Animal Genetics, Edinburgh, returning to America in 1940. He held a position at Amherst College, Massachusetts, from 1942 until 1945, when he became professor of zoology at Indiana University, remaining there for the rest of his life.

Muller made important theoretical contributions to genetics. He visualized the gene as the origin of life, because only genes can replicate themselves, and he believed all selection and therefore evolution acted at the level of the gene. He worried about the increasing number of mutations accumulating in human populations, which can survive because of modern medical technology, and proposed a program of eugenics to overcome the problem. He fully realized the harm to human chromosomes that can result from ionizing radiation and campaigned against excessive use of x-rays in medicine, careless handling of nuclear fuels, and testing of atomic bombs.

Muller is seen by many as the most influential geneticist of the 20th century, mainly through his appreciation of genetic mutation as fundamental to future genetic research. He published over 350 works, the most important paper being *Artificial Transmutation of the Gene* (1927).

Müller, Johannes Peter

(1801–1858)

GERMAN PHYSIOLOGIST

In intercourse with the external world we continually sense ourselves.
—*Zur vergleichenden Physiologie des Gesichtssinnes des Menschen und der Tiere* (1826; Comparative Physiology of the Sense of Sight in Humans and Animals)

Müller (**moo**-ler), a shoemaker's son from Koblenz in Germany, graduated in medicine from the University of Bonn in 1822. He worked as a pathologist in Bonn until 1833 when he moved to the University of

Berlin as professor of anatomy and physiology, a post he retained until his death.

Müller was the most important figure in 19th-century German physiology. Not only did he number among his pupils such figures as Hermann von Helmholtz, Carl Ludwig, Rudolf Virchow, and Max Schultze but those he did not teach were reached by his influential work, *Handbuch der Physiologie des Menschen* (2 vols., 1834–40; Handbook of Human Physiology).

It was in the field of neurophysiology that Müller made his major contribution to science. In 1831 he neatly and conclusively confirmed the law of Charles Bell and François Magendie, which first clearly distinguished between motor and sensory nerves. Using frogs and dogs, Müller cut through the posterior roots of nerves from a limb as they entered the spinal cord. The limb was insensible but not paralyzed. When however Müller severed the anterior root he found that the limb had become paralyzed but had not lost its sensibility.

He also worked on the cranial nerves and succeeded in showing that the first two branches of the trigeminal nerve are sensory while the third branch, to the jaw, contains motor fibers also. The vagus and the glossopharyngeal were, Müller claimed, mixed nerves.

Müller also formulated, in 1826, the law of specific nervous energies, which claimed that nerves are not merely passive conductors but that each particular type of nerve has its own special qualities. For example, the visual nerves, however they may be stimulated, are only capable of transmitting visual data. More specifically, if such a nerve is stimulated, whether by pressure, electric current, or a flashing light, the result will always be a visual experience.

After the completion of the *Handbuch* in 1840 Müller turned more to problems of anatomy and physiology. He worked with Robert Remak on embryological problems and was the first to describe what later became known as the "Müllerian duct." This is a tube found in vertebrate embryos, which develops into the oviduct in females; it is found only vestigially in males. He also spent a large amount of time collecting and classifying zoological specimens.

Müller was much given to fits of depression, frequently feeling that his own creativity was exhausted. Consequently when he was found dead in bed, although no autopsy was ever performed, it was widely assumed that he had died by his own hand.

Müller, Otto Friedrich

(1730–1784)

DANISH MICROSCOPIST

One of the earliest microscopists, Müller was among the first to study and describe microorganisms, such as bacteria, diatoms, and infusoria, of which he discovered many new species. He introduced the terms "bacillum" and "spirillum" for two groups of bacteria, and devised a system of classification of microscopic animals and plants, based on the Linnean system. Born in Copenhagen, Müller was professor of botany at the university there and a proponent of the theory of spontaneous generation. His published works include the continuation of Georg Christian Oeder's *Flora Danica* and other studies of Danish flora and fauna, including works on insects and earthworms.

Müller, Paul Hermann

(1899–1965)

SWISS CHEMIST

Müller, who was born in Olten, Switzerland, was educated at the University of Basel where he obtained his PhD in 1925. From then until 1961 when he retired Müller worked for the Swiss dye firm of J. R. Geigy as a research chemist.

In 1935 Müller began looking for a potent and persistent insecticide that would nevertheless be harmless to plants and warm-blooded animals. Five years later he took out a patent on a chemical that had first been prepared in 1873. The compound was dichlorodiphenyltrichloroethane which, not surprisingly, was soon abbreviated to DDT. It turned out to be cheap and simple to manufacture, requiring only chlorine, ethanol, benzene, and sulfuric acid, all of which were available in bulk from the heavy chemical industry.

It soon proved its effectiveness as an insecticide during the war. Müller thought it to be toxic only against insects and soon extravagant claims were being made about the elimination of arthropod-borne diseases. Before long, however, the insects appeared to be more resilient than chemists had supposed and DDT more destructive of life and ecosystems than they imagined. Several advanced countries were to ban it.

Müller was awarded the Nobel Prize for physiology or medicine in 1948 for his discovery.

Muller, Richard August

(1944–   )

AMERICAN PHYSICIST

Born in New York, Muller was educated at Columbia and at the University of California, Berkeley, where he completed his PhD in 1969. He has remained at Berkeley and was appointed professor of physics in 1980.

Muller has made numerous contributions to several areas of physics, including optics, astrophysics, and high-energy physics. In 1983, however, he began to work on a problem which brought him before a much wider audience. His colleague Luis Alvarez drew his attention to the claim made by the paleontologist David Raup that there were increased rates of extinction every 26 million years. What could possibly produce such periodicity?

One possibility was that the extinctions could be caused by collisions with other astronomical objects. Generally this would be random but Muller saw that there could be a way to produce periodic collisions with asteroids. If the Sun had a companion star that approached the earth every 26 million years bringing asteroids in its train, then the periodicity would be explained. Muller later thought the companion star, eventually to be named "Nemesis," brought with it comets from the Oort cloud rather than asteroids.

Muller found further evidence from a study of impact craters. If the craters were caused by the passage of Nemesis then they too would show an appropriate periodicity. Although the data was sketchy Muller found a fair enough fit to maintain his interest in the project. Despite some prolonged searches of the heavens, Nemesis has continued to remain undetected. In his own account of the issue, *Nemesis* (London, 1989), Muller, while still supporting periodic extinctions, sees his own work as "an elegant theory, a marvelous prediction, that needs verification."

Mulliken, Robert Sanderson

(1896–1986)

AMERICAN PHYSICIST AND CHEMIST

Mulliken was born in Newburyport, Massachusetts, the son of an organic chemist. He was educated at the Massachusetts Institute of Technology and at the University of Chicago, where he obtained his PhD in 1921. After working briefly at Washington Square College, New York, he was appointed to the staff of the University of Chicago, where he served as professor of physics from 1931 until he retired in 1961. From 1961 he was Distinguished Service Professor of Physics and Chemistry at Chicago and Distinguished Research Professor of Chemical Physics at Florida State University.

It was Mulliken, in 1922, who first suggested a method of isotope separation by evaporative centrifuging. Most of his research career was concerned with the interpretation of molecular spectra and with the application of quantum theory to the electronic states of molecules.

Mulliken, with Friedrich Hund, developed the molecular-orbital theory of chemical bonding, which is based on the idea that electrons in a molecule move in the field produced by all the nuclei. The atomic orbitals of isolated atoms become molecular orbitals, extending over two or more atoms in the molecule. He showed how the relative energies of these orbitals could be obtained from the spectra of the molecule.

Mulliken's approach to finding molecular orbitals was to combine atomic orbitals (LCAO, or linear combination of atomic orbitals). He showed that energies of bonds could be obtained by the amount of overlap of atomic orbitals.

Another of Mulliken's contributions is the application of electronegativity – the ability of a particular atom in a molecule to draw electrons to itself. He showed that this property was given by the formula $\frac{1}{2}(I + E)$, where I is the ionization potential of the atom and E is its electron affinity.

He also made major contributions to the theory and interpretation of molecular spectra. In 1966 he was awarded the Nobel Prize for chemistry for "his fundamental work concerning chemical bonds and the electronic structure of molecules by the molecular-orbital method."

Mullis, Kary Banks

(1944–   )

AMERICAN BIOCHEMIST

Born in Lenoir, North Carolina, Mullis was educated at Georgia Institute of Technology and at the University of California, Berkeley, where he completed his PhD in 1973. After postdoctoral periods at the University of Kansas Medical School and at the San Francisco campus of the University of California, Mullis joined the Cetus Corporation of Emeryville, California, in 1979.

One Friday night in April 1983 while driving to his weekend cabin, Mullis has recorded, it suddenly struck him that there was a method of producing unlimited copies of DNA fragments simply and *in vitro* (i.e., outside living cells). Previously, fragments could only be produced in limited numbers, in cells, and with much effort. Mullis named his method the "polymerase chain reaction" (PCR). The significance of the reaction can be judged by the price of $300 million placed by Cetus on the PCR patent sold to Hoffman-La Roche in 1991.

The first stage of the process is to heat DNA containing the required genetic segment in order to unravel the helix. Primers can then be added to mark out the target sequence. If, then, the enzyme DNA polymerase together with a number of free bases are added, two copies of the target sequence will be produced. These two copies can then be heated, separated, and once more produce two further copies each. The cycle, lasting no more than a few minutes, can be repeated as long as supplies last, doubling the target sequence each time. With geometric growth of this kind, more than 100 billion copies can be made in a few hours.

Relations between Mullis and Cetus quickly soured. He left the corporation in 1986 to work for a plastics manufacturer. But as the importance of his work began to be recognized Mullis found himself in sufficient demand to warrant his setting up as a consultant. One of his clients was Cetus as they fought off challenges to the PCR patent from DuPont and others. Mullis himself claims to be "tired of PCR" and more interested in "artificial intelligence, tunneling microscopes, science fiction, and surfing lessons."

Munk, Walter Heinrich

(1917–)

AMERICAN GEOPHYSICIST

Munk, who was born in the Austrian capital of Vienna, traveled to America in 1932; he was educated at the California Institute of Technology, graduating in 1939, and the University of California where he obtained his PhD in 1947. He taught initially at the Scripps Institution of Oceanography at the University of California before being appointed professor of geophysics there in 1954.

Munk's main fields of study have been the irregularities in the rotation of the Earth, tides, ocean waves, currents, and wind stress. Measurements made in the 19th century by such workers as Seth Chandler had made it clear that the Earth's rotation was far from uniform either in its rate or on its axis. By 1930 determinations of stellar transits made with pendulum clocks revealed that a January day exceeded a July day by two milliseconds. Such work was confirmed by the more accurate quartz-crystal clocks introduced in the 1950s.

With his colleagues at Scripps, Munk began a major survey of the problem of the Earth's rotation, which culminated in the publication, in collaboration with Gordon MacDonald, of the monograph, *The Rotation of the Earth: A Geophysical Discussion* (1961). Using evidence from ancient sources, from the International Latitude Service, and modern observations of the Moon they attributed variations in the length of the day to seasonal shifts in the terrestrial air masses, ocean tides, the distribution of glaciation, and changes within the Earth's core.

Murchison, Sir Roderick Impey

(1792–1871)

BRITISH GEOLOGIST

Murchison, the son of a Highland landowner from Tarradale in Scotland, was educated in Durham before entering the army at the age of 15. He served in the Napoleonic Wars, leaving the army after Waterloo, and settled in Durham where he intended to devote himself to a life of fox hunting. In 1824 his interest in science was aroused by his friendship with Humphry Davy; he moved to London and began attending lectures at the Royal Institution.

He became particularly interested in geology, learning field geology from William Buckland, and began exploring the main geological areas of Europe including Scotland, France, and the Alps. He was appointed president of the Geological Society in 1831 and in the same year concentrated his study on the Lower Paleozoic strata of South Wales. The strata he observed consisted chiefly of graywacke; he was soon able to establish that different beds of the graywacke were characterized by different fossils. His findings were outlined in *The Silurian System* (1839).

Together with Adam Sedgwick, Murchison also worked in southwest England where they identified the Devonian system. He went on an expedition to Russia in 1841 following which he proposed the Permian system based on the stratification of the Perm area of Russia. Noted for his obstinate nature, Murchison quarreled with Sedgwick and Henry De la Bech. He tried unsuccessfully to prevent his Silurian system being divided to form the Silurian, Ordovician, and Cambrian periods.

Murchison became director general of the Geological Survey in 1855. In 1871 he founded the chair of geology and mineralogy at the University of Edinburgh. The *Murchison Falls*, Uganda, were named for him, Murchison being president of the Royal Geographical Society at the time when Richard Burton, John Hanning Speke, and Samuel Baker were searching for the source of the River Nile.

Murphy, William Parry

(1892–1987)

AMERICAN PHYSICIAN

Murphy, the son of a congregational minister from Stoughton, Wisconsin, was educated at the University of Oregon and at Harvard where he obtained his MD in 1920. He then served on the staff of both the Harvard Medical School and the Peter Bent Brigham Hospital.

Murphy collaborated with George Minot in developing liver as a treatment of the then invariably fatal pernicious anemia. In 1934 he was able to report that 42 of the 45 patients originally treated in 1926 had been kept under observation. Of these 31 (75%) were alive and fit after ten years of treatment while the 11 who had died were victims of other complaints.

For this work Murphy shared the 1934 Nobel Prize for physiology or medicine with Minot and George Whipple.

Murray, Sir John

(1841–1914)

BRITISH MARINE ZOOLOGIST
AND OCEANOGRAPHER

Murray was born at Cobourg in Canada. A graduate of Edinburgh University, he was one of the naturalists on the *Challenger* expedition of 1872–76, the scientific reports of which he edited, becoming editor-in-chief in 1882. He completed much research on deep-sea deposits as well as observations of marine organisms such as foraminiferas and radiolarians. He was the inventor of a device for sounding and registering the temperature at great depths, conducting a bathymetrical survey of some of the freshwater lochs of Scotland. Murray took part in many other voyages, notably to the North Atlantic, the Faroe Channel, Spitzbergen and the Arctic, and to tropical Oceania. He wrote extensively on marine and freshwater biology, coral reef formation, and oceanography, including *The Ocean: A General Account of the Science of the Sea* (1913).

Murray, Joseph Edward

(1919–   )

AMERICAN SURGEON

Murray was born in Milford, Massachusetts. Educated at Holy Cross College and at Harvard University, he embarked on a career in medicine, specializing in plastic surgery. He worked at the Peter Bent Brigham

Hospital, Boston, becoming chief plastic surgeon (1964–86), held a similar position at the Children's Hospital Medical Center, Boston (1972–85), and served as professor of surgery at Harvard Medical School from 1970 to 1986.

Murray was a pioneer of kidney transplantation. In December 1954 he performed the first operation to implant a donor kidney into the pelvis of the recipient and attach it via the ureter to the bladder. Earlier attempts had placed the transplanted organ outside the body cavity, at sites such as the groin and armpit. The patient in Murray's operation was Richard Herrick, who received a kidney from his identical twin, Ronald.

The use of an organ from an identical sibling overcame the great obstacle of transplant surgery, namely rejection of the transplanted organ by the recipient's immune system. By receiving an organ of virtually identical tissue type, this first patient survived for eight years. For patients receiving organs from less closely related donors, the outlook was much worse.

Murray endeavored to improve the survival of the transplanted organ by suppressing the recipient's immune responses immediately prior to the operation. He conducted trials of the drug azathioprine, which killed cells of the immune system and so reduced the ability of the patient's own defense mechanism to reject the "foreign" tissue of a transplanted organ. Azathioprine had been developed by the British researcher, Roy Calne, working in collaboration with Murray at Boston. The drug proved to be an effective and much less hazardous alternative to Murray's initial method of using a massive dose of x-rays to suppress the recipient's immune system. (Azathioprine has now been superseded by cyclosporine, also developed by Calne.)

For his work in developing fundamental techniques in transplantation surgery, Murray was awarded the 1990 Nobel Prize for physiology or medicine, jointly with E. Donnall Thomas.

Muspratt, James

(1793–1886)

IRISH INDUSTRIAL CHEMIST

Muspratt, the son of a cork-cutter, was born and educated in Dublin before being apprenticed to a druggist. He developed an early interest in chemistry but before going into business he led an adventurous life and fought in Spain in the Peninsular War in both the army and the navy. He returned to Dublin in 1814 where, with the help of a small inheritance received in 1818, he manufactured various chemicals in a small way.

Muspratt moved to Liverpool, where he produced sulfuric acid, in 1822 and was quick to see the importance of the abolition in 1823 of the £30 per ton duty on salt. Cheap salt and the Leblanc process meant that a plentiful supply of soda could be produced for the large demands of the soap, glass, and dyeing industries. With this financial incentive Muspratt set up on Merseyside the third soda plant in Britain. Close to both the salt mines of Cheshire and the textile industry of Lancashire, he was ideally situated. The need for expansion drove him into partnership with Josias Gamble and they founded the alkali industry in St. Helens (1828), but two years later he moved to Newton-le-Willows on his own.

One of the major problems of the Leblanc process was its production of quantities of hydrochloric acid gas as a waste product. This pollution raised protests, such as the letters appearing in a Liverpool paper in 1827 lamenting that the local church could not be seen from a distance of 100 yards (91 m) and was rapidly turning a dark color. The move to St. Helens only delayed the inevitable prosecutions. Muspratt was unwilling to use William Gossage's tower and following litigation (1832–50) he was eventually successfully prosecuted by the neighboring farmers whose land was being destroyed. For this reason he moved his factories to Widnes and Flint in 1850. Following his retirement in 1857 they were run by his sons until in 1890 they became part of the United Alkali Company.

Musschenbroek, Pieter van

(1692–1761)

DUTCH PHYSICIST

Musschenbroek (**mu(r)s**-en-brook) came from a family of instrument makers in Leiden in the Netherlands. He studied at the University of Leiden, where he gained an MD in 1715 and a PhD in 1719. After holding a chair of medicine at Duisburg (1721–23) and of natural philosophy at Utrecht (1723–40), Musschenbroek returned to Leiden and served as professor of physics until his death.

On 20 April 1746 Musschenbroek reported in a letter to René Reaumur details of a new but dangerous experiment he had carried out. He had suspended, by silk threads, a gun barrel, which received static electricity from a glass globe rapidly turned on its axis and rubbed with the hands. From the other end he suspended a brass wire, which hung into a round glass bottle, partly filled with water. He was in fact trying to "preserve" electricity by storing it in a nonconductor.

When Musschenbroek held the bottle with one hand while trying to draw sparks from the gun-barrel he received a violent electric shock. He had accidentally made the important discovery of the Leyden jar – an early form of electrical capacitor. It was an event that captured both the popular and the scientific imagination and led to much effort by such scientists of the latter half of the 18th century as Benjamin Franklin to understand the nature and behavior of electricity. The German inventor Georg von Kleist independently discovered the Leyden jar in 1745.

Muybridge, Eadweard James

(1830–1904)

AMERICAN PHOTOGRAPHER

> He [Muybridge] invented one of the first high-speed shutters, and took a series of photos of a galloping horse by arranging a row of cameras beside the race track, operated by tapes which the horse ran through. This series...caused consternation, since it showed that all previous ideas of how a horse moves were incorrect...None of the photos showed the "hobbyhorse attitude," with front legs stretched forwards and hind legs stretched back, traditional in painting.
> —John Carey, *The Faber Book of Science* (1995)

Muybridge (**mI**-brij) was born Edward James Muggeridge at Kingston-on-Thames in Surrey, England. In his early twenties he changed his surname from Muggeridge to Muybridge and forename from Edward to Eadweard (Eadweard was the name of the Saxon kings who were crowned at Kingston in the 10th century). Although Muybridge spent much of his life in America, making his first trip there in 1852, he always retained links with his birthplace. Indeed, following a serious stagecoach accident in 1860 he returned to England to recuperate from his injuries.

By 1867 Muybridge was back in America, working as partner to the San Francisco-based photographer, Carleton E. Watson, and he quickly established a reputation as a skilled exponent of landscapes with a series of prints taken in California's Yosemite Valley. In 1868 he was appointed director of photographic surveys for the U.S. Government, and undertook photographic surveys of several remote regions, including the ports and harbors of newly purchased Alaska.

An interest in high-speed photography can be traced to the year 1872, when Muybridge was commissioned by the wealthy Californian race-horse owner, Leland Stanford, to attempt to settle the contentious issue of whether a trotting or galloping horse lifted all four feet clear of the ground at any point during its stride. Muybridge's attempts to capture this on film were of poor quality and less than convincing.

In October 1874 Muybridge's personal life was shattered when he was arrested for the murder of his wife's lover, whom Muybridge suspected was the father of the son born in April that year. Muybridge was held in prison for several months, but after a lengthy trial he was acquitted in February 1875. His wife, who had unsuccessfully sued for divorce, died later that year, leaving Muybridge to support the child.

Following a trip to Central America in 1875, and a dramatic panoramic sequence of pictures taken of San Francisco in 1877, Muybridge returned to his attempts at high-speed photography. He developed a more efficient shutter mechanism for the camera, and by using a battery of 12 cameras he was able to produce 12 sharply defined consecutive images of a galloping horse, all taken within half a second.

It was readily apparent that if such a sequence of pictures were viewed in rapid succession, the motion of the horse or other subject would be reproduced. Muybridge mounted the silhouettes of the horse on a glass disk, which was rotated and projected onto a screen through a device invented by the photographer and called a "zoopraxiscope." This was first demonstrated to the public in 1880, in what some would claim to be the first moving picture.

Muybridge's work was by now attracting considerable scientific interest, and in 1884 he began work at the University of Pennsylvania on what was to prove a celebrated series of high-speed studies of movement in both animals and human subjects. His new multilens camera could take 12 pictures on a single photographic plate in as little as one-fifth of a second. The results of this work were published in 11 volumes as *Animal Locomotion: an electro-photographic investigation of consecutive phases of animal movement* (1887). Included in this were his famous sequences of nude human subjects, often performing bizarre actions such as carrying a pan of water and sweeping with a broom.

The technique used by Muybridge could produce only very short sequences of moving pictures in the zoopraxiscope. However, the American inventor Thomas Edison was impressed by them, and may have found in them inspiration for his own invention, the cine camera and its perforated roll film. Certainly Muybridge and Edison collaborated on an abortive attempt to match sound to Muybridge's picture sequences.

Muybridge returned to Kingston in 1900, and spent his final years there. He bequeathed his zoopraxiscope and other effects to the public library in his home town.

Naegeli, Karl Wilhelm von

(1817–1891)

SWISS BOTANIST

Naegeli (**ne**-ge-lee), the son of a physician from Kilchberg in Switzerland, began medical studies at Zurich but went on to study botany under Alphonse de Candolle at Geneva. After graduating in 1840 he studied philosophy in Berlin but resumed his botanical studies in 1842, when he left for Jena to work with Matthias Schleiden.

In 1842 Naegeli published an essay on pollen formation in which he accurately described cell division, realizing that the wall formed between two daughter cells is not the cause but the result of cell division. He noted the division of the nucleus and recorded the chromosomes as "transitory cytoblasts." By 1846 these investigations had convinced him that Schleiden's theory of cells budding off the nuclear surface was incorrect.

Naegeli discovered the antherozoids (male gametes) in ferns and archegonia (female sex organs) in *Ricciocarpus* but did not realize the analogy of these to the pollen and ovary of seed plants. In 1845 he began investigating apical growth, which led to his distinguishing between formative (meristematic) and structural tissues in plants. Naegeli's micellar theory, formulated from studies on starch grains, gave information on cell ultrastructure.

In the taxonomic field, Naegeli made a thorough study of the genus *Hieracium* (hawkweeds), investigating crosses in the group. He had strong views on evolution and inheritance, which led him to reject Mendel's important work on heredity and hybrid ratios.

Nagaoka, Hantaro

(1865–1950)

JAPANESE PHYSICIST

Nagaoka (nah-gah-**oh**-ka) was born in Nagasaki, Japan, and educated at Tokyo University. After graduating in 1887 he worked with a visiting British physicist, C. G. Knott, on magnetism. In 1893 he traveled to Europe, where he continued his education at the universities of Berlin, Munich, and Vienna. He also attended, in 1900, the First International Congress of Physicists in Paris, where he heard Marie Curie lecture on radioactivity, an event that aroused Nagaoka's interest in atomic physics. Nagaoka returned to Japan in 1901 and served as professor of physics at Tokyo University until 1925.

Physicists in 1900 had just begun to consider the structure of the atom. The recent discovery by J. J. Thomson of the negatively charged electron implied that a neutral atom must also contain an opposite positive charge. In 1903 Thomson had suggested that the atom was a sphere of uniform positive electrification, with electrons scattered through it like currants in a bun.

Nagaoka rejected Thomson's model on the ground that opposite charges are impenetrable. He proposed an alternative model in which a positively charged center is surrounded by a number of revolving electrons, in the manner of Saturn and its rings. Nagaoka's model was, in fact, unstable and it was left to Ernest Rutherford and Niels Bohr, a decade later, to present a more viable atomic model.

Nambu, Yoichipo

(1921–)

JAPANESE PHYSICIST

Nambu (nahm-**boo**) was educated at the university in his native Tokyo, serving (1945–49) as a research assistant there before being appointed professor of physics at Osaka City University. He moved to America in 1952 and, after a two-year spell at the Institute of Advanced Studies, Princeton, he joined the University of Chicago and was appointed professor of physics in 1958, a position he held until his retirement in 1991.

In 1965 Nambu, in collaboration with M. Y. Han, tackled a major problem arising from the supposed nature of quarks. Baryons, that is, particles that interact by the strong force and have half-integer spin, were composed of three quarks. Thus the proton consists of two up and one down quark and consequently has a configuration written uud. But some baryons are composed of three identical quarks. The omega minus (Ω^-) particle, for example, is composed of three strange quarks with an sss configuration. Quarks, however, are fermions and are thus governed by the Pauli exclusion principle – i.e., no two identical particles can be in the same quantum state. As three s quarks will have the same quantum number, and as their spins can be aligned in only two ways, it seemed that at least two of the s quarks of the Ω^- particle occupy the same state.

Nambu proposed that quarks have an extra quantum number, which can take one of three possible values. The quantum number was arbitrarily referred to as "color," and the varieties equally arbitrarily as red, green, and blue. In this manner three up (uuu), down (ddd), or strange (sss) quarks could coexist without violating any quantum rules, as long as they had different colors. Nambu's work has been confirmed experimentally and is part of what is known as the standard model.

Nambu went on to consider the problem of quark confinement. How could it be, he asked, that free quarks were never encountered? When baryons decay they do not break down into quarks, but into different baryons and other particles. In response to this problem Nambu introduced string theory into physics in 1970. Particles were seen not as small spheres, but as massless rotating one-dimensional entities about 10^{-13} centimeter long, with an energy proportional to their length. The quarks are located at the string's ends. In the simplest case, a meson, a quark is located at one end and an antiquark at the other.

The quarks that make up a meson cannot be separated by stretching the string because the energy required rapidly increases with length. Nor would cutting the string suffice, for at the breaking point a newly created quark–antiquark pair would be created, yielding not a free quark but a further meson.

Though Nambu's string theory had its attractions as a theory of elementary particles it soon ran into other difficulties. Nonetheless, it has been revised by such theorists as John Schwarz in the form of superstring theory.

Nansen, Fridtjof

(1861–1930)

NORWEGIAN EXPLORER AND BIOLOGIST

Man wants to know, and when he ceases to do so, he is no longer man.
— Justifying polar explorations

One of the greatest men in Norway's history, Nansen (**nahn**-sen) is best remembered for his explorations of the Arctic, although he made many contributions to science, humanitarianism, and politics. Born at Store-Froen in Norway, he graduated in zoology from the University of Christiania, now Oslo. Nansen was appointed curator of the Bergen Natural History Museum in 1882, later becoming successively professor of zoology (1896) and professor of oceanography (1908) at the Royal Frederick University, Christiania. He helped found the International Commission for the Study of the Sea and was director of its Central Laboratory from 1901.

In 1888–89, after several preliminary expeditions, Nansen was the first to explore and describe the uncharted Greenland icecap, trekking from east to west and proving that the island is uniformly covered with an ice sheet. While wintering at Godthaab, Nansen spent some time studying the Eskimos, later publishing his observations as *Eskimoliv* (1891; Eskimo Life). Using a specially constructed ship, *Fram* (Forward), designed to withstand ice-pressure, Nansen then (1893–96) proceeded on his epic expedition to the North Pole. Allowing his ship to freeze in the ice, it drifted northwards (thus proving the existence of a warmer current from Siberia to Spitzbergen). Nansen left the ship and continued northward by sled to 86°14′N – only 200 miles (320 km) from the North Pole and further north than anyone had ever been before. Nansen described his Arctic journey in *Farthest North* (2 vols. 1897). He made further oceanographic expeditions to the northeast Atlantic, Spitzbergen, the Barents and Kara Seas, and to the Azores. In addition to explaining the nature of wind-driven sea currents and the formation of deep- and bottom-water, Nansen did much valuable work in improving and designing oceanographic instruments. In a quite different field his paper on the histology of the central nervous system is considered a classic.

In later life Nansen became a dedicated humanitarian. He assisted in famine relief and aid for refugees after World War I, for which he received the Nobel Peace Prize in 1922. As a politician, he influenced the separation of Norway from Sweden (1905), was a member of the Disarmament Committee (1927), and was Norway's first ambassador to Britain (1906–08).

Napier, John

(1550–1617)

SCOTTISH MATHEMATICIAN

[Napier] hath set my head and hands awork with his new and admirable logarithms. I hope to see him this summer, if it please God, for I never saw book which pleased me better and made me more wonder.
  —Henry Briggs, letter, 10 March 1615

Born in Edinburgh, Napier studied at the University of St. Andrews but left before taking his degree and then traveled extensively throughout Europe. He was a fervent Protestant and wrote a diatribe attacking

Catholics and others whose religious views he did not like. Napier was also very active in politics and he designed a number of war-engines of various kinds when it was believed that the Spanish were about to invade Scotland.

Napier devoted his spare time to mathematics, in particular to methods of computation. He introduced the concept of logarithms, publishing his work on this in *Mirifici logarithmorum canonis descriptio* (1614; Description of the Marvelous Canon of Logarithms). Napier's tables used natural logarithms, i.e., to base *e*, and soon after their publication the tables were slightly modified by Henry Briggs to base 10. Napier's further work on logarithms was published after his death in *Mirifici logarithmorum canonis constructio* (1619; Construction of the Marvelous Canon of Logarithms). Napier did some other mathematical work, in particular in spherical trigonometry and in perfecting the decimal notation.

Nasmyth, James

(1808–1890)

BRITISH ENGINEER

I also had the pleasure of showing him [Sir John Herschel] my experiment of cracking a glass globe filled with water and hermetically sealed. The water was then slightly expanded, on which the glass cracked. This was my method of explaining the action which, at some previous period of the cosmical history of the Moon, had produced those bright radiating lines that diverge from the lunar volcanic craters.

—*James Nasmyth, Engineer, an Autobiography*

Nasmyth demonstrated his mechanical expertise at an early age, producing model steam engines while only a boy. Born in the Scottish capital Edinburgh, he worked for two years in Henry Maudslay's machine shop in London and in 1836 set up his own foundry to make machine tools. When asked by Isambard Kingdom Brunel to make huge paddle wheels for a steamship, the *Great Britain*, he had to design the steam hammer to forge them (1839). Although the paddles were never made because screw propellers were used instead, the steam hammer was a crucial development in forging techniques.

Nasmyth retired from engineering at the age of 48 to study astronomy, especially the surface of the Moon.

Nathans, Daniel

(1928–)

AMERICAN MOLECULAR BIOLOGIST

Born in Wilmington, Delaware, Nathans was educated at the University of Delaware and at Washington University, St. Louis, where he obtained his MD in 1954. After first working at the Presbyterian Hospital and Rockefeller University in New York he moved in 1962 to Johns Hopkins as professor of microbiology.

With the identification of the first restriction enzyme by Hamilton Smith in 1970 it was clear to many microbiologists that at last a technique was available for the mapping of genes. Nathans immediately began working on the tumor-causing SV40 virus and by 1971 was able to show that it could be cleaved into 11 separate and specific fragments. In the following year he determined the order of such fragments, after which the way was clear for a full mapping. This also helped advance the techniques of DNA recombination.

It was for this work that Nathans shared the 1978 Nobel Prize for physiology or medicine with Smith and Werner Arber.

Natta, Giulio

(1903–1979)

ITALIAN CHEMIST

Natta (**naht**-ah), who was born at Imperia in Italy, was educated at the Milan Polytechnic Institute where he obtained his doctorate in chemical engineering in 1924. He was professor at the University of Pavia (1933–35), the University of Rome (1935–37), and the University of Turin (1937–38). Natta returned to Milan in 1939 as professor of industrial chemistry. In 1963 he became the first Italian to be awarded the Nobel Prize for chemistry, which he shared with Karl Ziegler for their development of *Ziegler–Natta catalysts*.

Natta's early work was on x-ray crystallography and on catalysis. In 1938 he began to organize research in Italy for the production of synthetic rubbers – work that led him on to his discoveries in polymer chemistry. Ziegler in 1953 had introduced catalysts for polymerizing ethene (ethylene) to polyethene (polythene) – these catalysts gave straight-chain polymers producing a superior form of polyethene. Natta applied these catalysts (and later improved catalysts) to propene (CH_3CHCH_2) to form polypropene. In 1954 he showed that polymers could be formed with regular structures with respect to the arrangement of the side groups (CH_3–) along the chain. These so-called stereospecific polymers had useful physical properties (strength, heat resistance, etc.). Natta extended the technique to the polymerization of other molecules.

Naudin, Charles

(1815–1899)

FRENCH EXPERIMENTAL BOTANIST AND HORTICULTURIST

> Happy is the professor who enjoys an assured income and whom the government
> provides with assistance and collaborators.
> —On his own difficulties in obtaining state funding

Born at Autun in eastern France, Naudin (noh-**dan**) received a sparse
formal education as a child; nevertheless, his will to learn led to him
earning the baccalaureate in science at Montpellier in 1837. He obtained
his doctorate in Paris in 1842 and held minor posts until 1846 when he
secured a teaching post in botany at the Natural History Museum, Paris.
However, two years later he was forced to abandon his public career due
to a severe nervous disorder that left him totally deaf. Eventually, in
1869, Naudin established a private experimental garden at Colliaure
and in 1878 he became director of a state-owned experimental garden at
Antibes.

Naudin's most significant work began in 1854 with experiments in
plant hybridization, from which he found that first-generation hybrids
display relative uniformity while second-generation hybrids obtained
by crossing within the first generation show great diversity of characters.
He recognized, in his theory of disjunction, that inheritance is particu-
late and not blending. However, unlike his contemporary Gregor
Mendel, he failed to recognize the statistical regularity with which different characters appear – a phenomenon now called segregation.

Naudin proposed hybridization to be the prime agent of evolutionary
change and not natural selection or environmental action. He held that
the present diversity of species is the product of a smaller number of
basic forms and might or might not exhibit permanence.

Needham, Dorothy Mary Moyle

(1896–1987)

BRITISH BIOCHEMIST

Needham, a Londoner, was educated at Cambridge University where she spent her whole career as a research worker at the Biochemistry Laboratory from 1920 until her retirement in 1963.

She worked extensively on the biochemistry of muscle and produced in her *Machina Carnis* (1971; Workings of the Flesh) the definitive history of the subject.

In 1948 Dorothy Needham was elected to the Royal Society, thus becoming one of the first female fellows. As her husband, Joseph Needham, had been a fellow since 1941, they were the first husband and wife members since Queen Victoria and Prince Albert.

Needham, John Turberville

(1713–1781)

BRITISH NATURALIST

Born in London and ordained as a Roman Catholic priest in France, Needham was founder and director of the Brussels Academy of Sciences. In 1740 he showed that pollen grains expanded in water, releasing their contents by means of papillae extruded at the pores. Like Lazzaro Spallanzani, Needham also demonstrated the revival ability of apparently dead microorganisms (e.g., rotifers and tardigrades) when placed in water. His most significant work, however, was concerned with what he thought to be spontaneous generation of living matter (1748). Having boiled meat broths and sealed them in apparently airtight containers, he later found them teeming with microorganisms. Spallanzani subsequently showed that Needham's experiments (conducted in collaboration with Georges Buffon) were faulty in that the broth had not been boiled long enough to kill the organisms previously present and that the containers had not been properly sealed.

Needham, Joseph

(1900–1995)

BRITISH BIOCHEMIST, HISTORIAN, AND SINOLOGIST

> I regarded the nature of biological organization as a purely philosophical question, and excluded it from scientific biology...I had not seen the full significance of the analogous science of crystallography. I am glad to have an opportunity of cancelling what I then said.
>
> —*Order and Life* (1936)

The son of a London physician, Needham was educated at Cambridge where he received his doctorate in 1924. He remained in Cambridge and began to work in the field of embryology, publishing in 1931 the comprehensive *Chemical Embryology* (3 vols.). He served as Dunn Reader in Biochemistry from 1933 until 1966, when he was appointed master of Gonville and Caius College.

Needham's life was radically changed in 1937 when three Chinese biochemistry students arrived in Cambridge. One of them, Lu Gwei-Djen, would become Needham's life-long collaborator and, in 1989, his second wife. At this point Needham became obsessed by Chinese culture and history. He began to learn the language and in 1942 was appointed scientific counsellor at the British embassy in Chungking. During his three-year stay in China he became aware of the enormous amount of material, virtually all unknown to the West, on science in China. He resolved that he would one day publish this material.

Needham had also spotted a major problem. It appeared to him that during much of its history Chinese science was more advanced than Western science. Yet, modern science arose in 17th-century Europe, not in China. The answer Needham suspected lies in the bureaucratic nature of Chinese society, and the rise of capitalism in the West.

After working briefly for UNESCO in Paris after the war, Needham returned to Cambridge and began to plan a multivolume work, *Science and Civilisation in China*. The first part appeared in 1954 and by the time of his death 16 substantial volumes of a planned 25 had been completed. From 1976 until his death Needham served as director of the East Asian History of Science Library, which was renamed the Needham Research Institute in 1986.

Néel, Louis Eugène Félix

(1904–)

FRENCH PHYSICIST

Néel (nay-**el**), who was born at Lyons in France, studied at the Ecole Normale Supérieure, later becoming professor of physics at the University of Strasbourg and subsequently at Grenoble. He became director of the Grenoble Polytechnic Institute in 1954 and director of the Center for Nuclear Studies there in 1956. He retired in 1976.

Most of his work has been concerned with the magnetic properties of solids. About 1930 he suggested that a new form of magnetic behavior might exist – called antiferromagnetism. This is exhibited by such substances as manganese(II) oxide (MnO), in which the magnetic moments of the Mn atoms and O atoms are equal and parallel but in opposite directions. Above a certain temperature (the *Néel temperature*) this behavior stops. More generally, Néel pointed out (1947) that materials could also exist in which the magnetic moments were unequal – the phenomenon is called ferrimagnetism.

Néel has also done considerable work on other magnetic properties, including an explanation of the weak magnetism of certain rocks that has made it possible to study the past history of the Earth's magnetic field. He was awarded the Nobel Prize for physics in 1970.

Ne'eman, Yuval

(1925–   )

ISRAELI PHYSICIST

Ne'eman (**nay**-man), who was born at Tel Aviv, was educated at the Israel Institute of Technology (Haifa) where he graduated in engineering in 1945. His academic career was interrupted by service in the Israeli army in the post-World War II troubles of Palestine.

In 1948, with the formation of the independent Israeli state, Ne'eman was able to return to his studies, while still serving with the Israeli defense forces. He went to the Ecole de Guerre in Paris and, while serving as a military attaché at the Israeli embassy in London, gained his PhD in physics from the University of London in 1962.

In 1961 Ne'eman and the American Murray Gell-Mann, working independently, developed a mathematical representation for the classification of elementary particles. This was known as the SU(3) theory and it successfully predicted the mass of the omega-minus particle observed for the first time in 1964. The theory was consolidated in a book by the two men with the title *The Eightfold Way* (1964) and later formed the basis of a further significant theoretical development – the "quark" hypothesis.

From 1961 to 1963 Ne'eman was scientific director of the Saraq Research Establishment of the Israeli Atomic Energy Commission, and from 1963 was head of the physics department and an associate professor at Tel Aviv University. In 1964 he became a full professor and vice-rector of the university.

Nef, John Ulric

(1862–1915)

AMERICAN CHEMIST

Nef was born at Herisau in Switzerland. In 1864 his father emigrated to America, where he became a superintendent of a textile factory; four years later Nef, aged six, joined him there. In 1880 he entered Harvard intending to study medicine but became interested in chemistry instead. Awarded a traveling fellowship he spent two years at Munich University where he gained his PhD in 1886. Returning to America, he first taught at Purdue and then Clark before he was finally appointed to the chair of chemistry at the University of Chicago in 1892.

Research on fulminates led Nef to speculate on the valence of carbon, one of the fundamental problems of late 19th-century chemistry. His work supported the theory of Archibald Couper that the carbon atom may sometimes have a valence of two, and Nef suggested the existence of the methylene radical, $:CH_2$. Nef's work also popularized Couper's method of representing the structure of carbon compounds, using dashes or dotted lines for carbon bonds.

Neher, Erwin

(1944–)

GERMAN BIOPHYSICIST

Neher (**nay**-er) was born in Landsberg, Germany. After attending the Technical University of Munich and the University of Wisconsin, he joined the Max Planck Institute of Psychiatry, Munich, in 1970, as a research associate. In 1972 he moved to the Max Planck Institute for Biophysical Chemistry in Göttingen, being appointed research director in 1983. Two periods of research in America took him to Yale University (1975–76) and the California Institute of Technology (1988–89).

Neher is best known for his studies of the minute channels in the membranes of living cells that allow ions to pass in and out of the cell. In the mid-1970s, working in collaboration with Bert Sakmann, Neher developed the so-called "patch-clamp technique" to detect the tiny electrical currents produced by the passage of ions through the membrane. Detection posed considerable technical challenges, given that the currents associated with each channel are of the order of 10^{-12} ampere, and the channels have a diameter comparable to the diameter of the ions.

The technique involved applying the tip of a saline-containing micropipette to the cell's membrane and applying suction to form a seal around the patch of membrane. The currents produced by the ions passing through the ion channel was monitored using a special amplifier. The technique had the great advantage of eliminating electrical noise generated by other parts of the membrane, which hitherto had obscured signals from any one channel.

Using their technique, Neher and Sakmann were able to demonstrate that the ion channels are either "open" or "shut," i.e., producing an "all or nothing" signal. Also, each channel is specific to a particular type of ion.

The patch-clamp technique has proved itself to be both sensitive and elegant, and has found application in many fields of basic and applied research. Ion channels are involved in a range of biological processes, such as the generation of nerve impulses, the fertilization of eggs, and the regulation of the heartbeat. The way in which their behavior is altered by disease or drugs can have far-reaching implications.

This crucial development in cellular research techniques earned Neher and Sakmann the 1991 Nobel Prize for physiology or medicine.

Neisser, Albert Ludwig Siegmund

(1855–1916)

GERMAN BACTERIOLOGIST

Neisser (**nI**-ser) was born in Schweidnitz (now Swidnica in Poland), the son of a physician. He was educated at Munsterberg and at Breslau, where he qualified in medicine (1877) and held the professorship of dermatology (from 1882).

In 1879 Neisser discovered the gonococcus, the causative agent of gonorrhea, which was named for him (*Neisseria*). In the same year he also identified the bacillus *Mycobacterium leprae* as the cause of leprosy, but in this he had been anticipated by Armauer Hansen. Neisser also worked on syphilis and collaborated with August von Wasserman in 1906 on the development of his diagnostic test.

Nernst, Walther Hermann

(1864–1941)

GERMAN PHYSICAL CHEMIST

> Knowledge is the death of research.
> —Quoted by C. G. Gillespie in *The Dictionary of Scientific Biography* (1981)

Nernst (nairnst), who was born at Briesen in Germany, studied at the universities of Zurich, Berlin, Würzburg, and Graz. After working as assistant to Wilhelm Ostwald in Leipzig from 1887 he became professor of chemistry at Göttingen in 1890. In 1904 he became professor of physical chemistry at Berlin and later was appointed director of the Institute for Experimental Physics there (1924–33). In 1933, out of favor with the Nazis, he retired to his country estate.

Nernst's early work was in electrochemistry – a field in which he made a number of contributions. Thus in 1889 he introduced the idea of the solubility product, i.e., the product of the concentrations of the different types of ions in a saturated solution. The product is a constant for sparingly soluble compounds (at constant temperature). Nernst also suggested (1903) the use of buffer solutions – mixed solutions of weak acids (or bases) and their salts, which resist changes in pH.

His main work, in 1906, was in thermodynamics. It came out of attempts to predict the course of chemical reactions from measurements of specific heats and heats of reaction. If heat is absorbed during a reaction, the amount absorbed falls with temperature and would become zero at absolute zero. Nernst postulated that the *rate* at which this reduction occurred would also become zero at absolute zero of temperature, and, as a consequence, derived the *Nernst heat theorem*, which states that if a reaction occurs between pure crystalline solids at absolute zero, then there is no change in entropy.

The theorem, stated in a slightly different form, is now known as the third law of thermodynamics. It is equivalent to the statement that absolute zero cannot be attained in a finite number of steps. At the time it allowed the calculation of absolute values of entropy (and then equilibrium constants), rather than changes in entropy. It is now known to be a consequence of the quantum statistics of the particles. For his work in thermodynamics, Nernst received the Nobel Prize for chemistry in 1920.

He also made contributions to photochemistry and, in addition, produced one of the standard texts of the period, *Theoretische Chemie* (1893; Theoretical Chemistry), which went through numerous editions and translations.

He managed to make a large fortune by the turn of the century by selling a form of electric light, which though superior to the Edison carbon-filament lamp soon became obsolete with the invention of the tungsten-filament lamp.

Newcomb, Simon

(1835–1909)

AMERICAN ASTRONOMER

The son of an itinerant teacher, Newcomb was born at Wallace in Nova Scotia and had little formal education. He was apprenticed to a herbalist in Nova Scotia but ran away to join his father in the United States. In 1857 he joined the American Nautical Almanac Office, and he graduated from Harvard in 1858. He joined the corps of professors of mathematics in the navy, and became professor of mathematics at the Naval Observatory in Washington in 1861. From 1884 to 1894 he was professor of mathematics and astronomy at Johns Hopkins University. He was also superintendent of the American Nautical Almanac from 1877 to 1897, retiring with the rank of rear admiral. In addition he was the editor of the *American Journal of Mathematics* and the author of over 350 scientific papers and a number of popular works on astronomy.

Newcomb worked for many years on new tables for the planets and the Moon, which were published in 1899. These, together with his organization of the Nautical Almanac, were his major astronomical work. His tables, the result of detailed observations and sophisticated mathematics, were the most accurate ever made and were in constant use until the middle of this century. Also of major importance was his production and promotion of a new, unified, and more accurate system of astronomical constants, which was adopted worldwide in 1896.

He did much to encourage younger scientists. Hearing the young Albert Michelson lecture to the American Association for the Advancement of Science on new methods for accurately determining the speed of light, he went out of his way to raise money for the unknown young scientist to continue with his work.

Newcomen, Thomas

(1663–1729)

BRITISH ENGINEER

Newcomen worked as an ironmonger in his home town of Dartmouth, Devon. His familiarity with the Cornish tin mines prompted him to try to improve the horse-driven pumps used to remove water from mines. Together with his assistant, a plumber by the name of John Calley, he built a pump based on the design developed and patented by Thomas Savery. In Newcomen's piston-operated steam engine, a counterweighted plunger was pushed to the top of a cylinder by steam pressure. Then, when the steam condensed, the partial vacuum created inside the piston caused the plunger to be pushed back down by atmospheric pressure. A water jet inside the cylinder condensed the steam at each stroke, and the design, unlike Savery's, included automatic valves. Newcomen's engine was the forerunner of James Watt's steam engine.

Newcomen entered into a partnership with Savery and they constructed their first engine near Dudley Castle, Staffordshire, in 1712. Versions of Newcomen's engine were being built until the 1800s and some were still in use at the beginning of the 20th century, both in mines and to power water wheels.

Newell, Allan

(1927–   )

AMERICAN COMPUTER SCIENTIST

Newell was born in San Fransisco, the son of a radiologist. He was educated at Princeton and at the Carnegie Institute of Technology, Pittsburgh, where he completed his PhD in 1957. After a period at RAND, Santa Monica, Newell returned to Carnegie in 1961 and was appointed professor of computer science in 1976.

In 1956 Newell helped to organize a seminal conference in Dartmouth, New Hampshire, on the subject of artificial intelligence (AI). Soon after, in collaboration with his RAND colleague Herbert Simon, Newell produced one of the early successes of the new discipline with Logic Theorist. This was a program written in IPL (Information Processing Language) designed to prove theorems in Russell and White-head's *Principia Mathematica*. They succeeded in deriving 38 of the first 52 theorems of the system. Further, because the proofs were produced in the main within a few minutes, they could not have been derived by any kind of purely random search; some kind of intelligence, it was argued, must have been deployed.

Encouraged by their success with Logic Theorist, Newell and his collaborators attempted to develop a successor, which they called General Problem Solver. It would be sufficiently flexible to play chess, break codes, solve mathematical problems, and deal with other diverse intellectual problems. Although some progress was made the program was eventually abandoned; the ability to solve problems proved to be not as general as was initially supposed. Further, other workers such as Edward Feigenbaum began to show in the 1970s that more progress could be made by preparing "expert systems."

Newlands, John Alexander Reina

(1837–1898)

BRITISH CHEMIST

Newlands, who was born in London, studied under August von Hofmann at the Royal College of Chemistry. In 1860, being of Italian ancestry, he fought with Giuseppe Garibaldi's army in its invasion of Naples. On his return from Naples he set up as a consultant with his brother in 1864 but, after the failure of his business, worked as an industrial chemist in a sugar refinery.

In various papers published in 1864 and 1865 Newlands stated his law of octaves and came close to discovering the periodic table. He claimed that if the elements were listed in the order of their atomic weights a pattern emerged in which properties seemed to repeat themselves after each group of seven elements. He pointed out the analogy of this with the intervals of the musical scale.

Newlands's claim to see a repeating pattern was met with savage ridicule on its announcement. His classification of the elements, he was told, was as arbitrary as putting them in alphabetical order and his paper was rejected for publication by the Chemical Society. It was not until Mendeleev's periodic table was announced in 1869 that the significance of Newlands's idea was recognized and he was able to publish his paper *On the Discovery of the Periodic Law* (1884).

Newton, Alfred

(1829–1907)

BRITISH ORNITHOLOGIST

Newton, the son of the member of Parliament for Ipswich, was born at Geneva in Switzerland and educated at Cambridge University. From 1854 until the early 1860s he traveled widely in Lapland, Iceland, the Caribbean, and America, making one of the first systematic studies of their birds. Thereafter he resided in Cambridge serving as the first occupant of the chair of zoology and comparative anatomy from 1866 until his death.

Newton developed ornithology in Britain into a serious scientific discipline, a cooperative and organized activity. It was, for example, in his Cambridge rooms in 1858 that the decision was made to found the important journal *Ibis*. He was also deeply involved in attempting to initiate bird censuses, the keeping of migration records, and the collecting of skins and eggs.

His own special interest lay with the great auk and dodo. He did, however, publish more general works such as the important *A Dictionary of Birds* (1893–96). Although noted for his reactionary views – he fought against the introduction of women and music into the college chapel with equal passion – he nonetheless had little difficulty in accepting the evolutionary theory of Darwin and of supporting the experimental physiology of Michael Foster.

Newton, Sir Isaac

(1642–1727)

ENGLISH PHYSICIST AND MATHEMATICIAN

I do not know what I may appear to the world, but to myself I seem to have been only like a boy playing on the sea-shore, and diverting myself in now and then finding a smoother pebble or a prettier shell than ordinary, whilst the great ocean of truth lay all undiscovered before me.

—Quoted by L. T. More in *Isaac Newton*

Newton's father, the owner of the manor of Woolsthorpe in Lincolnshire, England, died three months before Newton was born. The family had land but were neither wealthy nor gentry. Left by his mother in the care of his grandmother, the young Newton is reported to have been quiet, unwilling to play with the village boys, and interested in making things. His mother returned to Woolsthorpe in 1656 after the death of her second husband. By this time Newton was at school in Grantham where he stayed until 1658, lodging with a local apothecary. There is no evidence that he was especially gifted at this time, although he was certainly skillful for he made a water clock, sundials (which still survive at Woolsthorpe), and model furniture for his stepsisters. After two years helping his mother to run the family farm,

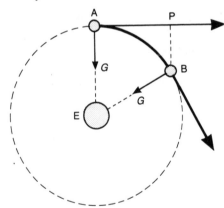

THE FALL OF THE MOON   The Moon at position A experiences a force of gravitational attraction toward the Earth E. In the absence of any force it would continue along a straight line AP. In fact it moves in a circular path AB. Newton saw that this is equivalent to the Moon "falling" toward the Earth – in the diagram the fall is the distance PB in the same direction as AE.

he went to Cambridge University in 1661, where he stayed for nearly 40 years.

Not much is known of Newton's student life. In 1665 he was forced by the plague to leave Cambridge and return to Woolsthorpe. Here, during his so-called *annus mirabilis* (miraculous year), he began to develop the ideas and insights for which he is so famous. Here he first began to think about gravity, and also devoted time to optics, grinding his own lenses and considering the nature of light. During this period he also worked out his mathematical ideas about "fluxions" (the calculus).

When he returned to Cambridge after the plague had died down he was elected a fellow of his college, Trinity, in 1667, and in 1669 he succeeded Barrow as Lucasian Professor. He served as member of parliament for the university for the periods 1689–90 and 1701–02, although he does not appear to have been politically very active. His public career was pursued through Charles Montague, first earl of Halifax, who was able to introduce Newton into court and society circles. When Montague became chancellor of the exchequer he was able to offer Newton the post of warden of the Mint in 1696. He was made master of the Mint in 1699 and knighted for his services in 1705. From this time he did virtually no new science apart from publishing and revising works already written. He did concern himself with the affairs of the Royal Society, of which he became president in 1703. He resigned his Cambridge post in 1701.

At the Mint, his first task was to supervise "the great recoinage" – the replacement of the old hammered coins with new pieces with milled edges. It was also Newton's business to pursue the counterfeiters and clippers of his day. As ever, he took his duties seriously and could be found regularly visiting suspects in Newgate and other prisons. Between June 1698 and Christmas 1699 he interviewed 200 witnesses on 123 separate occasions. In the same period 27 counterfeiters were executed. Other major tasks undertaken by Newton included the introduction of a union coinage in 1707 following the union of the Kingdoms of England and Scotland, the issue of new copper coins in 1718, the revaluation of the guinea to 21 shillings in 1717, and a general improvement in the assaying of the currency. The Mint made Newton a wealthy man. In addition to a salary of £600 a year he also received a commission on the amount of silver minted, which brought in on average £1,000 a year. At the time of his death Newton had accumulated £30,000 in cash and securities.

Much of Newton's later life was also spent in needless priority disputes. These arose largely through his reluctance to publish his own work. It was not until 1704, when Newton was over 60, that he actually published a mathematical text. Even then his main work on the calculus, *Methodis fluxionum* (Method of Fluxions), composed between 1670 and 1671, was only published posthumously in 1736. At the same time manuscripts of unpublished works were shown to friends and colleagues.

When, therefore, Leibniz published his own work on the differential and integral calculus in 1684, he felt no need to acknowledge any unpublished work of Newton. He had developed his methods and notation largely from his own vast intellectual resources. He had seen some Newtonian manuscripts on a visit to London in 1673, and letters from Newton in 1676 contained further details. None of this, it is now accepted, was sufficient to account for Leibniz's 1684 paper. The dispute began in 1700 when Leibniz objected to the practice of the Newtonians referring to him as the "second inventor" of the calculus. The dispute dragged on until the 1720s, long outlasting the death of Leibniz in 1716. After a decade of bitter and anonymous dispute Leibniz unaccountably applied to the Royal Society in 1712 to conduct an inquiry into the matter. Newton behaved quite shamelessly. He appointed the committee, decided what evidence it should see, and actually drafted the published report himself. Thereupon, in later stages of the dispute, he would appeal to the report, the *Commercium epistolicum* (1713; On the Exchange of Letters), as an independent justification of his position.

Newton is best known for his work on gravitation and mechanics. The most famous story in the history of science has the unusual distinction of being true, at least according to Conduit, who married Newton's niece Catherine. He reported that "In the year 1665, when he retired to his own estate on account of the plague, he first thought of his system of gravity, which he hit upon by observing an apple fall from a tree." His ideas were not published until 1684 when Edmond Halley asked Newton to find what force would cause a planet to move in an elliptical orbit. Newton replied that he already had the answer. Finding that he had lost his proof, he worked it out again.

His result was that two bodies – such as the Sun and a planet, or the Earth and the Moon – attract each other with a force that depends on the product of their masses and falls off as the square of their distance apart. Thus the force is proportional to $m_1 m_2/d^2$, where m_1 and m_2 are the masses and d is their distance apart. Originally he applied this to point masses but in 1685 he proved that a body acted as if its mass were a point mass of the same magnitude acting at the center of the body (for a symmetrical body).

Newton's original work on gravity, in 1665, had been applied to the motion of the Moon. His insight was that the Moon in its motion "falls" to the Earth under the same cause as the apple falls. His calculations at this time used an erroneously low value for the Earth's radius and it was possibly this that made him lay aside his calculations until 1684.

Then in 1684 he took up the subject again and began to write his great work *Philosophiae Naturalis Principia Mathematica* (Mathematical Principles of Natural Philosophy) – known as the *Principia*. The first edition was published in 1687. Here he set out his three laws of motion. His first law states that a body at rest or in uniform motion will continue in that state unless a force is applied. His second law gives a definition of force – that it equals the mass of a body multiplied by the acceleration it produces in the body. His third law puts forward the idea that if a body exerts a force (action) on another there is an equal but opposite force (reaction) on the first body.

What Newton did in his work in mechanics was to establish a unified system: one in which a simple set of basic laws explained a range of diverse phenomena – the motion of the Moon and planets, motion of the Earth, and the tides. Newton did not give any explanation of what gravity actually *is*. How it acts, its mechanism, and its cause were matters that Newton claimed we should not frame hypotheses on. That it has a cause Newton was sure of, for the idea that a body may act on another through a vacuum over a long distance "without the mediation of anything else...is to me so great an absurdity that I believe no man can ever fall into it. Gravity must be caused...but whether this agent be material or immaterial I have left to the consideration of my reader." Newton did not always obey his own injunction and in the 1713 edition of the *Principia* speculated about the existence of "certain very subtle spirits that pervade all dense bodies," which might explain light, electricity, sensation, and much besides.

Newton's reluctance to provide a gravitational mechanism was seen as a basic weakness of his system by the Cartesians. Whatever the defects of the physics of René Descartes at least he provided mechanisms, in the form of vortices, to explain all movements. To some Newton's gravity seemed a retrograde step in that it was reintroducing into physics the occult, meaningless forces that Descartes had recently eliminated. Nevertheless, Newton's system received great acclaim in England and was to become the model for all succeeding scientific theory.

Newton also worked extensively on light. He began by rejecting the Cartesian account of color. For Descartes white light was natural light; colored light was the modification produced in light by the medium through which it passes. Thus light passing through a prism is spread into a spectrum because the light has been differentially modified by the varying thickness of the prism.

Newton published his own account in 1672 in his first published paper, *New Theory about Light and Colours*. "I procured me a Triangular glass-Prisme to try therewith the celebrated Phenomena of Colours," he began. When he passed a ray of light through a prism he found that it formed an oblong, not a circular image, five times longer than its breadth. He found that, as was well known, light passing through a prism was dispersed and formed a colored spectrum. But when a second prism was taken and colored light rays passed through it, no further change was discernible. Red light remained red, and blue light blue. From this, his famous *experimentum crucis* (cross experiment), he derived two important conclusions: firstly, ordinary white light was composite, a mixture of the various colors of the spectrum; secondly, he concluded, "Light consists of Rays differently Refrangible," and it was this difference in refrangibility that produced the oblong image which had so puzzled Newton.

Newton's views found little favor and over the next few years he was repeatedly called upon to explain and defend his position. By 1676 he had had enough. "I see a man must either resolve to put out nothing new or become a slave to defend it," he wrote to Oldenburg, and published no more on light until 1704.

He had, however, already in 1675 sent a paper to the Royal Society entitled *An Hypothesis Explaining the Properties of Light*. He refused to allow it to be published and it first appeared in 1757, long after Newton's death. The paper contains Newton's analysis of light as "multitudes of unimaginable small and swift corpuscles of various sizes, springing from shining bodies." He dismissed the view that light, like sound, could consist of waves, because light unlike sound could not travel around corners. The paper also contained an account of what have since become known as *Newton's rings*. These consist of a series of concentric colored rings and can be produced by putting a plano-convex lens of large radius of curvature on a flat reflecting surface. They were explained by Newton with some ingenuity and some difficulty in terms of his corpuscular theory of light. Newton's mature views on these and many other matters were presented in his *Opticks* (1704).

Not all of Newton's work on light was of a theoretical kind. He was an extremely talented experimentalist and in the late 1660s he designed and built the first reflecting telescope. This involved grinding and polishing the mirrors himself. The idea of a reflecting telescope had occurred earlier to James Gregory but his attempts at constructing a model, despite receiving professional help, led nowhere. The advantage of the Newtonian telescope over the refractor of Galileo is that mirrors do not suffer from chromatic aberration.

But above all else Newton was a mathematician of incomparable power. In 1696 Johann Bernoulli posed a problem to the mathematicians of Europe, allowing them six months to solve it. Newton solved the problem in a single night and published the result anonymously in the *Transactions* of the Royal Society. Bernoulli was not fooled, claiming to recognize the author or, "the lion by his claw." Again in 1716 Leibniz issued another difficult problem, which Newton solved before going to bed after a day's work at the Mint.

Newton communicated the generalized form of the binomial theorem to Henry Oldenbourg in 1676. It was also in that year that he deposited with Oldenbourg his *epistola prior* (first letter) claiming discovery of his method of fluxions in an anagram. The terminology arose from his considering the path of a continuously moving body as a curve made by a continuously moving point. The moving point he called a fluent and its velocity he called a fluxion. This he symbolized by x and its acceleration as x. This, independently of Leibniz, was Newton's discovery of the calculus, although Leibniz's notation was the one eventually adopted.

Throughout his life Newton also displayed a deep interest in two other areas: religion and alchemy. At his death over 1,000 manuscript pages, running to nearly 1.5 million words, and two completed books were discovered, devoted entirely to religious matters. Newton was a unitarian, a matter kept fairly secret during his life as it would have excluded him from his Lucasian chair and his post at the Mint. Much of his life was spent on deep studies of church history, the Bible, and ancient chronology. His aim was to show that the text of the Bible had been corrupted by later trinitarian editors, and that the history of the early church revealed a similar corruption introduced by Athanasius in the fourth century. The matter was dealt with at length in his *Two Notable Corruptions of Scripture* (1754) and in numerous manuscripts.

Equally extensive were Newton's alchemical manuscripts. In his library were 138 books on alchemy, and his manuscripts on the subject ex-

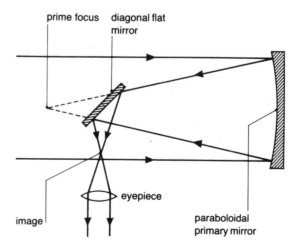

prime focus   diagonal flat mirror

eyepiece

image

paraboloidal primary mirror

NEWTONIAN TELESCOPE   *The ray path in the reflecting telescope first constructed by Newton.*

ceed 600,000 words. It is less clear, however, whether Newton was a genuine alchemist committed to dreams of transmutation and the philosopher's stone, or whether he was merely using whatever sources he could find to further his chemical interests. His interests in chemistry were sufficient to lead him to establish a laboratory in Trinity College and for a while in the 1680s, it was reported, "the laboratory fire scarcely went out night or day." He published during his life just one brief work on chemistry, *De natura acidorum* (1710; On the Nature of Acids). There are, however, several passages devoted to chemistry scattered among the *Queries* added by Newton to his *Opticks* (1704).

Newton died in 1727 at the age of 85 after a fairly short illness. He managed to preside over a meeting of the Royal Society a fortnight before his death. Shortly after he was diagnosed as having a stone in the bladder and seems to have spent the last days of his life in great pain. He was buried in Westminster Abbey where a most unattractive monument can still be seen. Many words have been written about his greatness as a scientist; the most apposite remain the often quoted words of Alexander Pope, composed for Newton's tomb but, for some reason, rejected:

Nature and Nature's laws lay hid in night:
God said, let Newton be! and all was light.

Nicholas of Cusa

(1401–1464)

GERMAN CARDINAL, MATHEMATICIAN, AND PHILOSOPHER

God has endowed every body with its own nature, orbit, and place, and has set the Earth in the middle of all, decreeing that it be heavy and deviate neither upward nor sideways.
—*De venatione sapientiae* (1463; On the Pursuit of Knowledge)

The son of a prosperous fisherman from Kues (Cusa), in Germany, Nicholas (**nik**-oh-las or nee-koh-**lah**-uus) studied at Heidelberg and Padua where he obtained an LLD in 1423. He rose through the hierarchy to become a cardinal in 1448 and a figure of some importance in the Church. His most lasting work was his *De docta ignorantia* (1440; On Learned Ignorance) in which he argued against the possibility of definitive knowledge. "Reason stands in the same relation to the truth as the polygon to a circle," he declared in a striking image. "The more vertices it has, the more it resembles a circle...yet never becomes a circle." Using metaphysical rather than astronomical arguments he was thus led to deny the standard picture of the universe as bounded by spheres with the Earth at the center. In its place he proposed a universe in which nothing is fixed, with no center or circumference yet not infinite, with everything in motion and a complexity beyond our understanding. He also proposed that the Earth revolved on its axis and around the Sun, and that the stars were other suns.

Not surprisingly, such an unorthodox construction had no impact on a conventional thinker like Nicolaus Copernicus. It did, however, help to overthrow in later minds the traditional idea of a "closed world" and prepare the way for the "infinite universe" of the 17th century.

In other areas of science, Nicholas is also said to have constructed spectacles for the nearsighted (with concave lenses) and to have thought that plants drew nourishment from the air.

Nicholson, Seth Barnes

(1891–1963)

AMERICAN ASTRONOMER

Nicholson was the son of a farmer from Springfield, Illinois. He graduated from Drake University, Des Moines, Iowa, in 1912 and in 1915 obtained his PhD from the University of California. From then until his retirement in 1957 he worked at the Mount Wilson Observatory, California.

While still a graduate student at the Lick Observatory, Nicholson discovered the ninth satellite of Jupiter (Sinope) in 1914, working close to the limits of resolution of the Lick telescope and the photographic plates then available. He went on to discover a further three satellites, Jupiter X (Lysithea) and XI (Carme) in 1938 and Jupiter XII (Ananke) in 1951. All four satellites are very small, about 15–20 kilometers (9–12 mi) in diameter.

Nicholson studied the surface features and spectrum of the Sun and also, in collaboration with Edison Petit, worked on planetary and lunar temperatures. Thus they showed in 1927 that the Moon undergoes enormous temperature changes, for in the course of an eclipse its surface temperature dropped from 160°F to –110°F (71°C to –79°C) in about an hour.

Nicholson, William

(1753–1815)

BRITISH CHEMIST

Nicholson was born in London, the son of a lawyer. In 1769, at the age of 16, he joined the East India Company, but left them in 1776 to become an agent in Europe for the pottery manufacturer Josiah Wedgwood. He then started a school of mathematics, as well as translating various scientific works into English. During his career he was also a patent agent, the engineer of the Portsmouth and Gosport waterworks, and the inventor of the hydrometer named for him for measuring the density of liquids.

In 1800 Nicholson heard of the invention of the electric battery by Alessandro Volta. Nicholson built the first voltaic pile in England and then discovered that when the leads from the battery were immersed in water the water broke up into bubbles of hydrogen and oxygen; he had discovered electrolysis.

Nicholson's importance also rests on the steady stream of textbooks that he produced, many of which were translations from the French. These included his *Introduction to Natural Philosophy* (1781), *First Principles of Chemistry* (1790), and *Dictionary of Chemistry* (1795). He also started the first independent scientific journal, the *Journal of Natural Philosophy, Chemistry, and the Arts*. Through publications of this kind the new artisans and industrialists learned much of the new chemistry, which they applied to the developing industries.

Nicol, William

(1768–1852)

BRITISH GEOLOGIST AND PHYSICIST

Little is known about Nicol's early life except that he was born in Scotland. Primarily a geologist, he lectured in natural philosophy at the University of Edinburgh where James Clerk Maxwell was probably one of his pupils. His first publication came when he was nearly 60.

Nicol is best remembered for his invention, announced in 1828, of the *Nicol prism*. This device, constructed from a crystal of Iceland spar (a natural form of calcium carbonate), made use of the phenomenon of double refraction discovered by Erasmus Bartholin. The crystal was split along its shorter diagonal and the halves cemented together in their original position by a transparent layer of Canada balsam. The ordinary ray was totally reflected at the layer of Canada balsam while the extraordinary ray, striking the cement at a slightly different angle, was transmitted. Nicol prisms made it easy to produce polarized light. For a long time they became the standard instrument in the study of polarization and played a part in the formation of theories of molecular structure.

Nicol also developed new techniques of preparing thin slices of minerals and fossil wood for microscopic examination. These techniques allowed the samples to be viewed through the microscope by transmitted light rather than by reflected light, which only revealed surface features. His lack of publications resulted in some 40 years elapsing before these techniques were incorporated into studies in petrology.

Nicolle, Charles Jules Henri

(1866–1936)

FRENCH BACTERIOLOGIST

Nicolle (nee-**kol**), the son of a physician, was born at Rouen in France and educated there and in Paris, where he obtained his MD in 1893. He returned to Rouen to join the faculty of the medical school but in 1902 moved to Tunis, where he served as director of the Pasteur Institute until his death.

In 1909 Nicolle revolutionized the study and treatment of typhus. He noticed that typhus patients outside the hospital transmitted the disease to their families, to the doctors who visited them, to the staff admitting them into hospital, to the personnel responsible for taking their clothes and linen, and to hospital laundry staff. But once admitted to the ward the typhus patients did not contaminate any of the other patients, the nurses, or the doctors. Since all newly admitted patients were stripped, washed, and changed, Nicolle concluded that the disease carrier was attached to the patient's skin and clothing and could be removed by washing. The obvious carrier was the louse.

Nicolle lost no time in providing experimental evidence for his reasoning. He transmitted typhus to a monkey by injecting it with blood from an infected chimpanzee. A louse was allowed to feed on the monkey and when transferred to another monkey succeeded in infecting it by its bite alone. It was for this work that Nicolle was awarded the Nobel Prize for physiology or medicine in 1928.

Nicolle actually considered his discovery of "apyretic typhus" the most important of his achievements. He found guinea pigs to be susceptible to typhus but that some of them, with blood capable of infecting other animals, showed no symptoms of the disease at all. He had in fact discovered the carrier state, which was to have significance for the emerging science of immunology.

Nicolle also attempted to develop vaccines against typhus and other infections. He was mildly successful in using serum from patients recovering from typhus and measles to induce a short-lasting passive immunity on those at risk.

Niepce, Joseph-Nicéphore

(1765–1833)

FRENCH INVENTOR

Niepce found that he could fix the camera image using a plate coated in bitumen that hardened on exposure to light. After taking the plate from the camera he washed off the unhardened bitumen in oil of lavender, so developing the picture. A murky view of a farmyard, photographed (with an eight-hour exposure) from his upstairs window, still survives.
—John Carey, *The Faber Book of Science* (1995)

Niepce (nyeps), who made the first permanent photographic image, came from a wealthy family in Châlon-sur-Saône, eastern France, that fled the French Revolution. He returned to serve with Napoleon Bonaparte's army, but after being dismissed because of ill health, went back to his birthplace (1801) to do scientific research.

With his brother, Niepce built an internal-combustion engine (1807) for boats using carbon and resin for fuel. In 1813 he started the attempt to record images, on paper coated with silver chloride. He produced his first image, a view from his workroom, in 1816, but was only able to fix this partially with nitric acid. In 1822 he produced a photographic copy of an engraving using a glass plate coated with bitumen of Judea. Later (1826) he used a pewter plate to make the first permanent camera photograph. He also devised the first mechanical reproduction process. The main difficulty was the long exposure times needed – over eight hours. Niepce formed a partnership with the Parisian painter, Louis-Jacques-Mandé Daguerre in 1826 to perfect the process of heliography but he died before seeing the final success of his efforts.

Nieuwland, Julius Arthur

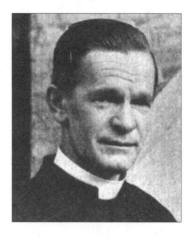

(1878–1936)

AMERICAN CHEMIST

Nieuwland (**nyoo**-land) was born at Hansbeke in Belgium and brought to America when three years old. He was educated at the University of Notre Dame, Indiana, obtaining his PhD on acetylene chemistry from there in 1904. His whole career was spent at Notre Dame, teaching botany from 1904 to 1918 and organic chemistry from 1918 to 1936. He entered the Roman Catholic priesthood in 1903.

Nieuwland made an important contribution to the chemistry of acetylene when, in 1925, he succeeded in making three molecules join together in a small chain to give divinylacetylene, which, to his surprise, produced a rubberlike solid on polymerization.

Working with chemists at Du Pont, Nieuwland found in 1929 that if monovinylacetylene is treated with acid it forms chloroprene, which can then be polymerized to give neoprene, the first synthetic rubber.

Nilson, Lars Fredrick

(1840–1899)

SWEDISH CHEMIST

Born at Östergötland in Sweden, Nilson (**nil**-son) studied at the University of Uppsala and was appointed professor of chemistry there in 1878. In 1883 he moved to the Agricultural Academy in Stockholm.

In 1879 he isolated a new element, which he named scandium after his native Scandinavia, from the rare earth ytterbia. His colleague, Per Cleve, showed that its properties were those of Dmitri Mendeleev's eka-boron, thus providing a second confirmation of the validity of the periodic table.

Nilson also made a significant contribution to agricultural chemistry by showing that the chalk moors of the island of Gotland would grow sugar beet if treated with a potash fertilizer.

Nirenberg, Marshall Warren

(1927–   )

AMERICAN BIOCHEMIST

Nirenberg, who was born in New York City, graduated from the University of Florida in 1948 and gained his PhD in biochemistry from the University of Michigan in 1957. He then joined the National Institutes of Health in Bethesda, Maryland, where he began the work that culminated in the cracking of the genetic code.

When Nirenberg began this research it had already been surmised that different combinations of three nucleotide bases (triplets) each coded for a specific amino acid and that through the operation of this "genetic code" amino acids are aligned in the right order to make proteins. As there are 64 possible triplets (from the combinations of the four bases present in DNA or RNA), the big question was: which triplets code for the 20 amino acids? Severo Ochoa's discovery of the technique to synthesize RNA artificially enabled Nirenberg to make an RNA molecule consisting entirely of uracil nucleotides. Thus the only triplet possible would be a uracil triplet (UUU of the code). Nirenberg found that the protein made by this RNA molecule consisted entirely of the amino acid phenylalanine, indicating that UUU must code for phenylalanine. With this first important step completed others were quick to unravel the rest of the code.

For this work, Nirenberg shared the 1968 Nobel Prize for physiology or medicine with Har Gobind Khorana and Robert Holley.

Nobel, Alfred Bernhard

(1833–1896)

SWEDISH CHEMIST, ENGINEER, AND INVENTOR

...to those who, during the preceding year, shall have conferred the greatest benefit on mankind.
—Clause in Nobel's will stipulating the beneficiaries of the annual prizes he endowed

Nobel (noh-**bel**) left Stockholm, where he was born, in 1842 to join his father, an engineer, who had moved to St. Petersburg. He was taught chemistry by his tutors and spoke fluently in English, French, German, Swedish, and Russian. In 1850 he went to Paris to study chemistry and then went on to America for four years, before returning to work in his father's factory in St. Petersburg.

In 1859 Nobel moved back to Sweden and set up a factory there (1864) to make nitroglycerin, a liquid explosive. After an explosion at the factory in 1864 in which his brother, Emil, and four others were killed, the Swedish government would not allow the factory to be rebuilt. Nobel then started to experiment to find a more stable explosive. Discovering that nitroglycerin was easily absorbed by a dry organic packing material, he invented dynamite and the detonating cap. These were patented in 1867 (UK) and 1868 (United States). From such work and from oil fields in Russia that he owned, Nobel amassed a vast fortune. He traveled widely and was a committed pacifist. He left the bulk of his money in trust for international awards – the Nobel Prizes for peace, literature, physics, chemistry, and medicine. The Nobel Prize for economics was introduced in his honor in 1969 and financed by the Swedish National Bank.

Nobili, Leopoldo

(1784–1835)

ITALIAN PHYSICIST

Nobili (**noh**-bee-lee) was born at Trassilico in Italy and, after a university education, served in the army as an artillery captain. He was later appointed professor of physics at the Florence Museum.

Nobili carried out pioneer work in the newly developing field of electrochemistry, publishing his results in 1828. He is known for his inventions of an astatic galvanometer (1825) and the thermocouple. His astatic galvanometer – a moving-magnet device constructed in such a way as to be independent of the Earth's magnetic field – was far more sensitive than existing instruments. Nobili's thermocouple – a device for measuring temperature – was based on the Seebeck effect. It consisted of two wires of different metals joined at each end with the junctions maintained at different temperatures; the temperature difference was determined by measuring the current flow. In 1829 Nobili made the first thermopile by joining in series six couples of antimony and bismuth. It was a cumbersome and fairly insensitive instrument. However, after later improvements by Macedonio Melloni it became fundamental to investigations of radiant heat.

Noddack, Ida Eva Tacke

(1896–1979)

GERMAN CHEMIST

Ida and Walter Noddack

Noddack (**nod**-ak), who was born at Lackhausen in Germany, was educated at the Technical University, Berlin, where she obtained her doctorate in 1921. After her marriage to the chemist Walter Noddack she worked at the same institutions as her husband.

In 1926 she collaborated with her husband and O. Berg in the discovery of rhenium. More intriguing, however, was her interpretation of a famous experiment of Enrico Fermi in which he had bombarded uranium with slow neutrons in the hope of producing artificial elements. Although their results were not particularly clear Noddack, in 1934, argued that "It is conceivable that in the bombardment of heavy nuclei with neutrons, these nuclei break up into several large fragments which are actually isotopes of known elements, not neighbors of the irradiated element." This is, in fact, the hypothesis of nuclear fission which, when it was published five years later by Otto Frisch, was immediately seen to be of fundamental importance.

Noddack's contribution seems rather to have passed unnoticed. Fermi was aware of her work as she had sent him a copy, but he remained unconvinced and continued to believe that he had made transuranic elements.

Noddack, Walter

(1893–1960)

GERMAN CHEMIST

Noddack was born in Berlin and educated at the university there, obtaining his doctorate in 1920. He worked first at the Physikalische Technische Reichsanstadt, the German national physical laboratory, until 1935, and then held chairs in physical chemistry at Freiburg and Strasbourg until, in 1946, he moved to Bamberg. Noddack taught chemistry at the local Hochschule there before serving as the director of the Bamberg Institute of Geochemistry (1955–60).

In 1926, in collaboration with his wife Ida Tacke, Noddack discovered the element rhenium. They thought that they had found element 43, which they named "masurium." In fact this element was correctly identified in 1937 by Emilio Segrè, who named it technetium.

Noddack is also remembered for arguing for a concept he called *allgegenwartskonzentration* or, literally, omnipresent concentration. This idea, somewhat reminiscent of the early Greek philosopher Anaxagoras, assumed that every mineral actually contained every element. The reason they could not all be detected was, of course, because they existed in too small quantities.

Noguchi, (Seisako) Hideyo

(1876–1928)

JAPANESE BACTERIOLOGIST

Noguchi (no-**goo**-chee) was born at Okinashimamura in Japan. In spite of a humble family background and a physical handicap caused by a childhood accident, he pursued a career in medicine. After considerable perseverance he entered medical school in Tokyo, obtaining his diploma in 1897. Three years later he traveled to America and commenced work at the University of Pennsylvania, studying animal venoms and their antivenins. In 1904, after a year spent in Copenhagen, Noguchi joined the Rockefeller Institute for Medical Research, New York. Here he successfully cultured the spirochete bacterium, *Treponema pallidum*, which causes syphilis. This enabled Noguchi to devise a diagnostic skin test for syphilis using an emulsion of his spirochete culture. He further showed that *T. pallidum* invades the nervous system as the disease progresses. In recognition of his work, Noguchi was awarded the Order of the Rising Sun in his home country in 1915.

Noguchi went on to study the possible causes of other diseases. After investigating Oroya fever in South and Central America, he showed that it was caused by a bacterium, *Bartonella bacilliformis*, which was transmitted to humans by sand flies. Between 1919 and 1922, Noguchi became certain that yellow fever also was caused by a bacterium. However, by 1927 this view had been discredited with the discovery that a virus was responsible.

In the same year, Noguchi went to West Africa and worked doggedly to prove to himself that yellow fever was in fact a virus disease. Within six months he had confirmed this but just before his departure for New York he contracted yellow fever himself and died shortly after.

Nollet, Abbé Jean Antoine

(1700–1770)

FRENCH PHYSICIST

No one ever saw him lose his composure or his unfailing consideration; he only became excited when he talked about physics.
—Grandjean de Fouchy, *Histoire de l'Académie des Sciences* (1770; History of the Academy of Sciences)

Born at Pimprez in France, Nollet (no-**lay**) was one of the great popularizers of the new electrical science in the salons and at the court of 18th-century France. He had collaborated with Charles Dufay in the period 1730–32 and tended to follow him in his electrical theory. Nollet saw electricity as a fluid, subtle enough to penetrate the densest of bodies. In 1746 he first formulated his theory of simultaneous "affluences and effluences" in which he assumed that bodies have two sets of pores in and out of which electrical effluvia might flow. He was later involved with Benjamin Franklin in a dispute over the nature of electricity.

After the discovery of the Leyden jar (a device for storing electrical charge) by Pieter van Musschenbroek in 1745, Nollet arranged some spectacular demonstrations of its power. He once gave a shock to 180 royal guards and, even more dramatically, joined 700 monks in a circle to a Leyden jar with quite startling results. Nollet also contributed to the theory of sound when he showed in 1743 that sound carried in water (he had taken care to expel the dissolved air from the water first).

Nordenskiöld, Nils Adolf Eric

(1832–1901)

FINNISH GEOLOGIST, EXPLORER, AND CARTOGRAPHER

Nordenskiöld (**noor**-den-shu(r)ld) was educated at the university in his native city of Helsinki where be obtained his PhD in 1857. Because of his hostility to the ruling Russians he emigrated to Sweden in 1858 where he became head of the mineralogy department of the National Museum.

As a geologist he made, between 1858 and 1872, five field trips to Spitsbergen, reaching as far north as latitude 81°. His most significant feat of exploration was his discovery and successful negotiation of the Northeast Passage between the Atlantic and Pacific oceans. He left Tromso, Norway, on board the *Vega* in July 1878, and after being trapped in ice near the Bering Strait throughout the winter entered the Pacific the following July.

Nordenskiöld also produced two works – *Facsimilie Atlas* (1889; Duplicate Atlas) and *Periplus* (1897; Circumnavigation) – which did much to stimulate the modern study of the history of cartography.

Norlund, Niels Erik

(1885–1981)

DANISH MATHEMATICIAN AND GEODESIST

Norlund (**nor**-luund), who was born at Stagelse in Denmark, studied at Soro High School and then worked as an assistant at the Copenhagen Observatory. His work there was to influence many of his subsequent scientific interests. After obtaining his doctorate in 1910 from the University of Copenhagen, Norlund took up a post in Sweden as professor of mathematics at Lund University. He remained there until 1922 when he returned to Denmark to become professor of mathematics at Copenhagen University, a post that he held until his retirement in 1956. He held many official posts, among them director of the Royal Geodesic Institute of Denmark (1923–55) and editor of the journal *Acta Mathematica*.

Norlund's interest in geodesy dates back to his time at the Copenhagen Observatory and his publications include works on the mapping of both Denmark and Iceland. He organized a new triangulation of Denmark from 1923, accompanied by gravity measurements and astronomical determinations of longitude, and also carried out a partial triangulation of Greenland. Among his more purely mathematical interests were differential equations and analysis.

Norman, Robert

(about 1580)

ENGLISH NAVIGATOR AND INSTRUMENT MAKER

Norman was described by William Gilbert as a "skilled navigator and ingenious artificer," and by himself as an "unlearned mechanician." By observing the downward tilt of the compass needle, Norman discovered the phenomenon of magnetic dip – the angle made by the Earth's magnetic field with the vertical at a point on the Earth's surface. He wrote a full account of it and published it in *The Newe Attractive* (1581).

Norrish, Ronald George Wreyford

(1897–1978)

BRITISH CHEMIST

Norrish was educated at the university in his native Cambridge. Apart from the war years, he spent his whole career there, serving as professor of physical chemistry from 1937 until 1965.

Norrish made his important contributions to chemistry in the fields of photochemistry and chemical kinetics, being introduced to these by Eric Rideal during his PhD work. From 1949 to 1965 he collaborated with his former pupil George Porter in the development of flash photolysis and kinetic spectroscopy for the investigation of very fast reactions. For their work they shared the 1967 Nobel Prize for chemistry with Manfred Eigen.

Norrish also made a significant contribution to chemistry when he showed the need to modify Draper's law. In the mid-19th century John Draper proposed his law that the amount of photochemical change is proportional to the intensity of the light multiplied by the time for which it acts. Norrish was able to show that the rate should be proportional to the square root of the light intensity.

Northrop, John Howard

(1891–1987)

AMERICAN CHEMIST

The son of biologists, Northrop was born in Yonkers, New York, and educated at Columbia, obtaining his PhD there in 1915. In 1917 he joined the Rockefeller Institute of Medical Research, only leaving on his retirement in 1961.

In the early 1930s Northrop confirmed some earlier results of James Sumner. Between 1930 and 1935 he and his coworkers succeeded in isolating a number of enzymes, including pepsin, trypsin, chymotrypsin, ribonuclease, and deoxyribonuclease, crystallizing them and unequivocally exhibiting their protein nature. This was sufficient finally to convince chemists that Sumner was correct, and Richard Willstätter had been wrong in his assertion that enzymes are nonprotein.

Using Northrop's techniques, Wendell Stanley was able in 1936 to isolate and crystallize the tobacco mosaic virus, and showed it to be composed of nucleoprotein. Subsequently (1938) Northrop isolated a bacteriophage (bacterial virus) and demonstrated that this also consisted of nucleoprotein. For such work on the isolation and crystallization of proteins and viruses, Northrop, Sumner, and Stanley shared the 1946 Nobel Prize for chemistry.

Norton, Thomas

(*c.* 1437–*c.* 1514)

ENGLISH ALCHEMIST

It is generally accepted that the anonymous work *The Ordinall of Alchimy* was written by Norton in about 1477. His authorship is revealed by an obvious cipher. The work was first published in a Latin translation by Maier in 1618 and, in its original English, was included in Elias Ashmole's *Theatrum chemicum Brittanicum* (1652; Exhibition of British Chemicals).

Norton claims in his poem to have learned the secrets of alchemy from his master, George Ripley, in 40 days. His objectives included the elixir of life and the philosopher's stone. His work contained much practical information on the craft of alchemy and is one of the classic alchemical works. Norton recognized the importance of color, odor, and taste as guides to chemical analysis.

Noyce, Robert Norton

(1927–1990)

AMERICAN PHYSICIST

Noyce was the son of a congregational minister from Denmark, Iowa. He was educated at Grinnell College, Iowa, and at the Massachusetts Institute of Technology, where he obtained his PhD in 1953. After working briefly for Philco, Philadelphia, Noyce moved to Mountain View, California, to work for William Shockley, coinventor of the transistor, at his Semiconductor Laboratory. Noyce and a number of colleagues decided to set up in business themselves. Financed by the Fairchild Corporation of New York, they set up Fairchild Semiconductor in the Santa Clara Valley, fifty miles south of San Francisco, a site better known today as "Silicon Valley."

The first major success was the integrated circuit, the foundation of the modern electronics industry. Noyce filed his patent in April 1959, some six weeks after a similar patent had been filed by Jack Kilby at Texas Instruments. Although Noyce's design was more advanced, priority seemed to lie with Kilby. Yet in 1968 the Supreme Court awarded all rights to Noyce and Fairchild on the grounds that Kilby's patent application lacked sufficient clarity.

Whereas Kilby's circuit had used the silicon mesa transistor, Noyce opted for a planar model. Unlike the mesa, Noyce's model had no raised parts to attract contaminants and was more easily protected by a layer of silicon dioxide. Parts were no longer connected by wires but by evaporating the aluminum wires onto the insulating surface. As an extra bonus it also proved much easier to mass-produce planar transistors.

At this point Noyce was able to sell back to Fairchild his initial investment of $500 for $250,000. He went on in 1968 to found Intel (Integrated Electronics). It gained an early success with the production of a one-kilobyte RAM chip. Further improvements were quickly made and, with the 1973 launch of a 4K RAM chip, sales soared above $60 million. Intel's success rapidly made Noyce one of Silicon Valley's first multimillionaires; it continued with the production of the 486 chip in 1989 and the 60 MHz Pentium chip in 1993.

Noyes, William Albert

(1857–1941)

AMERICAN CHEMIST

Noyes, born the son of a farmer in Independence, Iowa, was educated at Johns Hopkins University where he obtained his PhD in 1882. After working at the University of Tennessee (1883–86) and Rose Polytechnic, Terre Haute, Indiana (1886–1903), he held the post of chief chemist at the Bureau of Standards (1903–06). He then moved to the University of Illinois where he served as professor of chemistry until his retirement in 1926.

Noyes is mainly remembered for his careful and accurate determination of certain crucial atomic weights while at the Bureau of Standards. His measurement of the hydrogen-to-oxygen ratio as 1.00787:16 differs only at the fourth decimal place from currently accepted values. He also, in addition to writing a number of textbooks, founded *Chemical Abstracts* in 1907 and was the first editor of *Chemical Reviews* (1924–26).

Nüsslein-Volhard, Christiane

(1942–)

GERMAN BIOLOGIST

Nüsslein-Volhard (noos-lIn-**fol**-hart) was educated at the University of Tübingen. After a spell at the European Molecular Biology Laboratory at Heidelberg, she moved in 1981 to the Max Planck Institute for Development, Tübingen, where she has served since 1990 as the director of the department of genetics.

From 1978 to 1981 Nüsslein-Volhard collaborated with Eric Wieschaus on identifying the genetic factors responsible for the development of the fruit fly *Drosophila melanogaster*. After examining many thousands of specially bred mutant flies they had managed by 1980 to identify the main development sequence in *Drosophila*.

Nüsslein-Volhard also succeeded in illuminating the general process of development. It had long been thought that differentiation in early embryos – anterior from posterior, for example, or dorsal from ventral – was caused by varying concentrations of substances along the axes of the egg. The theory of morphological gradients, as it is known, has recently been supported by experimental work carried out by Nüsslein-Volhard and her Tübingen colleagues.

Nüsslein-Volhard shared the 1995 Nobel Prize for physiology or medicine with Edward Lewis and Eric Wieschaus for their work on the development of *Drosophila*.

Oakley, Kenneth Page

(1911–1981)

BRITISH PHYSICAL
ANTHROPOLOGIST

Oakley, the son of a physician, was educated at University College, London, where he obtained his PhD in 1938. After a brief period with the Geological Survey, Oakley joined the British Museum (Natural History); he remained there for his whole career and served as deputy keeper (anthropology) from 1959 until his retirement in 1969.

Oakley, much concerned with the accurate dating of human and animal remains, had developed by the late 1940s a method of dating them by measuring the amount of fluorine present. The technique received considerable publicity in the early 1950s when it was used to discredit Piltdown man, the skull and jaw supposedly discovered by Charles Dawson and Arthur Woodward in 1912.

Oberth, Hermann Julius

(1894–1989)

GERMAN ROCKET SCIENTIST

We shall make every effort so that the greatest dream of mankind might be fulfilled.
—On manned space flight. Letter to
Konstantin Tsiolkovsky (1929)

The son of a surgeon, Oberth (**oh**-bairt or **oh**-bert) was born in Hermannstadt (then in Austria–Hungary; now Sibiu in Romania). He began by studying medicine in Munich but after the interruption caused by World War I decided to study the exact sciences. This he did at Munich, Göttingen, and Heidelberg, qualifying as a teacher in 1922. He taught first in Romania then in 1938 joined the faculty of the Technical University in Vienna. He became a German citizen in 1940. In 1941 he was transferred to the rocket development center at Peenemünde, on the Baltic Sea, where he worked under Wernher von Braun, and in 1943 was sent to another rocket-research location. After the war he settled for varying periods in Switzerland, Italy, and America before returning to Germany in 1958. He appears to have been deliberately misleading and secretive about his activities in this period.

Like the other space pioneers, Robert Goddard and Konstantin Tsiolkovsky, the passion for space travel came to him early. He related reading Jules Verne's *From the Earth to the Moon* so frequently as a child that he knew it by heart. He calculated quite early that only with a rocket engine powered by liquid propellants would it be theoretically possible to reach the escape velocity of 25,000 mph (11.2 km/s). Oberth also worked out the equations for practical flight and submitted them to the University of Heidelberg in 1922 for his doctorate. They were rejected but Oberth went ahead and published the thesis in 1923 as *Die Rakete zu den Planetenräumen* (The Rocket into Interplanetary Space). He was unaware of similar calculations by Tsiolkovsky and Goddard but later acknowledged their precedence in the field.

Unlike Goddard and Tsiolkovsky, Oberth's work was greeted enthusiastically by an admittedly small band of devotees. There were certainly enough of them to form a society, the *Verein für Raumschiffahrt*, or Society for Space Travel, by the end of the decade. This partly explains why, when war came in 1939, Germany could so quickly organize an efficient and competent research team. It was made up of people who had worked on and thought of little else other than rockets since the late 1920s.

Oberth almost got a rocket in the air in the 1920s. He was acting as scientific adviser to Fritz Lang who was making a film, *Frau im Mond* (Lady in the Moon), and was persuaded that publicity would flow to the film if rocket flight could be publicly demonstrated just before its opening. Oberth, who was no engineer, confidently accepted Lang's finance, promising a rocket within a year. The flight never materialized, with Oberth disappearing at a crucial moment, exhausted and depressed after nearly having been blinded in an explosion while testing various mixtures of gasoline and liquid air.

Occhialini, Giuseppe Paolo Stanislao

(1907–)

ITALIAN PHYSICIST

Occhialini (ohk-ya-**lee**-nee) was born at Fossombrone in Italy and educated at the University of Florence, where he also taught from 1932 to 1937. He belonged to a small group of creative physicists, which, centered on Enrico Fermi, emerged in Italy during the interwar period. Like most of his colleagues he fled from Italy with the growth of fascism, and he taught at São Paulo, Brazil, from 1937 to 1944, at Bristol University, England, from 1944 to 1947, and at the University of Brussels from 1948 to 1950. He then returned to Italy where he has held chairs of physics at the University of Genoa (1950–52) and at the University of Milan since 1952.

Occhialini was involved in two major discoveries with his collaborators, both of whom were later awarded Nobel prizes. In 1933 with Patrick Blackett he obtained cloud-chamber photographs that showed tracks due to the positive electron (or positron).

In 1947 Occhialini and Cecil Powell, examining the tracks of cosmic rays in photographic emulsions, noted the track of a particle that was some 300 times more massive than an electron. The particle broke down into the already familiar mu meson (muon); it was in fact the pi meson or pion.

Ochoa, Severo

(1905–1993)

SPANISH–AMERICAN BIOCHEMIST

Born at Luarca in Spain, Ochoa (oh-**choh**-a) graduated from Málaga University in 1921 and then proceeded to study medicine at Madrid University, receiving his MD in 1929. Having held research positions in Germany, Spain, and England, he became a research associate in medicine at New York University in 1942, taking American citizenship in 1956. He became a full professor in 1976 and in 1985 was appointed honorary director of the center for molecular biology, University of Madrid.

Ochoa was one of the first to demonstrate the role of high-energy phosphates, e.g., adenosine triphosphate, in the storage and release of the body's energy. While investigating the process of oxidative phosphorylation, in which such triphosphates are formed from diphosphates, he discovered the enzyme polynucleotide phosphorylase. This can catalyze the formation of ribonucleic acid (RNA) from appropriate nucleotides and was later used for the synthesis of artificial RNA. Ochoa was awarded the 1959 Nobel Prize for physiology or medicine for this discovery, sharing the prize with Arthur Kornberg, who synthesized deoxyribonucleic acid (DNA). Ochoa also isolated two enzymes catalyzing certain reactions of the Krebs cycle.

Odling, William

(1829–1921)

BRITISH CHEMIST

Odling, the son of a London surgeon, studied medicine at London University before moving into chemistry. He studied in Paris under Charles Gerhardt and in 1863 was appointed professor of chemistry at St. Bartholomew's Hospital, London. In 1867 he succeeded Michael Faraday as Fullerian Professor at the Royal Institution, London, and in 1872 he moved to Oxford University to take up the Waynflete Chair of Chemistry until his retirement in 1912.

Odling was one of the pioneers of the valence theory first propounded by Edward Frankland in 1852. Although the term "valence" was not in use in 1854 when Odling first wrote on the topic, he had a clear idea of the concept, which he referred to as replaceable or representative value. Odling, like many of his contemporaries, was skeptical of the existence of atoms, and it was not until the 1890s that his misgivings were overcome. From his work on atomic weights he was led to suggest that the atomic weight of oxygen should be 16, not 8. In 1861 he was able to clear up a troublesome problem over oxygen by suggesting that ozone was triatomic; this was later confirmed by J. Soret in 1866. Odling also studied and classified silicates.

Oersted, Hans Christian

(1777–1851)

DANISH PHYSICIST

> Spirit and nature are one, viewed under two different aspects. Thus we cease to wonder at their harmony.
> —*The Soul in Nature* (1852)

Oersted (**er**-sted) was born at Rudkjöbing in Denmark and studied at Copenhagen University, where he received a PhD in 1799 for a thesis defending Kantian philosophy. To complete his scientific training he then traveled through Europe visiting the numerous physicists working on aspects of electricity. On his return to Denmark he started giving public lectures, which were so successful that, in 1806, he was offered a professorship at Copenhagen. Here he became well known as a great teacher and did much to raise the level of Danish science to that of the rest of Europe.

It was while lecturing that he actually first observed electromagnetism (although for years he had believed in its existence) by showing that a needle was deflected when brought close to a wire through which a current was flowing. By the summer of 1820 he had confirmed the existence of a circular magnetic field around the wire and published his results. They produced an enormous flurry of new activity in the scientific world, which up to that time had accepted Coulomb's opinion that electricity and magnetism were completely independent forces.

Ohm, Georg Simon

(1787–1854)

GERMAN PHYSICIST

Ohm (ohm), who was born at Erlangen in Germany, seems to have acquired his interest in science from his father, a skilled mechanic. He studied at the University of Erlangen and then taught at the Cologne Polytechnic in 1817. From 1826 to 1833 he taught at the Military Academy in Berlin, moving to the Polytechnic at Nuremburg before finally obtaining a chair in physics at Munich in 1849.

Despite the fact that he published his famous law in 1827 in his *Die galvanische Kette mathematisch bearbeitet* (The Galvanic Circuit Investigated Mathematically) he received no recognition or promotion for more than twenty years. Ohm seems to have been stimulated by the work on heat of Joseph Fourier. The flow of heat between two points depends on the temperature difference and the conductivity of the medium between them. So too, argued Ohm, with electricity. If this line of thought is pursued it soon leads to the general form of *Ohm's law* that the current is proportional to the voltage. Using wires of different sizes he was able to show that the resistance was proportional to the cross-sectional area of the wire and inversely proportional to its length.

Ohm also worked on sound, suggesting in 1843 that the ear analyzes complex sounds into a combination of pure tones. This result was rediscovered by Hermann von Helmholtz in 1860.

In Ohm's honor the unit of electrical resistance, the ohm, was named for him.

O'Keefe, John Aloysius

(1916–   )

AMERICAN ASTRONOMER AND GEOPHYSICIST

O'Keefe was born in Lynn, Massachusetts, and studied at Harvard, gaining his BA in 1937, and at the University of Chicago where he obtained his PhD in 1941. He worked as a mathematician in the Army Map Service from 1945 to 1958. Since then he has been with the National Aeronautics and Space Administration at their Goddard Space Flight Center in Maryland.

Once with NASA O'Keefe started work on the Vanguard project, which was part of the American program for International Geophysical Year. The first Vanguard satellite was launched in March 1958, two months after the launch of Explorer 1, America's first satellite. Both craft were tracked over a long period – Vanguard 1 transmitted signals for six years – and O'Keefe used the satellite positions to check the size and shape of the Earth. By making careful observations of the orbits adopted by the satellites it is possible to reconstruct the detailed figure of the attracting mass, in this case, the Earth.

The 18th-century surveyors had confirmed the predictions of Newton that the Earth was an oblate spheroid, i.e., its equatorial diameter was longer than its polar diameter (by about 26.5 miles or 42.7 km). O'Keefe showed that while this is true in general there are a few modifications that need to be added. In particular he showed that the north pole is about 100 feet (30 m) further from the Earth's center than the south pole (both poles considered to be at sea level) and that the equatorial bulge is not completely symmetrical for its highest points lie a little south of the equator. This means that the Earth is slightly pear-shaped, which has been verified by more recent satellite observations.

Oken, Lorenz

(1779–1851)

GERMAN NATURE PHILOSOPHER

> In August 1806, while walking in a forest in the Harz Mountains, I saw at my feet a [sheep's] skull bleached by time. This, I cried out, is a vertebral column!
> —On his theory that the skull is composed of a number of vertebrae. Quoted by René Taton in *Science in the Nineteenth Century* (1965)

Oken (**oh**-ken), a farmer's son from Bohlsbach in Germany, was one of the most influential adherents of the system termed "nature philosophy," a school of thought established in Germany at the beginning of the 19th century. Oken's numerous clashes with the authorities over his strongly held political and scientific beliefs meant that he was frequently changing jobs until he finally settled at Zurich University in 1832. He nevertheless managed to found the reputable biological journal *Isis*, and he was also instrumental in organizing regular scientific congresses for biological and medical scientists.

Oken is remembered mainly for the theory proposing that the skull is formed from the fusion of several vertebrae – an idea for which Wolfgang von Goethe also claimed priority. The theory was later disproved by T. H. Huxley, but it served some purpose in preparing people for the evolutionary ideas put forward by Charles Darwin.

Olah, George Andrew

(1927–)

HUNGARIAN–AMERICAN
CHEMIST

Olah gained his PhD from the Technical University, Budapest, in 1949. He moved to Canada in 1956 following the Hungarian uprising and joined the staff of the Dow Chemical Company in Ontario. In 1964 he moved to the U.S. and in 1965 joined the faculty of the Case Western Reserve University, Cleveland, Ohio. In 1977 he moved to the University of Southern California, becoming director of the Loker Hydrocarbon Research Institute in 1991. Olah became a naturalized American citizen in 1970.

In certain chemical reactions involving hydrocarbons, extremely short-lived highly reactive positively charged carbon intermediates are often formed. These have a positive charge on the carbon atom and are known as "carbonium ions" or "carbocations." Because of their short lifetime, little had been established about these intermediates.

Olah, while working at Dow, discovered a way to preserve the intermediates and to allow their properties to be investigated. He found that solutions of a very strong acid, variously described as a "superacid" or a "magic acid," would preserve carbocations for months at a time and thus allow their structure to be determined with such techniques as nuclear magnetic resonance spectroscopy (NMR). Olah's superacids were formed by dissolving compounds such as antimony pentafluoride in water at low temperature. The result was an acid some 10^{18} times stronger than sulfuric acid. The stable carbocations formed in this way proved to be quite unusual, with structures quite unlike the more familiar tetrahedral forms. Olah's work quickly found important applications in industry; it has, for example, been widely used in synthesizing high-octane gasoline.

For his work on carbocations Olah was awarded the 1995 Nobel Prize for chemistry.

Olbers, Heinrich

(1758–1840)

GERMAN ASTRONOMER

> He [Olbers] was to me the most noble friend.
> With wise and fatherly counsel he guided my
> youth.
> —Friedrich Wilhelm Bessel, obituary
> notice of Olbers (1840)

Olbers (**ohl**-bers), who was born at Arbegen in Germany, was a physician who practiced medicine at Bremen. He became a good amateur astronomer, and converted part of his house into an observatory. He became interested in searching for a planet in the "gap" between Mars and Jupiter, and rediscovered the first minor planet (or asteroid) Ceres after it had been lost by its discoverer Giuseppe Piazzi. In 1802 he discovered the second asteroid, Pallas, and in 1807 the fourth, Vesta. He also devised a method of calculating comet orbits, called *Olbers's method*, and discovered five comets. The one named for him was last seen in 1956.

Olbers's modern fame, however, rests on his statement of a very simple problem, the solution of which has had a profound impact on modern cosmology. He asked the naive question: why is the sky dark at night? Olbers assumed that the heavens are infinite and unchanging and that the stars are evenly distributed. The amount of light reaching the Earth from very distant stars is very small – in fact, the illumination decreases with the square of the distance. On the other hand, this is compensated for by the increased number of stars – the average number at a given distance increases with the square of the distance. The result is that the whole sky should be about as bright as our Sun. Olbers's solution to this problem was that the light is absorbed by dust in space, but this is an unsatisfactory explanation since the dust would eventually become incandescent and radiate energy. In the 20th century it became clear that the solution lies in the fact that the universe is not uniform, infinite in time, or unchanging; the red shift of the light from distant galaxies results in a reduction of the energy of the radiation from stars. The paradox had been discussed earlier (1744) by J. P. L. Chesaux.

Oldham, Richard Dixon

(1858–1936)

BRITISH SEISMOLOGIST AND
GEOLOGIST

Oldham's father, Thomas, was professor of geology at Trinity College, Dublin, and director of the Geological Surveys of India and Ireland. Oldham, who was born in Dublin, was educated at the Royal School of Mines; in 1879 he followed his father in joining the Geological Survey of India, rising to the rank of superintendent. He retired in 1903 and became director of the Indian Museum in Calcutta.

Oldham made two fundamental discoveries. He made a detailed study of the Assam earthquake of 1897 and, in 1900, was the first to identify clearly the primary (P) and secondary (S) seismic waves transmitted through the Earth, which had been predicted by the mathematician Siméon Poisson on theoretical grounds. Secondly, in 1906 he provided the first clear evidence that the Earth had a central core. He found that the arrival of the primary, or compressional, waves was delayed at places opposite to the focal point of an earthquake. He deduced from this that the Earth contains a central core that is less dense and rigid than the rocks of the mantle, and through which compressional waves would travel less fast. A detailed analysis of the arrival and distortion of the P and S waves that had traveled through or near to the center of the Earth later provided much insight into the structure of the Earth.

Oliphant, Marcus Laurence Elwin

(1901–   )

AUSTRALIAN PHYSICIST

Born in Adelaide, Oliphant was educated at the university there and at Cambridge University, England, where he obtained his PhD in 1929. He then worked at the Cavendish Laboratory in Cambridge before being appointed (1937) to the Poynting Professorship of Physics at Birmingham University. Oliphant returned to Australia in 1950 and held research chairs at the Australian National University, Canberra, until his retirement in 1967.

Hydrogen, the simplest of all atoms, normally has a nucleus of a single proton, but in 1932 Harold Urey had discovered a heavier form that he called deuterium, with a nucleus consisting of a proton and a neutron. The enlarged nucleus became known as the deuteron. In 1934 Oliphant and his collaborator Paul Harteck produced an even heavier form of hydrogen by bombarding deuterium with deuterons. This new isotope has a nucleus consisting of one proton and two neutrons (hydrogen–3). They named it "tritium" and called the nucleus a "triton." The isotope is radioactive with a half-life of 12.4 years and for this reason is not found in significant amounts in nature.

During the war Oliphant did important work on the development of radar. It was in his laboratory that two German refugees, Rudolf Peierls and Otto Frisch, made some of the vital calculations and experiments that revealed the real possibility of an atomic bomb.

Olsen, Kenneth Harry

(1926–   )

AMERICAN COMPUTER ENGINEER AND ENTREPRENEUR

Born in Bridgeport, Connecticut, Olsen studied electrical engineering at the Massachusetts Institute of Technology (MIT). He remained at MIT after graduating, joining the Digital Computer Laboratory directed by Jay Forrester. While there Olsen worked on the design and construction of the first computers to adopt magnetic-core memory systems.

In 1957 Olsen left MIT to set up Digital Equipment Corporation in partnership with his brother Stan Olsen and a colleague, Harlan Anderson. The company was partly financed by the Boston firm American Research and Development who, for a stake of $70,000, took some 60% of the equity. When they sold their stake in 1972 it was worth $350 million.

The foundation for Digital's success lay with the development of the first minicomputer, the PDP-1 (Programmed Data Processor). Before Olsen the computer market was dominated by mainframe computers built by IBM and Sperry Rand. They cost millions to produce and operated by selling time to their clients. Olsen saw that few organizations needed such computing power, but could readily use a smaller and cheaper model to calculate their payroll, monitor sales, or analyze data. The PDP-1 sold for $120,000; the PDP-8, introduced in 1963 and incorporating magnetic cores and integrated circuits, was about the size of a refrigerator and sold for $18,000. Under Olsen's direction Digital grew into one of the largest computer companies in the world generating by the mid-1980s sales in excess of $4 billion.

Omar Khayyam

(*c.* 1048–*c.* 1122)

PERSIAN ASTRONOMER, MATHEMATICIAN, AND POET

> The majority of the people who imitate philosophers confuse the true with the false...they do nothing but deceive and pretend knowledge, and they do not use what they know of the sciences except for base and material purposes.
> —Quoted by H. J. J. Winter and W. 'Arafat in *Journal of the Royal Asiatic Society of Bengal Science* (1950)

Omar Khayyam (oh-**mar** kI-**yahm**), who was born at Nishapur (now in Iran), produced a work on algebra that was used as a textbook in Persia until this century. He gave a rule for solving quadratic equations, he could solve special cases of the cubic, and – in a last work – seemed to have some inkling of the binomial theorem. He also worked on the reform of the Persian calendar, which was basically the Egyptian one of 365 days, introducing a sixth epagomenic (extra) day and obtaining an accurate estimate of the tropical year.

Onsager, Lars

(1903–1976)

NORWEGIAN–AMERICAN CHEMIST

Born at Christiania (now Oslo) in Norway, Onsager (on-**sah**-ger) was educated at the Norwegian Institute of Technology. He moved to America in 1928 and obtained his PhD at Yale in 1935. He spent virtually his whole career at Yale, serving as J. W. Gibbs Professor of Theoretical Chemistry from 1945 until 1972.

Onsager made two important contributions to chemical theory. In 1926 he showed the need to modify the equation established by Peter

Debye and Erich Hückel in 1923, which described the behavior of ions in a solution, by taking Brownian motion into consideration.

Onsager's main work, however, was in the foundation of the study of nonequilibrium thermodynamics. Here an attempt is made to apply the normal laws of thermodynamics to systems that are not in equilibrium – where there are temperature, pressure, or potential differences of some kind. For his work in this field Onsager was awarded the Nobel Prize for chemistry in 1968. The study of nonequilibrium thermodynamics was further developed by Ilya Prigogine.

Oort, Jan Hendrik

(1900–1992)

DUTCH ASTRONOMER

The son of a physician from Franeker in the Netherlands, Oort (ohrt) was educated at the University of Gröningen where he worked under Jacobus Kapteyn and gained his PhD in 1926. After a short period at Yale University in America he was appointed to the staff of the University of Leiden where he was made professor of astronomy in 1935 and from 1945 to 1970 served as director of the Leiden Observatory. He also served as director of the Netherlands Radio Observatory.

Oort's main interest was in the structure and dynamics of our Galaxy. In 1927 he succeeded in confirming the hypothesis of galactic rotation proposed by Bertil Lindblad. He argued that just as the outer planets appear to us to be overtaken and passed by the less distant ones in the solar system, so too with the stars if the Galaxy really rotated. It should then be possible to observe distant stars appearing to lag behind and be overtaken by nearer ones. Extensive observation and statistical analysis of the results would thus not only establish the fact of galactic rotation but also allow something of the structure and mass of the Galaxy to be deduced.

Oort was finally able to calculate, on the basis of the various stellar motions, that the Sun was some 30,000 light-years from the center of the

Galaxy and took about 225 million years to complete its orbit. He also showed that stars lying in the outer regions of the galactic disk rotated more slowly than those nearer the center. The Galaxy does not therefore rotate as a uniform whole but exhibits what is known as "differential rotation."

Oort was also one of the earliest of the established astronomers to see the potential of the newly emerging discipline of the 1940s, radio astronomy. As one of the few scientists free to do pure research in the war years, he interested Hendrik van de Hulst in the work that finally led to the discovery in 1951 of the 21-centimeter radio emission from neutral interstellar hydrogen.

By measuring the distribution of this radiation and thus of the gas clouds Oort and his Leiden colleagues lost little time in tracing the spiral structure of the galactic arms and made substantial improvements to the earlier work of William Morgan. They were also able to make the first investigation of the central region of the Galaxy: the 21-centimeter radio emission passed unabsorbed through the gas clouds that had hidden the center from optical observation. They found a huge concentration of mass there, later identified as mainly stars, and also discovered that much of the gas in the region was moving rapidly outward away from the center.

Oort made major contributions to two other fields of astronomy. In 1950 he proposed that a huge swarm of comets surrounded the solar system at an immense distance and acted as a cometary reservoir. A comet could be perturbed out of this *Oort cloud* by a star and move into an orbit taking it toward the Sun. In 1956, working with Theodore Walraven, he studied the light emitted from the Crab nebula, a supernova remnant. The light was found to be very strongly polarized and must therefore be synchrotron radiation produced by electrons moving at very great speed in a magnetic field.

Oparin, Aleksandr Ivanovich

(1894–1980)

RUSSIAN BIOCHEMIST

Oparin (o-**pa**-rin), who was born at Uglich near Moscow, studied plant physiology at the Moscow State University, where he later served as professor. He helped found, with the botanist A. N. Bakh, the Bakh Institute of Biochemistry, which the government established in 1935. Oparin became director of the institute in 1946. As early as 1922 Oparin was speculating on how life first originated and made the then controversial suggestion that the first organisms must have been heterotrophic – that is, they could not make their own food from inorganic starting materials, but relied upon organic substances. This questioned the prevailing view that life originated with autotropic organisms, which, like present-day plants, could synthesize their food from simple inorganic materials. Oparin's view has gradually gained acceptance in many circles. Oparin did much to stimulate research on the origin of life and organized the first international meeting to discuss the problem, held in Moscow in 1957.

Opie, Eugene Lindsay

(1873–1971)

AMERICAN PATHOLOGIST

Born in Staunton, Virginia, Opie was educated at Johns Hopkins University, where he gained his MD in 1897. He worked at the Rockefeller Institute from 1904 until 1910 when he moved to St. Louis as professor of pathology at Washington University. He later held similar appointments at the University of Pennsylvania (1923–32) and Cornell from 1932 until his retirement in 1941.

It had been shown by Oskar Minkowski in 1889 that removal of the pancreas leads to fatal diabetes. Opie, in 1900, made the further advance of implicating the pancreatic islets of Langerhans in the disease. He pointed out that they showed a characteristic degeneration found only in the pancreas of diabetic patients. It was left to Frederick Banting and Charles Best in 1921 to show that it was the failure of the islets to secrete insulin that caused the complaint. Opie also did important work on the epidemiology of tuberculosis and demonstrated that the level of tuberculosis in a population can be accurately assessed from the tuberculin reaction.

Oppenheimer, Julius Robert

(1904–1967)

AMERICAN PHYSICIST

The physicists have known sin; and this is a knowledge which they cannot lose.
—*Open Mind* (1955)

The scientist is not responsible for the laws of nature, but it is a scientist's job to find out how these laws operate. It is the scientist's job to find ways in which these laws can serve the human will. However, it is not the scientist's job to determine whether a hydrogen bomb should be used. This responsibility rests with the American people and their chosen representatives.
—Quoted by L. Wolpert and A. Richards in *A Passion for Science* (1988)

Oppenheimer came from a wealthy New York City family. He was educated at Harvard, at Cambridge, England, and at Göttingen where he obtained his PhD in 1927. From 1929 to 1942 he was at the University of California, and while there accepted the post of director of the Los Alamos laboratory where he worked on the development of the atom bomb. After the war in 1947 he was appointed director of the Institute for Advanced Studies at Princeton, a post he held until his death. He also served (1947–52) as chairman of the important General Advisory Committee of the Atomic Energy Commission.

He is mainly remembered, however, for his work on the Los Alamos project. It has been argued that only Oppenheimer could have made Los Alamos viable for only he could have commanded the allegiance of the world's best talents in physics, who gathered around him in the New Mexico desert. It was also only Oppenheimer who had sufficient independence and authority to persuade the military and General Groves, his superior, to grant sufficient freedom to the scientists to make the project workable.

Freeman Dyson, who saw Oppenheimer in the early 1950s at Princeton with some of his old colleagues, caught in their talk "a glow of pride and nostalgia. For every one of these people the Los Alamos days had been a great experience, a time of hard work and comradeship and deep happiness." But Oppenheimer stayed on after the war when, by all accounts, there was little comradeship, much divisiveness and, ultimately, tragedy for Oppenheimer and some of his friends. In 1948 he was on the cover of *Time* magazine; four years later he was summarily dismissed from his post with the Atomic Energy Commission.

Oppenheimer had actually been under investigation since 1942, first as a matter of routine and then more rigorously when reports critical of his loyalty began to arrive at the office of Colonel Pash, who was responsible for security at Los Alamos. It should be emphasized that at no time has any evidence been published to suggest that Oppenheimer was disloyal to his country. Suspicions were aroused because some of his friends had been members of the Communist party and because he had moved freely in left-wing circles. Both his wife and brother were well-known left-wing sympathizers, if not communists. Before long the suspicions became more precise: it was felt that a Russian agent had made an approach to Oppenheimer and although he had not responded he was guilty of failing to report the approach to the authorities.

Oppenheimer finally admitted that an approach had been made to him but he refused to disclose any names for he felt the man was no longer involved and in any case had merely been a messenger. In a classic dialogue with his inquisitor he kept insisting that, "I feel that I should not give it. I don't mean that I don't hope that if he's still operating that you will find it ... But I would just bet dollars to doughnuts that he isn't still operating."

Finally, at the end of 1943, the Army lost patience and Groves put it clearly to Oppenheimer that he must either provide names or go. He named Haakon Chevalier, a professor of romance languages at the University of California whom he had known since 1938. Chevalier was of course ruined and, although no charges were ever laid against him, it became impossible for him to find academic employment ever again in America. Whether Oppenheimer had behaved honorably by his own judgment is far from clear as there is too much conflicting evidence about the crucial approach. For some, Chevalier was a totally innocent man maligned by a man consumed by ambition; for others Chevalier was a Russian agent who was lucky not to collect a heavy sentence. Where precisely the truth lies must await the release of further documentation.

Oppenheimer was thus free to develop the bomb and at 5.30 a.m. on 16 July 1945 the first bomb was tested. When Oppenheimer saw the huge cloud rising over the desert, he later reported, a passage from the *Bhagavad Gita* came to him: "I am become Death, the shatterer of worlds." A move by senior scientists led by James Franck and Leo Szilard to arrange for a public demonstration of the bomb's power rather than its military use on a Japanese city was referred to Oppenheimer for comment. He was in favor of using it on a Japanese town.

After the war, when he could reasonably have left Government service and devoted himself to theoretical physics, he – for reasons that are not clear – remained as the leading adviser on nuclear weapons, taking responsibility for the development of the hydrogen bomb. Oppenheimer had made many enemies and when accusations were made that he had in fact obstructed the program to build the fusion bomb they were more than willing to work for his downfall. A commission to investigate his loyalty reported in 1954 that "Dr. Oppenheimer did not show the enthusiastic support for the Super (H-bomb) program which might have been expected of the chief adviser of the Government" and rendered its judgment that he was unfit to serve his country. Although Oppenheimer never regained his security clearance, peace of a sort was made with the authorities when in 1963 he received the Fermi award from President Kennedy. Four years later, after bearing his illness with great courage, he died of cancer of the throat.

Ortelius, Abraham

(1527–1598)

FLEMISH CARTOGRAPHER

Ortelius (or-**tee**-lee-us) was the son of a local merchant from Antwerp, which is now in Belgium. At the age of 20 he began to illustrate maps and, in 1564, issued his first world map. His most famous work, *Theatrum orbis terrarum* (Theater of the Whole World), a collection of 70 maps, was the first modern atlas of the world. Published in 1570, it went through 41 editions and appeared in 7 languages.

The maps in it were quite conventional as Ortelius was neither an explorer nor a scientist. He was prepared to collect and produce the best maps of his day and thus uncritically represented such terrestrial additions as "the great southern continent."

Osborn, Henry Fairfield

(1857–1935)

AMERICAN PALEONTOLOGIST

Osborn was born in Fairfield, Connecticut, and educated at Princeton. He held professorships firstly in comparative anatomy at Princeton and then in biology followed by zoology at Columbia University. He was curator of the American Museum of Natural History's vertebrate paleontology department, and was also a member of the United States and Canadian geological surveys. Chairman of the executive committee of the New York Zoological Society (1896–1903), Osborn was among the founders of the society's renowned zoological park. At the American Museum of Natural History he built up one of the world's finest collections of vertebrate fossils. Like Ernst Mayr he was a proponent of adaptive radiation – the theory that one species may eventually develop into several different species through individuals dispersing from a common center and subsequently developing different characters in adaptation to new environments. Osborn was a successful popularizer of paleontology and wrote extensively on aspects of evolution.

Osler, Sir William

(1849–1919)

CANADIAN PHYSICIAN

Patients should have rest, food, fresh air, and exercise – the quadrangle of health.
　　　　　　　　—Aphorisms

In science the credit goes to the man who convinces the world, not to the man to whom the idea first occurs.
　　　　　　　　—Books and Men

Born at Bond Head, in Ontario, Osler studied medicine at Toronto Medical School and McGill University, obtaining his degree in 1872. In the following year he discovered the minute bodies in blood, known as platelets, that are involved in the clotting mechanism. After a time spent studying and traveling in Europe, he returned to McGill University and was appointed professor in 1875. Following a spell (1884–88) as professor of clinical medicine at the University of Pennsylvania, Philadelphia, Osler was appointed as the first professor of medicine to the newly founded Johns Hopkins University, Baltimore. Here he pioneered new teaching methods in medicine, including tuition on the wards and an emphasis on laboratory techniques. He also wrote a perennially popular medical textbook, *The Principles and Practice of Medicine* (1892).

In 1905 Osler moved to England as professor of medicine at Oxford University, where he lectured and wrote on medical history. He was made a baronet in 1911.

Ostwald, Friedrich Wilhelm

(1853–1932)

GERMAN CHEMIST

If my ideas should prove worthless, they will be put on the shelf here [Britain] more quickly than anywhere else, before they can do harm.
—Faraday Lecture to fellows of the Chemical Society (1904)

Ostwald (**ost**-vahlt) was born of German parents who had settled at Riga, now in Latvia. He was educated at the University of Dorpat and the Riga Polytechnic, where he was professor of physics from 1881 until he left to take the chair of physical chemistry at Leipzig in 1887. He retired from his chair in 1906 and spent the rest of his life mainly in literary, philosophical, and editorial work.

Ostwald probably did more than anyone else to establish the new discipline of physical chemistry. He was a great teacher and built up an important research school at Leipzig through which most of the major chemists passed at some time in their career. He founded in 1887 the *Zeitschrift für physikalische Chemie* (Journal of Physical Chemistry), the first journal in the world devoted to the new discipline, translated the writings of the American physical chemist Josiah Willard Gibbs into German in 1892, and also produced an inspiring two-volume textbook on the subject, *Lehrbuch der allgemeinen Chemie* (1885, 1887; Textbook of General Chemistry).

Ostwald's own research was mainly on catalysts, for which he received the Nobel Prize for chemistry in 1909. He defined catalysis in 1894 as "the acceleration of a chemical reaction, which proceeds slowly, by the presence of a foreign substance." He emphasized that the catalyst for the reaction does not alter the general energy relations or the position of equilibrium. In 1888 he formulated his dilution law, which allows the degree of ionization of a weak electrolyte to be calculated with reasonable accuracy. The *Ostwald process* (patented in 1902) was an industrial process for oxidizing ammonia to nitric acid.

Philosophically Ostwald was a positivist and denied the reality of atoms until well into the 20th century. The chemist, he argued, does not observe atoms but studies the simple and comprehensive laws to which the weight and volume ratios of chemical compounds are subject. He believed that atoms were a hypothetical conception but by 1908 he had been converted to atomism.

Ostwald's son, Wolfgang, also became a chemist of some note.

Otto, Nikolaus

(1832–1891)

GERMAN MECHANICAL ENGINEER
AND INVENTOR

The son of a farmer from Holzhausen in Germany, Otto (**ot**-oh) was very much the self-taught engineer. He left school at sixteen to begin work in a merchant's office, progressing to the position of a traveling salesman. During his work he became aware of the gas engines developed by Jean Lenoir, and Lenoir's attempt to use them to power vehicles. Otto also began to experiment with engines. In 1864 he joined with the industrialist Eugen Langen to design and manufacture engines. A factory was built near Cologne in 1869 and engineers hired, one of whom was Gottlieb Daimler (1834–1900).

In 1876 Otto took out a patent on a new engine design. Like the Lenoir engine, it was powered by coal gas but it operated with a four-stroke cycle. Lenoir had used, in the manner of a steam engine, a two-stroke cycle. Otto's four-stroke cycle of intake, compression, expansion, and exhaust had originally seemed a backward step producing only one power stroke for every two revolutions of the crank. Further, it was tied to an external gas supply and very heavy, and clearly unsuitable to power a vehicle. A further problem arose when it was discovered that the four-stroke cycle had been patented in 1862 by A. B. Rochas, thus depriving Otto of his own patent.

Despite this the engine was adaptable enough to be used for lifting and pulling a variety of goods. Some 30,000 were sold before Otto's death in 1891. Thereafter, suitably modified by Daimler to consume gasoline, millions of Otto's engines would eventually be sold each year.

Oughtred, William

(1575–1660)

ENGLISH MATHEMATICIAN

> The *Clavis* [The Key (to Mathematics) by Oughtred] doth in as little room deliver as much of the fundamental and useful parts of geometry (as well as of arithmetic and algebra) as any book I know.
> —John Wallis, *Algebra* (1695)

Oughtred (**aw**-tred) was born at Eton in England and educated at the famous school there (where his father taught writing) and at Cambridge University. He was ordained a priest in 1603 and eventually became rector of Albury.

Despite his clerical post he found time to work on mathematics and he produced what was to become a very famous book on mathematics, the *Clavis mathematicae* (1631; The Key to Mathematics). This work dealt with arithmetic and algebra, and it is of historical importance because Oughtred managed to put into it more or less everything that was known at that time in those areas of mathematics. It rapidly became an influential and widely used textbook and held in high regard by mathematicians of the stature of Isaac Newton and John Wallis, himself a pupil of Oughtred. A number of mathematical symbols that are still used were first introduced by Oughtred. Among these were the sign "×" for multiplication and the "sin" and "cos" notation for trigonometrical functions. Oughtred also invented the earliest form of the slide rule in 1622 but only published this discovery in 1632. As a result he became embroiled in a violent dispute with one of his former students, Richard Delamain, who had made the same invention independently.

Oughtred's religious views were conservative and he was a staunch supporter of the Royalist party, but during the time of Cromwell and the Commonwealth he was able to retain his post as vicar. He lived just long enough to see Charles II installed on the throne.

Owen, Sir Richard

(1804–1892)

BRITISH ANATOMIST AND PALEONTOLOGIST

Sir Richard Owen, best and brightest of Victorian anatomists, coined the term "Dinosauria," from Greek roots meaning "terrible lizard," in 1842. When Owen first penned the word "dinosaurs," paleontology was still a brand-new science. Owen invented the term...to describe the huge *land* animals of this age. And his original definition is still good.
—Robert Bakker, *The Dinosaur Heresies* (1986)

Owen studied medicine in his native city of Lancaster (where he was apprenticed), at Edinburgh University, and at St. Bartholomew's Hospital, London. He then practiced and lectured at St. Bartholomew's under the eminent surgeon John Abernethy. In 1826 Owen was appointed curator of the Hunterian Collection of anatomical specimens of the Royal College of Surgeons. He was Hunterian Professor in 1836, and in the following year became the Royal College's professor of comparative anatomy and physiology and also Fullerian Professor of Comparative Anatomy at the Royal Institution. In 1856 Owen was appointed superintendent of the natural history department of the British Museum, and from then until his retirement in 1883 was responsible for the transfer of specimens to and organization of the new Natural History Museum at South Kensington, London (opened to the public in 1881).

The chief anatomist of his day, Owen gained much of his extensive knowledge of comparative anatomy from studies of the Hunterian Collection, which he described in a series of catalogs published from 1833 to 1840. In 1830–31 he had also studied specimens in the Natural History Museum, Paris, attending lectures by Georges Cuvier. Prompted largely by his interest in the structure and origin of mammalian teeth, he turned his attention to fossil forms, reconstructing a large number of extinct animals, including giant flightless toothed birds. He obtained for the British Museum the first specimen of the earliest known fossil bird, *Archaeopteryx*, describing it in the *Philosophical Transactions of the Royal Society of London* (1863). However reexamination of the specimen in 1954 brought to light errors in Owen's reconstruction. Owen early recognized the difference between homologous (real) and analogous (apparent) structures in different animals, constructing a hypothetical vertebrate ancestor. His thesis that the vertebrate skull derived from modified vertebrae was demolished by T. H. Huxley and others.

Owen was a bitter opponent of Darwin and his theory of natural selection. He published anonymously a damaging and slanted review of *The Origin of Species* in *The Edinburgh Review* (1860), but subsequently changed his views to partial and then total acceptance as support for Darwin grew.

Owen's other publications include the classic *Memoir on the Pearly Nautilus* (1832), which established his name, and *On the Anatomy and Physiology of Vertebrates* (1866–68). He also wrote pioneering works on parthenogenesis and on extinct mammals and wingless birds of Australia and New Zealand.

Palade, George Emil

(1912–   )

ROMANIAN–AMERICAN
PHYSIOLOGIST AND CELL
BIOLOGIST

Palade (pa-**lah**-dee) was born at Iasi in Romania. Educated at Bucharest University, where he was professor of physiology during World War II, he emigrated to America in 1946, becoming a naturalized citizen in 1952. He worked at the Rockefeller Institute for Medical Research, New York, becoming professor of cytology there (1958–72). In 1972 he became director of studies in cell biology at Yale University's medical school. In 1990 he was appointed dean of scientific affairs at the University of California at San Diego.

Palade's work has been primarily concerned with studies of the fine structure of animal cells, although he has also investigated the nature of plant chloroplasts. He has shown that minute semisolid structures in cells, known as mitochondria, have an enzymic effect, oxidizing fats and sugars and releasing energy. His discovery of even smaller bodies called microsomes, which function independently of the mitochondria (of which they were previously thought to be part), showed them to be rich in ribonucleic acid (RNA) and therefore the site of protein manufacture. The microsomes were subsequently renamed ribosomes. For his work in cellular biology, Palade received, with Albert Claude and Christian de Duve, the Nobel Prize for physiology or medicine (1974).

Paley, William

(1743–1805)

BRITISH NATURAL PHILOSOPHER

> I take my stand in human anatomy...the necessity, in each particular case, of an intelligent designing mind for the contriving and determining of the forms which organized bodies bear.
>
> —*Natural Theology* (1802)

Born the son of a headmaster in Peterborough, eastern England, Paley graduated from Cambridge in 1763. He taught theology at Cambridge until 1776, after which time he held a number of livings in the Church of England in Westmorland, Carlisle, and Lincoln.

In 1802 Paley published one of the most successful works of the century, *Natural Theology, or Evidence of the Existence and Attributes of the Deity Collected from the Appearances of Nature*; twenty editions were called for before 1820. He began by contrasting the significance between finding a stone and a watch on the heath. The presence of the stone can be explained by saying "it had lain there forever." But the mechanism of the watch is such that we must conclude that there is a maker "who formed it for the purpose which we find it actually to answer."

He went on to argue that if a watch led to a designer then, as "the contrivances of nature surpass the contrivances of art," nature should lead more firmly to a designer. The eye, for example, is more clearly made for vision than a telescope. Throughout the book Paley deploys the facts of anatomy and physiology of a variety of animals and plants to this end.

A number of specific mechanisms were identified. By a process of "compensation" the shortness of an elephant's neck is overcome by the length of its trunk. Unnecessary organs such as fetal lungs display "prospective contrivance."

The bulk of Paley's argument derived from the living world. The heavens, he found, were too simple, showing nothing but bright points. He conceded, however, that if they did not lead to the Creator's existence, they did show something of His magnificence.

Paley was not the first to present the argument from design. Nor was he the last. A generation later, eight of the leading British scientists of the day would be commissioned by the Earl of Bridgewater to demonstrate how "the Power, Wisdom, and Goodness of God" can be seen in nature. In more recent times something of Paley's approach can be seen in the writings of Sir Fred Hoyle, Freeman Dyson, and Bernard Lovell.

The approach has also aroused considerable scientific opposition. Most recently a strong attack on Paley has been launched by Richard Dawkins in his appropriately titled *The Blind Watchmaker* (1986).

Palmieri, Luigi

(1807–1896)

ITALIAN GEOPHYSICIST AND METEOROLOGIST

Palmieri (pahl-**myair**-ee), who was born at Faicchio in Italy and educated at the University of Naples, became professor of physics there in 1847. He later joined the staff of the Mount Vesuvius Observatory where he was made director in 1854.

He is mainly remembered for his introduction of improved versions of such instruments as the seismograph and the rain gage. He also produced, in 1854, a two-volume work on experimental meteorology.

Paneth, Friedrich Adolf

(1887–1958)

AUSTRIAN CHEMIST

Paneth (**pah**-nayt), the son of a Viennese physiologist, was educated at Munich, Glasgow, and Vienna where he obtained his PhD in 1910. After working at the Institute for Radium Research in Vienna from 1912 to

1918 he taught in Germany at the universities of Hamburg, Berlin, and Königsberg until he fled to England in 1933. There he worked at Imperial College, London, and in 1939 was appointed to the professorship of chemistry at the University of Durham. In 1953 he returned to Germany to the post of director of the Max Planck Institute.

In 1913 Paneth collaborated with Georg von Hevesy on the possibility of using radioisotopes as tracers. He later, in 1929, advanced the work of Moses Gomberg when he demonstrated the existence of the free methyl radical ($\cdot CH_3$). He found that by heating lead tetramethyl vapor in a tube, one of the products of the decomposition was a very reactive material that attacked metal films and turned out to be the methyl radical. Unlike the triphenyl methyl of Gomberg, this free radical was short-lived.

In the late 1920s Paneth used chemical techniques to determine the age of meteorites. As uranium in its disintegration produces a fixed amount of helium at a constant rate then by establishing the uranium:helium ratio of a sample it should be possible to date it. Paneth's calculations of meteorites eventually yielded a date ranging from 10^9 to 3×10^9 years, which agreed reasonably well with dates established by Arthur Holmes for the age of the Earth.

Panofsky, Wolfgang Kurt Hermann

(1919–)

GERMAN–AMERICAN PHYSICIST

Panofsky (pa-**nof**-skee) was born in Berlin, Germany. He was brought to America in 1934 and studied at Princeton University, where he graduated in 1938, and at the California Institute of Technology, where he gained his PhD in 1942. In the same year he became a naturalized American citizen. He helped America's wartime research efforts, working for the Office of Scientific Research and Development (1942–43) and on the Manhattan project in Los Alamos (1943–45).

After World War II, Panofsky worked as a physicist at the Radiation Laboratory of the University of California at Berkeley (1945–46). He then moved to Stanford University, where he rose to become professor of physics in 1951. During the 1940s and 1950s, Panofsky did a series of high-energy physics experiments in which the fundamental nature of the pion particle was uncovered, and another series that probed the connection between pions and the electromagnetic field.

In 1953 he was made director of the High-Energy Physics Laboratory at Stanford and made many contributions to the design of accelerators for fundamental particles and instruments for their detection. In 1961 he was appointed director of the Stanford Linear Accelerator Center, a post he held until his retirement in 1984.

Pantin, Carl Frederick Abel

(1899–1967)

BRITISH PHYSIOLOGIST AND MARINE BIOLOGIST

Pantin was born in London. Following a brief period of service with the Royal Engineers in World War I, he entered Cambridge University to study zoology, graduating in 1922. He then worked at the Marine Biological Association's laboratory at Plymouth until 1929, when he returned to Cambridge as a lecturer in zoology. Pantin's research concentrated on marine invertebrates, particularly sea anemones and crabs. He demonstrated that the primitive nerve net found in sea anemones behaves in a way essentially identical to the nervous system of higher animals. His work on crabs, however, emphasized their dissimilarities from other animals.

Papin, Denis

(1647–*c*. 1712)

FRENCH PHYSICIST AND INVENTOR

Papin (pa-**pan**), who was born at Blois in France, graduated with a medical degree from the University of Angers in 1669. Preferring physics to medicine, he started as an assistant in the laboratory of Christiaan Huygens in Paris in 1671. As a Protestant, Papin was attracted to England in 1675 where he worked as an assistant to Robert Boyle. From 1687 to 1696 he was professor of mathematics at Marburg in Germany. He then worked in Cassel until 1707, when he returned to England.

In 1679 while working with Boyle he invented his steam digester – an early and very efficient pressure cooker or, as he described it, "an Engine for softening bones." It was a container with a tightly fitting lid – the enclosed steam generated a high pressure that raised the boiling point of the water – and a lever-type safety valve, which he also invented.

His most important work however was his description of "a new method of obtaining very great moving power at small cost." This was a simple form of steam engine whereby the condensation of steam under a piston allowed atmospheric pressure to raise a weight of 60 pounds (27 kilograms). This was described in his *Ars nova ad aquam ignis adminiculo efficacissime elevandum* (1707; The New Art of Pumping Water by Using Steam). Papin's design was never developed commercially.

Pappenheimer, John Richard

(1915–   )

AMERICAN PHYSIOLOGIST

Born in New York City, Pappenheimer was educated at Harvard and in England at Cambridge University, where he obtained his PhD in 1940. After teaching at the College of Physicians and Surgeons, New York, and the University of Pennsylvania he joined the staff of the Harvard Medical School in 1946, serving since 1969 as professor of physiology.

The idea that the brain might secrete daily a chemical that will naturally produce sleep at the appropriate time was first investigated by H. Pieron in 1913. He kept dogs awake for ten days, extracted cerebrospinal fluid from them, and injected it into normal dogs. Pieron claimed that such dogs would sleep for several hours while other dogs used as controls, receiving fluid from regular dogs, would behave just as any other animal.

In 1965 Pappenheimer took up the problem, aiming this time to actually "identify the sleep-promoting factor." After three years' work on 20 sleep-deprived goats Pappenheimer had some six liters of fluid for purification. Eventually he could claim that "a concentrated solution of cerebrospinal fluid...was found to reduce the nocturnal activity of rats to half the normal level for 12 hours." That such power could be destroyed by a proteolytic enzyme indicated that the sleep-factor probably contained an amino acid.

As so little of the factor remains after purification, little more can be said as yet of its chemical constitution. Pappenheimer however claims to have established that the factor is not species specific.

Pappus of Alexandria

(about 320)

GREEK MATHEMATICIAN

> I declare God to be one in form but not in number, the maker of heaven and
> Earth, as well as the tetrad of the elements and things formed from them, who
> has further harmonized our rational and intellectual souls with our bodies, and
> who is borne upon the chariots of the cherubim and hymned by angelic throngs.
> —Oath attributed to Pappus

Pappus (**pap**-us) was the last notable Greek mathematician and is
chiefly remembered because his writings contain reports of the work of
many earlier Greek mathematicians that would otherwise be lost. His
chief work, *Synagogue* (*c.* 340; Collection), consisted of eight books of
which the first and part of the second are now lost. It was intended as a
guide to the whole of Greek mathematics and this is what makes it such
a significant historical source. Among the mathematicians whose work
Pappus expounds are Euclid, Apollonius of Perga, Aristaeus, and Era-
tosthenes. Pappus did contribute some original work, however, notably
in projective geometry.

As with many Greek mathematicians Pappus was as interested in astronomy as in pure mathematics and his other work included comments
on Ptolemy's astronomical system contained in the *Almagest*.

Paracelsus, Philippus Aureolus

(1493–1541)

GERMAN PHYSICIAN, CHEMIST, AND ALCHEMIST

> Medicine is not only a science; it is also an art. It does not consist of compounding pills and plasters; it deals with the very processes of life, which must be understood before they may be guided.
>
> —*Die grosse Wundarznei* (The Great Surgeons)

Paracelsus (pa-ra-**sel**-sus), born Theophrastus Bombastus von Hohenheim in Einsiedeln, Switzerland, was the son of a physician from whom he received his early training in medicine and alchemy. His assumed name stems from his claim to have surpassed the Roman physician Celsus. He traveled with his father to Villach in Austria where he worked as an apprentice in the mines and acquired much of his practical knowledge of mineralogy and metallurgy. He left the mines in 1507, attended various German universities, and may have obtained an MD from Ferrara. After practicing medicine in Sweden, Strasbourg, Basel, Nuremburg, and a host of other places, in 1540 Paracelsus settled in Salzburg where he died in the following year.

Paracelsus was the first to reject totally the authority of antiquity, suggesting its replacement by nature and experiment. To show his seriousness he burned the great medieval compilation of medical knowledge, the *Canon* of Avicenna, before his students. In Basel he was lucky enough to cure the infected limb of an influential publisher Frebenius, for which orthodox physicians had recommended amputation. This led to his appointment as professor of medicine and city physician at Basel.

His contempt for traditional learning and the reason the medical authorities found him so distasteful is best conveyed by his much quoted riposte to them: "Let me tell you this: every little hair on my neck knows more than you and all your scribes, and my shoe-buckles are more learned than your Galen and Avicenna, and my beard has more experience than all your high colleges." The alternative proposed by Paracelsus contained a number of not particularly coherent strands. There was much in his work that belonged to, or at least overlapped with, the occult tradition but there was an eagerness to embrace new sources of knowledge. He would willingly learn his chemistry from the craftsmen in the mines and claimed to gain knowledge from gypsies, magicians, and elderly country folk.

His greatest influence on 16th-century science arose from his chemical philosophy in which he posed the "tria prima": salt, sulfur, and mercury. These terms were meant to emphasize the principles of solidity, combustibility, and liquidity inherent in any substance. It was by following through the implications of such schemes that later chemists such as Robert Boyle were led to the corpuscular view of matter.

In medicine Paracelsus took the revolutionary step of introducing chemically prepared drugs rather than persisting exclusively with the herbal medicines or "simples" of antiquity. While he was perhaps not the first to use such new remedies as mercury, sulfur, potassium, and antimony his dramatic use of them, often with supposedly verified cures, brought them sharply before the attention of the public. It is from this work that medicine begins to take on its modern aspect as being concerned with the discovery of specialized drugs providing complete and harmless cures.

Pardee, Arthur Beck

(1921–   )

AMERICAN BIOCHEMIST

Born in Chicago, Pardee was educated at the University of California, Berkeley, and at the California Institute of Technology where he obtained his PhD in chemistry under Linus Pauling in 1947. He taught at Berkeley until 1961, taking a year off (1957–58) to work with Jacques Monod at the Pasteur Institute. He was then appointed professor of biochemical science at Princeton and in 1975 joined the Harvard Medical School as professor of pharmacology.

In the 1950s and 1960s Pardee was involved in a number of major advances in the new discipline of molecular biology, for example his demonstration in 1955 with R. Litman of the mutagenic effect on the virus bacteriophage T2 of 5-bromouracil. This was followed in 1958 by his publication with François Jacob and Jacques Monod of their classic paper announcing the results of the so-called PaJaMo experiment. Using a mutant bacterium, which was able to synthesize β-galactosidase without any outside stimulation, they crossed this (by conjugation) with a normal bacterium, which had to be induced to make β-galactosidase, and found that the normal process is dominant to the mutant; that is inducibility is dominant to constitutivity. It was this experiment that led them to formulate the concept of a "repressor molecule" suppressing the production of β-galactosidase by the gene.

Pardee threw considerable light on the control of enzyme synthesis by the cell. The process of end-product feedback by which a metabolic pathway is inhibited by its own end product had been clearly shown to apply to a number of synthetic processes by numerous workers. An elegant development of this mechanism was revealed by Pardee in collaboration with John Gerhart in 1959. They showed that the output of pyrimidine is controlled not only by its own end product but also by the independent purine production line. As both were essential constituents of nucleic acid such a mechanism was presumably designed to keep their production in phase.

Just how the process of feedback inhibition is controlled was proposed by Pardee and Gerhart in 1962; their work was, however, superseded by a more general account of allosteric proteins published by Jacob, Monod, and J.-P. Changeux in 1963.

Paré, Ambroise

(1510–1590)

FRENCH SURGEON

I dressed him, God cured him.
—Motto referring to his surgery

Paré (pa-**ray**), the son of an artisan from Bourg-Hersent in France, received his medical training as an apprentice to a barber-surgeon. He first worked at the Hôtel-Dieu, a large Paris hospital, but beginning with the Italian campaign of 1536, spent much time as a surgeon with the French army. He also served as a surgeon at the courts of Henri II, Charles IX, and Henri III.

Paré's fame as a surgeon rests mainly on his abandonment of the practice of cauterizing gunshot wounds and the introduction of surgical ligatures. He introduced his first innovation during the 1536 campaign to relieve Turin. He had accepted the orthodox view that as gunpowder was poisonous, gunshot wounds should be cauterized with boiling oil. However on one occasion, because of an unusually large number of wounded, Paré found himself running out of boiling oil so instead he dressed the wounds with an ointment. To his surprise the following day revealed a number of such patients with uninflamed wounds while those with cauterized wounds were feverish and in great pain, with the region around their wounds swollen. He thus decided never again to cauterize gunshot wounds, publishing his findings in his *La Méthode de traicter les ployes faites par les arquebuses et autres bastons a feu* (1545; The Method of Treating Wounds Made by Arquebuses and Other Guns).

His second main innovation, the practice of tying rather than cauterizing blood vessels, has been described as the greatest improvement ever in operative surgery but the improvement was only widely adopted after a delay of centuries. The initial advantage in using ligatures was that it permitted more selective surgery for there was a limit to the areas that could be cauterized. The disadvantages were however many. Cauterization was simple, swift, and could be practiced single handed; ligatures were time consuming, requiring many stitches for the amputation of a limb necessitating skilled assistance, and the cooperation of a patient willing to accept long operations. It was only with the invention of the screw tourniquet by Jean Petit in the early 18th century that ligatures became widely used in surgery.

Parkes, Alexander

(1813–1890)

BRITISH CHEMIST AND INVENTOR

Parkes, the son of a Birmingham lock manufacturer, was apprenticed to a brass founder and started his career in charge of the casting department at Elkington. He took out his first patent, which was for electroplating delicate objects such as works of art, in 1841. Eventually Parkes took out over 50 patents in this field; when the prince consort, Prince Albert, visited Elkington, Parkes presented him with a silver-plated spider's web. In metallurgy, Parkes also invented a process for removing silver from lead by extraction with molten zinc (the *Parkes process*).

He also worked on rubber and plastics. In 1846 he discovered the cold vulcanization process, which was important in the manufacture of thin-walled rubber articles. In 1855 he took out a number of patents on a new product initially called xylonite (or parkesine). Aiming to produce a synthetic form of horn, Parkes found that if the recently discovered nitrocellulose was mixed with camphor and alcohol, a hornlike substance was produced. It was not fully developed by Parkes however and was left to the Hyatt brothers of New Jersey to develop it as celluloid, the first synthetic plastic material.

Parkinson, James

(1755–1824)

BRITISH PHYSICIAN AND PALEONTOLOGIST

The son of a London surgeon, Parkinson practiced medicine in his native city and engaged in radical politics such as campaigning for universal suffrage. He was the author of a number of pamphlets advocating political reform under the pseudonym "Old Hubert" and, in 1794, was thought by the authorities to be involved in the so-called pop-gun plot to assassinate George III with a poisoned dart. He was called to give evidence before the Privy Council but they failed to implicate him.

In 1817 he published his most significant work, *An Essay on the Shaking Palsy*, which described the disease he referred to as paralysis agitans but is now more commonly known as Parkinson's disease. He also gave, in 1812, the first description in English of appendicitis and established perforation as the cause of death. Parkinson was also a well-known paleontologist. He was one of the founder members of the London Geological Society in 1807 and author of the influential *Organic Remains of a Former World* (3 vols. 1804–11).

Parmenides of Elea

(*c.* 515 BC–*c.* 450 BC)

GREEK PHILOSOPHER

Virtually nothing is known about the early life of Parmenides (par-**men**-i-deez) except that he was born in Elea (now Velia) in southern Italy. He was the founder of the Eleatic school, one of the leading pre-Socratic forms of Greek thought, and wrote the remarkable poem *On Nature*, 155 lines of which survive. It is generally accepted as the first extended philosophical text in which an idea, however obscure, is argued for instead of the isolated assertions contained in the surviving fragments of earlier thinkers.

The poem argues for an austere Monism, a universe that must necessarily be uncreated, uniform, changeless, complete, and without motion. The dialectic used in the poem awakened the minds of the Greeks to the power of reason as no other work had done; used by another Eleatic, Zeno, it produced a number of deep paradoxes.

Parsons, Sir Charles Algernon

(1854–1931)

BRITISH ENGINEER

Parsons, a Londoner, was educated at Cambridge University and in 1877 became an engineer at an engineering plant. In 1884 he invented the multistage steam turbine and in 1889 set up his own engineering plant at Newcastle upon Tyne to produce turbines and dynamos. The dynamo was first used in a steamship in 1897 and revolutionized ship design. It was also crucial to the development of electricity generators. Parsons became a fellow of the Royal Society in 1898, was awarded the Rumford Medal in 1902, and was knighted in 1911.

Sources and Further Reading

MAXWELL

Goldman, Martin. *The Demon in the Aether*. Edinburgh: Paul Harris, 1983.

Hunt, Bruce J. *The Maxwellians*. Ithaca, NY: Cornell University Press, 1991.

McCLINTOCK

Keller, E. F. *A Feeling for the Organism: The Life and Work of Barbara McClintock*. San Francisco, CA: Freeman, 1983.

MEDAWAR

Medawar, Peter. *Memoir of a Thinking Radish*. Oxford: Oxford University Press, 1986.

——. *The Threat and the Glory: Reflections on Science and Scientists*. New York: Harper-Collins, 1990.

MENDEL

Olby, Robert C. *The Origins of Mendelism*. New York: Schoken Books, 1966.

Orel, Viezslav. *Mendel*. New York: Oxford University Press, 1984.

MENDELEEV

Brock, William A. *The Norton History of Chemistry*. New York: W. W. Norton, 1993.

MERCATOR

Wilford, John Noble. *The Mapmakers*. New York: Alfred A. Knopf, 1981.

MERTON, Robert

Merton, R. K. *The Sociology of Science*. Chicago, IL: Chicago University Press, 1973.

MESSIER

Mallas, J. H., and E. Kreimer, eds. *The Messier Album*. New York: Cambridge University Press, 1979.

MICHELSON

Jaffe, Bernard. *Michelson and the Speed of Light*. Garden City, NY: Doubleday, Anchor Books, 1960.

Livingston, D. M. *The Master of Light: A Biography of Albert A. Michelson*. Chicago, IL: Chicago University Press, 1973.

MILLIKAN

Kargon, Robert Hugh. *The Rise of Robert Millikan: Portrait of a Life in American Science*. Ithaca, NY: Cornell University Press, 1982.

Kevles, Daniel J. *The Physicists: The History of a Scientific Community in Modern America*. Cambridge, MA: Harvard University Press, 1987.

MINSKY

Minsky, Marvin. *The Society of Mind*. New York: Simon and Schuster, 1987.

Minsky, Marvin, and Seymour Papert. *Perceptions*. Cambridge, MA: MIT Press, 1968.

MÖBIUS

Fauvel, J., R. Flood, and R. J. Wilson, eds. *Möbius and his Band: Mathematics and Astronomy in 19th Century Germany*. Oxford: Oxford University Press, 1993.

MONOD

Monod, Jacques. *Chance and Necessity: An Essay on the Natural Philosophy of Modern Biology*. New York: Alfred A. Knopf, 1971.

Lwoff, A., and A. Ullmann. *The Origins of Molecular Biology: A Tribute to Jacques Monod*. New York: Academic Press, 1979.

MORGAN, Thomas Hunt

Allen, G. E. *Thomas Hunt Morgan: The Man and His Science*. Princeton, NJ: Princeton University Press, 1978.

MOSELEY

Jaffe, Bernard. *Moseley and the Numbering of the Elements*. New York: Doubleday, 1971.

MULLER, Richard

Muller, Richard. *Nemesis: The Death Star*. New York: Weidenfeld and Nicolson, 1988.

MURCHISON

Stafford, Robert A. *Scientist of the Empire: Sir Roderick Murchison, Scientific Exploration and Victorian Imperialism*. New York: Cambridge University Press, 1989.

MUYBRIDGE

Scharf, Aaron. *Art and Photography*. New York: Viking Penguin, 1986.

NAPIER

Hooper, Alfred. *Makers of Mathematics*. New York: Random House, 1948.

NEEDHAM, Joseph

Needham, Joseph. *The Grand Titration: Science and Society in East and West*. London: Allen and Unwin, 1969.

——. *Clerks and Craftsmen in China and the West*. New York: Cambridge University Press, 1970.

NERNST

Mendelsson, Kurt. *The World of Walther Nernst*. Pittsburgh, PA: Pittsburgh University Press, 1973.

NEWCOMEN

Rolt, L. T. C. *Thomas Newcomen: The Prehistory of the Steam Engine*. London: David and Charles, 1963.

NEWTON, Sir Isaac

Fauvel, J., R. Flood, M. Shortland, and R. Wilson, eds. *Let Newton Be!* New York: Oxford University Press, 1988.

Manuel, Frank. *A Portrait of Isaac Newton.* Cambridge, MA: Harvard University Press, 1968.

Westfall, Richard S. *Never at Rest.* New York: Cambridge University Press, 1980.

NOBEL

Zuckerman, Harriet. *Scientific Elites.* New York: The Free Press, 1977.

NOYCE

Reid, T. R. *Microchip: The Story of a Revolution and the Men Who Made It.* London: Collins, 1985.

OLBERS

Harrison, Edward. *Darkness at Night: A Riddle of the Universe.* New York: Cambridge University Press, 1987.

OPPENHEIMER

Goodchild, Peter. *J. Robert Oppenheimer: "Shatterer of Worlds."* London: BBC, 1980.

Rhodes, Richard. *The Making of the Atom Bomb.* New York: Simon and Schuster, 1986.

———. *Dark Sun: The Making of the Hydrogen Bomb.* New York: Simon and Schuster, 1995.

OWEN

Desmond, Adrian. *Archetypes and Ancestors.* Chicago, IL: University of Chicago Press, 1984.

PALEY

Brooke, John Hedley. *Science and Religion, Some Historical Perspectives.* New York: Cambridge University Press, 1991.

PARACELSUS

Pachter, Henry M. *Paracelsus: Magic into Science.* New York: Henry Schuman, 1951.

Pagel, W. *Paracelsus: An Introduction to Philosophical Medicine.* New York: Karger, 1958.

PARÉ

Paré, Ambroise. *The Apologie and Treatise.* New York: Dover Publications, 1968.

———. *On Monsters and Marvels.* Chicago, IL: University of Chicago Press, 1982.

Glossary

absolute zero The zero value of thermodynamic temperature, equal to 0 kelvin or −273.15°C.

acceleration of free fall The acceleration of a body falling freely, at a specified point on the Earth's surface, as a result of the gravitational attraction of the Earth. The standard value is 9.80665 m s^{-2} (32.174 ft s^{-2}).

acetylcholine A chemical compound that is secreted at the endings of some nerve cells and transmits a nerve impulse from one nerve cell to the next or to a muscle, gland, etc.

acquired characteristics Characteristics developed during the life of an organism, but not inherited, as a result of use and disuse of organs.

adrenaline (epinephrine) A hormone, secreted by the adrenal gland, that increases metabolic activity in conditions of stress.

aldehyde Any of a class of organic compounds containing the group –CHO.

aliphatic Denoting an organic compound that is not aromatic, including the alkanes, alkenes, alkynes, cycloalkanes, and their derivatives.

alkane Any of the saturated hydrocarbons with the general formula C_nH_{2n+2}.

alkene Any one of a class of hydrocarbons characterized by the presence of double bonds between carbon atoms and having the general formula C_nH_{2n}. The simplest example is ethylene (ethene).

alkyne Any one of a class of hydrocarbons characterized by the presence of triple bonds between carbon atoms. The simplest example is ethyne (acetylene).

allele One of two or more alternative forms of a particular gene.

amino acid Any one of a class of organic compounds that contain both an amino group (–NH$_2$) and a carboxyl group (–COOH) in their molecules. Amino acids are the units present in peptides and proteins.

amount of substance A measure of quantity proportional to the number of particles of substance present.

anabolism The sum of the processes involved in the synthesis of the constituents of living cells.

androgen Any of a group of steroid hormones with masculinizing properties, produced by the testes in all vertebrate animals.

antibody A protein produced by certain white blood cells (lymphocytes) in response to the presence of an antigen. An antibody forms a complex with an antigen, which is thereby inactivated.

antigen A foreign or potentially harmful substance that, when introduced into the body, stimulates the production of a specific antibody.

aromatic Denoting a chemical compound that has the property of aromaticity, as characterized by benzene.

asteroid Any of a large number of small celestial bodies orbiting the Sun, mainly between Mars and Jupiter.

atomic orbital A region around the nucleus of an atom in which an electron moves. According to wave mechanics, the electron's location is described by a probability distribution in space, given by the wave function.

ATP Adenosine triphosphate: a compound, found in all living organisms, that functions as a carrier of chemical energy, which is released when required for metabolic reactions.

bacteriophage A virus that lives and reproduces as a parasite within a bacterium.

bacterium (*pl.* **bacteria**) Any one of a large group of microorganisms that all lack a membrane around the nucleus and have a cell wall of unique composition.

band theory The application of quantum mechanics to the energies of electrons in crystalline solids.

baryon Any of a class of elementary particles that have half-integral spin and take part in strong interactions. They consist of three quarks each.

beta decay A type of radioactive decay in which an unstable nucleus ejects either an electron and an antineutrino or a positron and a neutrino.

black body A hypothetical body that absorbs all the radiation falling on it.

bremsstrahlung Electromagnetic radiation produced by the deceleration of charged particles.

carbohydrate Any of a class of compounds with the formula $C_nH_{2m}O_m$. The carbohydrates include the sugars, starch, and cellulose.

carcinogen Any agent, such as a chemical or type of radiation, that causes cancer.

catabolism The sum of the processes involved in the breakdown of molecules in living cells in order to provide chemical energy for metabolic processes.

catalysis The process by which the rate of a chemical reaction is increased by the presence of another substance (the catalyst) that does not appear in the stoichiometric equation for the reaction.

cathode-ray oscilloscope An instrument for displaying changing electrical signals on a cathode-ray tube.

cellulose A white solid carbohydrate, $(C_6H_{10}O_5)_n$, found in all plants as the main constituent of the cell wall.

chelate An inorganic metal complex in which there is a closed ring of atoms, caused by attachment of a ligand to a metal atom at two points.

chlorophyll Any one of a group of green pigments, found in all plants, that absorb light for photosynthesis.

cholesterol A steroid alcohol occurring widely in animal cell membranes and tissues. Excess amounts in the blood are associated with atherosclerosis (obstruction of the arteries).

chromatography Any of several related techniques for separating and analyzing mixtures by selective adsorption or absorption in a flow system.

chromosome One of a number of threadlike structures, consisting mainly of DNA and protein, found in the nucleus of cells and constituting the genetic material of the cell.

codon The basic coding unit of DNA and RNA, consisting of a sequence of three nucleotides that specifies a particular amino acid in the synthesis of proteins in a cell.

collagen A fibrous protein that is a major constituent of the connective tissue in skin, tendons, and bone.

colligative property A property that depends on the number of particles of substance present in a substance, rather than on the nature of the particles.

continental drift The theory that the Earth's continents once formed a single mass, parts of which have drifted apart to their present positions.

cortisone A steroid hormone, produced by the cortex (outer part) of the adrenal gland, that regulates the metabolism of carbohydrate, fat, and protein and reduces inflammation.

critical mass The minimum mass of fissile material for which a chain reaction is self-sustaining.

cryogenics The branch of physics concerned with the production of very low temperatures and the study of phenomena occurring at these temperatures.

cyclotron A type of particle accelerator in which the particles move in spiral paths under the influence of a uniform vertical magnetic field and are accelerated by an electric field of fixed frequency.

cytoplasm The jellylike material that surrounds the nucleus of a living cell.

dendrochronology A method of dating wooden specimens based on the growth rings of trees. It depends on the assumption that trees grown in the same climatic conditions have a characteristic pattern of rings.

dialysis The separation of mixtures by selective diffusion through a semipermeable membrane.

diffraction The formation of light and dark bands (diffraction patterns) around the boundary of a shadow cast by an object or aperture.

diploid Describing a nucleus, cell, or organism with two sets of chromosomes, one set deriving from the male parent and the other from the female parent.

DNA Deoxyribonucleic acid: a nucleic acid that is a major constituent of the chromosomes and is the hereditary material of most organisms.

dissociation The breakdown of a molecule into radicals, ions, atoms, or simpler molecules.

distillation A process used to purify or separate liquids by evaporating them and recondensing the vapor.

ecology The study of living organisms in relation to their environment.

eigenfunction One of a set of allowed wave functions of a particle in a given system as determined by wave mechanics.

electrolysis Chemical change produced by passing an electric current through a conducting solution or fused ionic substance.

electromagnetic radiation Waves of energy (electromagnetic waves) consisting of electric and magnetic fields vibrating at right angles to the direction of propagation of the waves.

electromotive force The energy supplied by a source of current in driving unit charge around an electrical circuit. It is measured in volts.

electromotive series A series of the metals arranged in decreasing order of their tendency to form positive ions by a reaction of the type $M = M^+ + e$.

electron An elementary particle with a negative charge equal to that of the proton and a rest mass of 9.1095×10^{-31} kilograms (about 1/1836 that of the proton).

electron microscope A device in which a magnified image of a sample is produced by illuminating it with a beam of high-energy electrons rather than light.

electroweak theory A unified theory of the electromagnetic interaction and the weak interaction.

enthalpy A thermodynamic property of a system equal to the sum of its internal energy and the product of its pressure and its volume.

entomology The branch of zoology concerned with the study of insects.

entropy A measure of the disorder of a system. In any system undergoing a reversible change the change of entropy is defined as the energy absorbed divided by the thermodynamic temperature. The entropy of the system is thus a measure of the availability of its energy for performing useful work.

escape velocity The minimum velocity that would have to be given to an object for it to escape from a specified gravitational field. The escape velocity from the Earth is 25,054 mph (7 miles per second).

ester A compound formed by a reaction between an alcohol and a fatty acid.

estrogen Any one of a group of steroid hormones, produced mainly by the ovaries in all vertebrates, that stimulate the growth and maintenance of the female reproductive organs.

ethology The study of the behavior of animals in their natural surroundings.

excitation A change in the energy of an atom, ion, molecule, etc., from one energy level (usually the ground state) to a higher energy level.

fatty acid Any of a class of organic acids with the general formula R.CO.OH, where R is a hydrocarbon group.

fermentation A reaction in which compounds, such as sugar, are broken down by the action of microorganisms that form the enzymes required to catalyze the reaction.

flash photolysis A technique for investigating the spectra and reactions of free radicals.

free energy A thermodynamic function used to measure the ability of a system to perform work. A change in free energy is equal to the work done.

free radical An atom or group of atoms that has an independent existence without all its valences being satisfied.

fuel cell A type of electric cell in which electrical energy is produced directly by electrochemical reactions involving substances that are continuously added to the cell.

fungus Any one of a group of spore-producing organisms formerly classified as plants but now placed in a separate kingdom (Fungi). They include the mushrooms, molds, and yeasts.

galaxy Any of the innumerable aggregations of stars that, together with gas, dust, and other material, make up the universe.

gene The functional unit of heredity. A single gene contains the information required for the manufacture, by a living cell, of one particular polypeptide, protein, or type of RNA and is the vehicle by which such information is transmitted to subsequent generations. Genes correspond to discrete regions of the DNA (or RNA) making up the genome.

genetic code The system by which genetic material carries the information that directs the activities of a living cell. The code is contained in the sequence of nucleotides of DNA and/or RNA (*see* codon).

genome The sum total of an organism's genetic material, including all the genes carried by its chromosomes.

global warming *See* greenhouse effect.

glycolysis The series of reactions in which glucose is broken down with the release of energy in the form of ATP.

greenhouse effect An effect in the Earth's atmosphere resulting from the presence of such gases as CO_2, which absorb the infrared radiation produced by the reradiation of solar ultraviolet radiation at the Earth's surface. This causes a rise in the Earth's average temperature, known as "global warming."

half-life A measure of the stability of a radioactive substance, equal to the time taken for its activity to fall to one half its original value.

halogens The nonmetallic elements fluorine, chlorine, bromine, iodine, and astatine.

haploid Describing a nucleus or cell that contains only a single set of chromosomes; haploid organisms consist exclusively of haploid cells. During sexual reproduction, two haploid sex cells fuse to form a single diploid cell.

heat death The state of a closed system when its total entropy has increased to its maximum value. Under these conditions there is no available energy.

histamine A substance released by various tissues of the body in response to invasion by microorganisms or other stimuli. It triggers inflammation and is responsible for some of the symptoms (e.g., sneezing) occurring in such allergies as hay fever.

histology The study of the tissues of living organisms.

hormone Any of various substances that are produced in small amounts by certain glands within the body (the endocrine glands) and released into the bloodstream to regulate the growth or activities of organs and tissues elsewhere in the body.

hydrocarbon Any organic compound composed only of carbon and hydrogen.

hydrogen bond A weak attraction between an electronegative atom, such as oxygen, nitrogen, or fluorine, and a hydrogen atom that is covalently linked to another electronegative atom.

hysteresis An apparent lag of an effect with respect to the magnitude of the agency producing the effect.

ideal gas An idealized gas composed of atoms that have a negligible volume and undergo perfectly elastic collisions. Such a gas would obey the gas laws under all conditions.

immunology The study of the body's mechanisms for defense against disease and the various ways in which these can be manipulated or enhanced.

insulin A hormone that is responsible for regulating the level of glucose in the blood, i.e., "blood sugar." It is produced by certain cells in the pancreas; deficiency causes the disease diabetes mellitus.

integrated circuit An electronic circuit made in a single small unit.

interferon Any one of a group of proteins, produced by various cells and tissues in the body, that increase resistance to invading viruses. Some types are synthesized for use in medicine as antiviral drugs.

internal energy The total energy possessed by a system on account of the kinetic and potential energies of its component molecules.

ion An atom or group of atoms with a net positive or negative charge. Positive ions (cations) have a deficiency of electrons and negative ions (anions) have an excess.

ionizing radiation Electromagnetic radiation or particles that cause ionization.

ionosphere A region of ionized air and free electrons around the Earth in the Earth's upper atmosphere, extending from a height of about 31 miles to 621 miles.

isomerism The existence of two or more chemical compounds with the same molecular formula but different arrangements of atoms in their molecules.

isotope Any of a number of forms of an element, all of which differ only in the number of neutrons in their atomic nuclei.

ketone Any of a class of organic compounds with the general formula RCOR′, where R and R′ are usually hydrocarbon groups.

kinetic energy The energy that a system has by

virtue of its motion, determined by the work necessary to bring it to rest.

kinetic theory Any theory for describing the physical properties of a system with reference to the motion of its constituent atoms or molecules.

laser A device for producing intense light or infrared or ultraviolet radiation by stimulated emission.

latent heat The total heat absorbed or produced during a change of phase (fusion, vaporization, etc.) at a constant temperature.

lepton Any of a class of elementary particles that have half-integral spin and take part in weak interactions; they include the electron, the muon, the neutrino, and their antiparticles.

lipid An ester of a fatty acid. Simple lipids include fats and oils; compound lipids include phospholipids and glycolipids; derived lipids include the steroids.

liquid crystal A state of certain molecules that flow like liquids but have an ordered arrangement of molecules.

macromolecule A very large molecule, as found in polymers or in such compounds as proteins.

magnetohydrodynamics The study of the motion of electrically conducting fluids and their behavior in magnetic fields.

meiosis A type of nuclear division, occurring only in certain cells of the reproductive organs, in which a diploid cell produces four haploid sex cells, or gametes.

meson Any member of a class of elementary particles characterized by a mass intermediate between those of the electron and the proton, an integral spin, and participation in strong interactions. They consist of two quarks each.

metabolism The totality of the chemical reactions taking place in a living cell or organism.

mitosis The type of nuclear division occurring in the body cells of most organisms, in which a diploid cell produces two diploid daughter cells.

moderator A substance used in fission reactors to slow down fast neutrons.

monoclonal antibody Any antibody produced by members of a group of genetically identical cells (which thus constitute a "clone"). Such antibodies have identical structures and each combines with the same antigen in precisely the same manner.

morphology The study of the form of organisms, especially their external shape and structure.

muon An elementary particle having a positive or negative charge and a mass equal to 206.77 times the mass of the electron.

mutation Any change in the structure of a gene, which can arise spontaneously or as a result of such agents as x-rays or certain chemicals. It may have a beneficial effect on the organism but most mutations are neutral, harmful, or even lethal. Mutations affecting the germ cells can be passed on to the organism's offspring.

natural selection The process by which the individuals of a population that are best adapted to life in a particular environment tend to enjoy greater reproductive success than members which are less well adapted. Hence, over successive generations, the descendants of the former constitute an increasing proportion of the population.

neutrino An elementary particle with zero rest mass, a velocity equal to that of light, and a spin of one half.

nuclear fission The process in which an atomic nucleus splits into fragment nuclei and one or more neutrons with the emission of energy.

nuclear fusion A nuclear reaction in which two light nuclei join together to form a heavier nucleus with the emission of energy.

nuclear winter The period of darkness and low temperature, predicted to follow a nuclear war, as a result of the obscuring of sunlight by dust and other debris.

nucleic acid Any of a class of large biologically important molecules consisting of one or more chains of nucleotides. There are two types: deoxyribonucleic acid (DNA) and ribonucleic acid (RNA).

nucleotide Any of a class of compounds consisting of a nitrogen-containing base (a purine or pyrimidine) combined with a sugar group (ribose or deoxyribose) bearing a phosphate group. Long chains of nucleotides form the nucleic acids, DNA and RNA.

nucleon A particle that is a constituent of an atomic nucleus; either a proton or a neutron.

nucleus 1. The positively charged part of the atom about which the electrons orbit. The nucleus is composed of neutrons and protons held together by strong interactions. **2.** A prominent body found in the cells of animals, plants, and other organisms (but not bacteria) that contains the chromosomes and is bounded by a double membrane.

oncogene A gene, introduced into a living cell by certain viruses, that disrupts normal metabolism and transforms the cell into a cancer cell.

optical activity The property of certain substances of rotating the plane of polarization of plane-polarized light.

osmosis Preferential flow of certain substances in solution through a semipermeable membrane. If the membrane separates a solution from a pure solvent, the solvent will flow through the membrane into the solution.

oxidation A process in which oxygen is combined with a substance or hydrogen is removed from a compound.

ozone layer A layer containing ozone in the Earth's atmosphere. It lies between heights of 9 and 19 miles and absorbs the Sun's higher-energy ultraviolet radiation.

parity A property of elementary particles depending on the symmetry of their wave function with respect to changes in sign of the coordinates.

parthenogenesis A form of reproduction in which a sex cell, usually an egg cell, develops into an embryo without fertilization. It occurs in certain plants and invertebrates and results in offspring that are genetically identical to the parent.

pathology The study of the nature and causes of disease.

peptide A compound formed by two or more amino acids linked together. The amino group ($-NH_2$) of one acid reacts with the carboxyl group (–COOH) of another to give the group –NH–CO–, known as the "peptide linkage."

periodic table A tabular arrangement of the elements in order of increasing atomic number such that similarities are displayed between groups of elements.

pH A measure of the acidity or alkalinity of a solution, equal to the logarithm to base 10 of the reciprocal of the concentration of hydrogen ions.

photocell Any device for converting light or other electromagnetic radiation directly into an electric current.

photoelectric effect The ejection of electrons from a solid as a result of irradiation by light or other electromagnetic radiation. The number of electrons emitted depends on the intensity of the light and not on its frequency.

photolysis The dissociation of a chemical compound into other compounds, atoms, and free radicals by irradiation with electromagnetic radiation.

photon A quantum of electromagnetic radiation.

photosynthesis The process by which plants, algae, and certain bacteria "fix" inorganic carbon, from carbon dioxide, as organic carbon in the form of carbohydrate using light as a source of energy and, in green plants and algae, water as a source of hydrogen. The light energy is trapped by special pigments, e.g., chlorophyll.

piezoelectric effect An effect observed in certain crystals in which they develop a potential difference across a pair of opposite faces when subjected to a stress.

pion A type of meson having either zero, positive, or negative charge and a mass 264.2 times that of the electron.

plankton The mass of microscopic plants and animals that drift passively at or near the surface of oceans and lakes.

plasma 1. An ionized gas consisting of free electrons and an approximately equal number of ions. 2. Blood plasma: the liquid component of blood, excluding the blood cells.

plate tectonics The theory that the Earth's surface consists of lithospheric plates, which have moved throughout geological time to their present positions.

polypeptide A chain of amino acids held together by peptide linkages. Polypeptides are found in proteins.

potential energy The energy that a system has by virtue of its position or state, determined by the work necessary to change the system from a reference position to its present state.

probability The likelihood that an event will occur. If an event is certain to occur its probability is 1; if it is certain not to occur the probability is 0. In any other circumstances the probability lies between 0 and 1.

protein Any of a large number of naturally occurring organic compounds found in all living matter. Proteins consist of chains of amino acids joined by peptide linkages.

proton A stable elementary particle with a positive electric charge equal to that of the electron. It is the nucleus of a hydrogen atom and weighs 1,836 times the mass of the electron.

protozoa A large group of minute single-celled organisms found widely in freshwater, marine, and damp terrestrial habitats. Unlike bacteria they possess a definite nucleus and are distinguished from plants in lacking cellulose.

pulsar A star that acts as a source of regularly fluctuating electromagnetic radiation, the period of the pulses usually being very rapid.

quantum electrodynamics The quantum theory of electromagnetic interactions between particles and between particles and electromagnetic radiation.

quantum theory A mathematical theory involving the idea that the energy of a system can change only in discrete amounts (quanta), rather than continuously.

quark Any of six elementary particles and their corresponding antiparticles with fractional charges that are the building blocks of baryons and mesons. Together with leptons they are the basis of all matter.

quasar A class of starlike astronomical objects with large redshifts, many of which emanate strong radio waves.

radioactive labeling The use of radioactive atoms in a compound to trace the path of the compound through a biological or mechanical system.

radioactivity The spontaneous disintegration of the nuclei of certain isotopes with emission of beta rays (electrons), alpha rays (helium nuclei), or gamma rays.

radio astronomy The branch of astronomy involving the use of radio telescopes.

radiocarbon dating A method of dating archeological specimens of wood, cotton, etc., based on the small amount of radioactive carbon (carbon–14) incorporated into the specimen when it was living and the extent to which this isotope has decayed since its death.

radioisotope A radioactive isotope of an element.

recombination The reassortment of maternally derived and paternally derived genes that occurs during meiosis preceding the formation of sex cells. Recombination is an important source of genetic variation.

redox reaction A reaction in which one reactant is oxidized and the other is reduced.

redshift The displacement of the spectral lines emitted by a moving body towards the red end of the visual spectrum. It is caused by the Doppler effect and, when observed in the spectrum of distant stars and galaxies, it indicates that the body is receding from the earth.

reduction A process in which oxygen is removed from or hydrogen is combined with a compound.

reflex An automatic response of an organism or body part to a stimulus, i.e., one that occurs without conscious control.

refractory A solid that has a high melting point and can withstand high temperatures.

relativistic mass The mass of a body as predicted by the theory of relativity. The relativistic mass of a particle moving at velocity v is $m_0(1 - v^2/c^2)^{-1/2}$, where m_0 is the rest mass.

rest mass The mass of a body when it is at rest relative to its observer, as distinguished from its relativistic mass.

retrovirus A type of virus whose genome, consisting of RNA, is transcribed into a DNA version and then inserted into the DNA of its host. The flow of genetic information, from RNA to DNA, is thus the reverse of that found in organisms generally.

RNA Ribonucleic acid: any one of several types of nucleic acid, including messenger RNA, that process the information carried by the genes and use it to direct the assembly of proteins in cells. In certain viruses RNA is the genetic material.

semiconductor A solid with an electrical conductivity that is intermediate between those of insulators and metals and that increases with increasing temperature. Examples are germanium, silicon, and lead telluride.

semipermeable membrane A barrier that permits the passage of some substances but is impermeable to others.

serum The fraction of blood plasma excluding the components of the blood-clotting system.

sex chromosome A chromosome that participates in determining the sex of individuals. Humans have two sex chromosomes, X and Y; females have two X chromosomes (XX) and males have one of each (XY).

sex hormone Any hormone that controls the development of sexual characteristics and regulates reproductive activity. The principal human sex hormones are progesterone and estrogens in females, testosterone and androsterone in males.

simple harmonic motion Motion of a point moving along a path so that its acceleration is directed towards a fixed point on the path and is directly proportional to the displacement from this fixed point.

SI units A system of units used, by international agreement, for all scientific purposes. It is based on the meter-kilogram-second (MKS) system and consists of seven base units and two supplementary units.

soap A salt of a fatty acid.

solar cell Any electrical device for converting solar energy directly into electrical energy.

solar constant The energy per unit area per unit time received from the Sun at a point that is the Earth's mean distance from the Sun away. It has the value 1,400 joules per square meter per second.

solar wind Streams of electrons and protons emitted by the Sun. The solar wind is responsible for the formation of the Van Allen belts and the aurora.

solid-state physics The experimental and theoretical study of the properties of the solid state, in particular the study of energy levels and the electrical and magnetic properties of metals and semiconductors.

speciation The process in which new species evolve from existing populations of organisms.

specific heat capacity The amount of heat required to raise the temperature of unit mass of a substance by unit temperature; it is usually measured in joules per kilogram per kelvin.

spectrometer Any of various instruments used for producing a spectrum (distribution of wavelengths of increasing magnitude) and measuring the wavelengths, energies, etc.

speed of light The speed at which all electromagnetic radiation travels; it is the highest speed attainable in the universe and has the value 2.998×10^8 meters per second in a vacuum.

standing wave A wave in which the wave profile remains stationary in the medium through which it is passing.

state of matter One of the three physical states – solid, liquid, or gas – in which matter may exist.

stereochemistry The arrangement in space of the groups in a molecule and the effect this has on the compound's properties and chemical behavior.

steroid Any of a group of complex lipids that occur widely in plants and animals and include various hormones, such as cortisone and the sex hormones.

stimulated emission The process in which a photon colliding with an excited atom causes emission of a second photon with the same energy as the first. It is the basis of lasers.

stoichiometric Involving chemical combination in exact ratios.

strangeness A property of certain hadrons that causes them to decay more slowly than expected from the energy released.

strong interaction A type of interaction between elementary particles occurring at short range (about 10^{-15} meter) and having a magnitude about 100 times greater than that of the electromagnetic interaction.

sublimation The passage of certain substances from the solid state into the gaseous state and then back into the solid state, without any intermediate liquid state being formed.

substrate A substance that is acted upon in some way, especially the compound acted on by a catalyst or the solid on which a compound is adsorbed.

sugar Any of a group of water-soluble simple carbohydrates, usually having a sweet taste.

sunspot A region of the Sun's surface that is much cooler and therefore darker than the surrounding area, having a temperature of about 4,000°C as opposed to 6,000°C for the rest of the photosphere.

superconductivity A phenomenon occurring

in certain metals and alloys at temperatures close to absolute zero, in which the electrical resistance of the solid vanishes below a certain temperature.

superfluid A fluid that flows without friction and has extremely high thermal conductivity.

supernova A star that suffers an explosion, becoming up to 10^8 times brighter in the process and forming a large cloud of expanding debris (the supernova remnant).

surfactant A substance used to increase the spreading or wetting properties of a liquid. Surfactants are often detergents, which act by lowering the surface tension.

symbiosis A long-term association between members of different species, especially where mutual benefit is derived by the participants.

taxonomy The science of classifying organisms into groups.

tensile strength The applied stress necessary to break a material under tension.

thermal conductivity A measure of the ability of a substance to conduct heat, equal to the rate of flow of heat per unit area resulting from unit temperature gradient.

thermal neutron A neutron with a low kinetic energy, of the same order of magnitude as the kinetic energies of atoms and molecules.

thermionic emission Emission of electrons from a hot solid. The effect occurs when significant numbers of electrons have enough kinetic energy to overcome the solid's work function.

thermodynamics The branch of science concerned with the relationship between heat, work, and other forms of energy.

thermodynamic temperature Temperature measured in kelvins that is a function of the internal energy possessed by a body, having a value of zero at absolute zero.

thixotropy A phenomenon shown by some fluids in which the viscosity decreases as the rate of shear increases, i.e., the fluid becomes less viscous the faster it moves.

transducer A device that is supplied with the energy of one system and converts it into the energy of a different system, so that the output signal is proportional to the input signal but is carried in a different form.

transistor A device made of semiconducting material in which a flow of current between two electrodes can be controlled by a potential applied to a third electrode.

tribology The study of friction between solid surfaces, including the origin of frictional forces and the lubrication of moving parts.

triple point The point at which the solid, liquid, and gas phases of a pure substance can all coexist in equilibrium.

tritiated Denoting a chemical compound containing tritium (^3H) atoms in place of hydrogen atoms.

ultracentrifuge A centrifuge designed to work at very high speeds, so that the force produced is large enough to cause sedimentation of colloids.

unified-field theory A theory that seeks to explain gravitational and electromagnetic interactions and the strong and weak nuclear interactions in terms of a single set of equations.

vaccine An antigenic preparation that is administered to a human or other animal to produce immunity against a specific disease-causing agent.

valence The combining power of an element, atom, ion, or radical, equal to the number of hydrogen atoms that the atom, ion, etc., could combine with or displace in forming a compound.

valence band The energy band of a solid that is occupied by the valence electrons of the atoms forming the solid.

valence electron An electron in the outer shell of an atom that participates in the chemical bonding when the atom forms compounds.

vector 1. A quantity that is specified both by its magnitude and its direction. 2. An agent, such as an insect, that harbors disease-causing microorganisms and transmits them to humans, other animals, or plants.

virtual particle A particle thought of as existing for a very brief period in an interaction between two other particles.

virus A noncellular agent that can infect a living animal, plant, or bacterial cell and use the apparatus of the host cell to manufacture new virus particles. In some cases this causes disease in the host organism. Outside the host cell, viruses are totally inert.

viscosity The property of liquids and gases of resisting flow. It is caused by forces between the molecules of the fluid.

water of crystallization Water combined in the form of molecules in definite proportions in the crystals of many substances.

wave equation A partial differential equation relating the displacement of a wave to the time and the three spatial dimensions.

wave function A mathematical expression giving the probability of finding the particle associated with a wave at a specified point according to wave mechanics.

wave mechanics A form of quantum mechanics in which particles (electrons, protons, etc.) are regarded as waves, so that any system of particles can be described by a wave equation.

weak interaction A type of interaction between elementary particles, occurring at short range and having a magnitude about 10^{10} times weaker than the electromagnetic force.

work function The minimum energy necessary to remove an electron from a metal at absolute zero.

x-ray crystallography The determination of the structure of crystals and molecules by use of x-ray diffraction.

zero point energy The energy of vibration of atoms at the absolute zero of temperature.

zwitterion An ion that has both a positive and negative charge.

INDEX

Chinese pharmacologist: **6**: 121
Chittenden, Russell Henry **2**: 150
Chladni, Ernst Florens **2**: 151
Chlorophyll: **3**: 212; **8**: 19, 212; **10**: 142, 167
Cholera: **6**: 4; **9**: 90
Cholesterol: **1**: 204; **2**: 62, 87, 190; **4**: 134; **8**: 204; **10**: 150, 167
Chou Kung 2: 152
Christie, Sir William Henry Mahoney **2**: 152
Chromatography: **10**: 1
Chromosomes: **4**: 6; **7**: 103; **9**: 127, 145
Chu, Paul Ching-Wu **2**: 153
Chu Shih-Chieh 2: 154
Civil Engineer: **3**: 140
Clairaut, Alexis Claude **2**: 155
Claisen, Ludwig **2**: 156
Clark, Alvan Graham **2**: 157
Clarke, Sir Cyril Astley **2**: 158
Claude, Albert **2**: 159
Claude, Georges **2**: 160
Clausius, Rudolf **2**: 161
Clemence, Gerald Maurice **2**: 162
Cleve, Per Teodor **2**: 163
Climate: **3**: 14; **6**: 48
Cloud chamber: **1**: 198; **10**: 145
Cloud formation: **1**: 164
Coblentz, William Weber **2**: 164
Cockcroft, Sir John **2**: 164
Cocker, Edward **2**: 165
Coenzymes: **3**: 168; **4**: 207; **9**: 181, 205; **10**: 74
Cohen, Paul Joseph **2**: 166
Cohen, Seymour Stanley **2**: 166
Cohen, Stanley **2**: 167
Cohn, Ferdinand Julius **2**: 168
Cohnheim, Julius **2**: 169
Colloids: **4**: 153; **10**: 198
Colombo, Matteo Realdo **2**: 170
Comets: **7**: 195; **10**: 112
Compton, Arthur Holly **2**: 171
Computer Scientists: **1**: 18, 41, 76, 96; **2**: 49, 90; **3**: 116, 190; **4**: 15; **5**: 71, 76, 90, 153, 176, 204; **6**: 2, 106; **7**: 10, 24, 81, 151, 192; **9**: 12, 131, 138; **10**: 133, 151, 200
Comte, Auguste Isidore **2**: 172
Conant, James Bryant **2**: 174
Conon of Samos 2: 174
Continental drift: **1**: 198; **2**: 76; **3**: 109; **5**: 80, 148; **8**: 191; **10**: 88
Contraceptive pill: **8**: 48; **9**: 100
Conway, John Horton **2**: 175
Conybeare, William **2**: 177
Cook, James **2**: 178
Cooke, Sir William **2**: 179
Cooper, Leon Neil **2**: 180
Cope, Edward Drinker **2**: 181
Copernicus, Nicolaus **2**: 182
Corey, Elias James **2**: 184
Cori, Carl Ferdinand **2**: 185
Cori, Gerty Theresa **2**: 186
Coriolis, Gustave-Gaspard **2**: 187
Cormack, Allan Macleod **2**: 188
Corner, Edred **2**: 189
Cornforth, Sir John **2**: 190
Correns, Karl Erich **2**: 190

Cort, Henry **2**: 191
Corvisart, Jean-Nicolas **2**: 192
Cosmic background radiation: **3**: 69; **8**: 25
Cosmic rays: **1**: 198; **2**: 17, 171; **5**: 41; **7**: 73; **8**: 80
Cosmologists: **2**: 4; **3**: 3; **4**: 173; **5**: 2, 99; **6**: 102
Coster, Dirk **2**: 193
Cottrell, Sir Alan **2**: 193
Coulomb, Charles Augustin de **2**: 194
Coulson, Charles Alfred **2**: 196
Couper, Archibald Scott **2**: 197
Cournand, André **2**: 198
Courtois, Bernard **2**: 199
Cousteau, Jacques Yves **2**: 200
Crafts, James Mason **2**: 201
Craig, Lyman Creighton **2**: 201
Cram, Donald James **2**: 202
Crick, Francis **2**: 203
Croatian earth scientist: **7**: 88
Croatian mathematician: **7**: 68
Croll, James **2**: 205
Cronin, James Watson **2**: 206
Cronstedt, Axel Frederic **2**: 207
Crookes, Sir William **2**: 207
Cross, Charles Frederick **2**: 208
Crum Brown, Alexander **2**: 209
Crutzen, Paul **2**: 210
Crystallographers: **1**: 168; **5**: 178; **6**: 159; **10**: 179
Crystallography: **9**: 125
Cuban physician: **3**: 206
Cugnot, Nicolas-Joseph **2**: 211
Culpeper, Nicholas **2**: 211
Curie, Marie Skłodowska **2**: 212
Curie, Pierre **2**: 215
Curtis, Heber Doust **2**: 217
Curtius, Theodor **2**: 218
Cushing, Harvey **2**: 218
Cuvier, Baron Georges **2**: 219
Cybernetics: **10**: 125
Cytologists: **1**: 159; **2**: 114; **3**: 103; **4**: 6, 136; **7**: 56
Czech chemist: **5**: 47
Czech physiologist: **8**: 100

d'Abano, Pietro **3**: 1
Daguerre, Louis-Jacques-Mandé **3**: 2
d'Ailly, Pierre **3**: 3
Daimler, Gottlieb Wilhelm **3**: 4
Dainton, Frederick Sydney **3**: 5
Dale, Sir Henry Hallett **3**: 6
d'Alembert, Jean Le Rond **3**: 7
Dalén, Nils Gustaf **3**: 8
Dalton, John **3**: 9
Dam, Carl Peter Henrik **3**: 11
Dana, James Dwight **3**: 12
Daniell, John Frederic **3**: 13
Daniels, Farrington **3**: 14
Danish anatomist: **9**: 125
Danish archeologists: **9**: 188; **10**: 169
Danish astronomers: **2**: 35; **3**: 94; **5**: 36; **8**: 167; **9**: 141
Danish bacteriologist: **4**: 154
Danish biochemist: **3**: 11
Danish biologist: **9**: 22
Danish botanist: **5**: 154
Danish chemists: **1**: 195; **2**: 57; **5**: 216; **9**: 103, 189

Danish earth scientists: **6**: 96; **7**: 173; **9**: 125
Danish geneticist: **5**: 154
Danish immunologist: **5**: 152
Danish mathematicians: **1**: 129; **7**: 173
Danish meteorologist: **3**: 14
Danish physicians: **3**: 203, 207
Danish physicists: **1**: 215, 216; **7**: 112, 120, 184
Danish physiologist: **6**: 27
Danish zoologist: **9**: 122
Dansgaard, Willi **3**: 14
Darby, Abraham **3**: 15
Dark matter: **8**: 187
Darlington, Cyril Dean **3**: 16
Dart, Raymond Arthur **3**: 17
Darwin, Charles Robert **3**: 18
Darwin, Erasmus **3**: 21
Darwin, Sir George **3**: 22
Daubrée, Gabriel Auguste **3**: 23
Dausset, Jean **3**: 24
Davaine, Casimir Joseph **3**: 25
Davenport, Charles **3**: 26
Davis, Raymond **3**: 26
Davis, William Morris **3**: 27
Davisson, Clinton Joseph **3**: 28
Davy, Sir Humphry **3**: 29
Dawes, William Rutter **3**: 31
Dawkins, Richard **3**: 32
Day, David Talbot **3**: 33
Deacon, Henry **3**: 34
de Bary, Heinrich Anton **3**: 34
De Beer, Sir Gavin **3**: 35
Debierne, André Louis **3**: 36
de Broglie, Prince Louis Victor Pierre Raymond **3**: 37
Debye, Peter **3**: 38
Dedekind, (Julius Wilhelm) Richard **3**: 39
de Duve, Christian René **3**: 40
Deficiency diseases: **3**: 130; **4**: 56, 130; **6**: 131
De Forest, Lee **3**: 41
De Geer, Charles **3**: 42
Dehmelt, Hans Georg **3**: 43
De la Beche, Sir Henry **3**: 44
Delambre, Jean Baptiste **3**: 45
De la Rue, Warren **3**: 45
Delbrück, Max **3**: 46
D'Elhuyar, Don Fausto **3**: 48
DeLisi, Charles **3**: 49
Del Rio, Andrès Manuel **3**: 50
De Luc, Jean André **3**: 50
Demarçay, Eugene Anatole **3**: 52
Demerec, Milislav **3**: 52
Democritus of Abdera 3: 53
De Moivre, Abraham **3**: 54
Dempster, Arthur Jeffrey **3**: 55
Dendrochronologist: **3**: 90
Dentists: **7**: 107; **10**: 98
Derham, William **3**: 56
Desaguliers, John **3**: 57
Desargues, Girard **3**: 57
Descartes, René du Perron **3**: 58
Desch, Cyril Henry **3**: 60
de Sitter, Willem **3**: 61
Desmarest, Nicolas **3**: 61
Désormes, Charles Bernard **3**: 62
Deville, Henri **3**: 63
de Vries, Hugo **3**: 64
Dewar, Sir James **3**: 65

Goddard, Robert 4: 121
Gödel, Kurt 4: 122
Godwin, Sir Harry 4: 124
Goeppert-Mayer, Maria 4: 125
Goethe, Johann Wolfgang von 4: 126
Gold, Thomas 4: 128
Goldberger, Joseph 4: 130
Goldhaber, Maurice 4: 131
Goldschmidt, Johann Wilhelm 4: 132
Goldschmidt, Victor 4: 132
Goldstein, Eugen 4: 133
Goldstein, Joseph 4: 134
Golgi, Camillo 4: 136
Gomberg, Moses 4: 137
Good, Robert Alan 4: 138
Goodall, Jane 4: 139
Goodman, Henry Nelson 4: 141
Goodpasture, Ernest 4: 142
Goodrich, Edwin Stephen 4: 143
Goodricke, John 4: 144
Gordan, Paul Albert 4: 144
Gorer, Peter Alfred 4: 145
Gorgas, William 4: 146
Gossage, William 4: 147
Goudsmit, Samuel 4: 148
Gould, Benjamin 4: 149
Gould, Stephen Jay 4: 150
Graaf, Regnier de 4: 151
Graebe, Karl 4: 152
Graham, Thomas 4: 152
Gram, Hans Christian 4: 154
Granit, Ragnar Arthur 4: 155
Grassi, Giovanni Battista 4: 156
Gray, Asa 4: 157
Gray, Harry Barkus 4: 158
Gray, Stephen 4: 159
Greek anatomists: 3: 154; 5: 25
Greek astronomers: 1: 65; 2: 93, 174; 3: 155, 165; 5: 23, 57; 7: 57; 8: 78, 102; 9: 177
Greek botanist: 9: 180
Greek earth scientists: 1: 56; 9: 177
Greek explorer: 8: 102
Greek-French astronomer: 1: 55
Greek geographers: 3: 67; 5: 7, 57; 9: 137
Greek inventor: 5: 25
Greek mathematicians: 1: 56, 62; 2: 174; 3: 73, 163, 165; 5: 25, 131; 7: 214; 8: 101
Greek philosophers: 1: 24, 45, 46, 65; 3: 53, 67, 146, 152; 5: 23; 6: 108; 7: 219; 8: 40, 55, 78, 91, 101; 9: 93, 140, 177, 180; 10: 181, 192
Greek physicians: 1: 24; 3: 73, 154; 4: 62; 5: 25, 58; 8: 82
Greek scientists: 1: 65; 8: 41
Green, George 4: 159
Greenhouse effect: 8: 134
Greenstein, Jesse Leonard 4: 160
Gregor, William 4: 160
Gregory, James 4: 161
Griess, Johann Peter 4: 162
Griffin, Donald Redfield 4: 163
Griffith, Fred 4: 164
Grignard, François 4: 165
Grimaldi, Francesco 4: 166
Group theory: 1: 6; 4: 72; 5: 161
Grove, Sir William 4: 166

Guericke, Otto von 4: 167
Guettard, Jean Etienne 4: 168
Guillaume, Charles 4: 169
Guillemin, Roger 4: 170
Guldberg, Cato 4: 171
Gullstrand, Allvar 4: 172
Gutenberg, Beno 4: 172
Guth, Alan Harvey 4: 173
Guthrie, Samuel 4: 174
Guyot, Arnold Henry 4: 175
Guyton de Morveau, Baron Louis Bernard 4: 176

Haber, Fritz 4: 177
Hadamard, Jacques 4: 178
Hadfield, Sir Robert 4: 179
Hadley, George 4: 180
Hadley, John 4: 180
Haeckel, Ernst Heinrich 4: 181
Hahn, Otto 4: 183
Haken, Wolfgang 4: 185
Haldane, John Burdon Sanderson 4: 186
Haldane, John Scott 4: 187
Hale, George Ellery 4: 189
Hales, Stephen 4: 191
Hall, Asaph 4: 192
Hall, Charles Martin 4: 193
Hall, Edwin Herbert 4: 194
Hall, James 4: 195
Hall, Sir James 4: 195
Hall, Marshall 4: 196
Haller, Albrecht von 4: 197
Halley, Edmond 4: 198
Halsted, William Stewart 4: 200
Hamilton, William 4: 201
Hamilton, Sir William Rowan 4: 202
Hämmerling, Joachim 4: 203
Hammond, George Simms 4: 204
Hansen, Gerhard Henrik 4: 205
Hantzsch, Arthur Rudolf 4: 206
Harcourt, Sir William 4: 206
Harden, Sir Arthur 4: 207
Hardy, Godfrey Harold 4: 208
Hardy, Sir William Bate 4: 209
Hare, Robert 4: 210
Hargreaves, James 4: 211
Hariot, Thomas 4: 211
Harkins, William Draper 4: 212
Harris, Geoffrey Wingfield 4: 213
Harrison, Ross Granville 4: 214
Hartline, Haldan Keffer 4: 215
Hartmann, Johannes 4: 215
Harvey, William 4: 216
Hassell, Odd 4: 218
Hatchett, Charles 4: 219
Hauksbee, Francis 4: 219
Hauptman, Herb Aaron 4: 220
Haüy, René Just 5: 1
Hawking, Stephen William 5: 2
Haworth, Sir (Walter) Norman 5: 5
Hays, James Douglas 5: 6
Heat: 1: 197; 3: 163; 8: 190
Heaviside, Oliver 5: 7
Hecataeus of Miletus 5: 7
Hecht, Selig 5: 8
Heezen, Bruce Charles 5: 8
Heidelberger, Michael 5: 9
Heisenberg, Werner Karl 5: 10
Helmholtz, Hermann Ludwig

von 5: 13
Helmont, Jan Baptista van 5: 14
Hemoglobin: 2: 174; 5: 135; 8: 33; 10: 113
Hempel, Carl Gustav 5: 15
Hench, Philip Showalter 5: 17
Henderson, Thomas 5: 18
Henle, Friedrich 5: 19
Henry, Joseph 5: 20
Henry, William 5: 21
Hensen, Viktor 5: 22
Heracleides of Pontus 5: 23
Heraclitus of Ephesus 5: 23
Herbalist: 4: 101
Hermite, Charles 5: 24
Hero of Alexandria 5: 25
Herophilus of Chalcedon 5: 25
Héroult, Paul 5: 26
Herring, William Conyers 5: 27
Herschbach, Dudley 5: 28
Herschel, Caroline 5: 29
Herschel, Sir (Frederick) William 5: 30
Herschel, Sir John Frederick William 5: 31
Hershey, Alfred Day 5: 32
Hertz, Gustav 5: 33
Hertz, Heinrich Rudolf 5: 34
Hertzsprung, Ejnar 5: 36
Herzberg, Gerhard 5: 38
Hess, Germain Henri 5: 39
Hess, Harry Hammond 5: 39
Hess, Victor Francis 5: 40
Hess, Walter Rudolf 5: 42
Hevelius, Johannes 5: 43
Hevesy, George Charles von 5: 44
Hewish, Antony 5: 45
Heymans, Corneille 5: 46
Heyrovský, Jaroslav 5: 47
Higgins, William 5: 48
Higgs, Peter Ware 5: 48
Hilbert, David 5: 49
Hildebrand, Joel Henry 5: 52
Hilditch, Thomas Percy 5: 53
Hill, Archibald Vivian 5: 54
Hill, James Peter 5: 55
Hillier, James 5: 55
Hinshelwood, Sir Cyril 5: 56
Hipparchus 5: 57
Hippocrates of Cos 5: 58
Hirsch, Sir Peter Bernhard 5: 60
Hirst, Sir Edmund 5: 60
His, Wilhelm 5: 61
Hisinger, Wilhelm 5: 62
Histologists: 4: 136; 6: 11, 204; 8: 108, 114; 9: 106
Hitchings, George Herbert 5: 63
Hittorf, Johann Wilhelm 5: 64
Hitzig, Eduard 5: 65
HIV: 4: 70; 7: 98
Hjelm, Peter Jacob 5: 66
Hoagland, Mahlon Bush 5: 66
Hodge, Sir William 5: 67
Hodgkin, Sir Alan Lloyd 5: 68
Hodgkin, Dorothy 5: 69
Hodgkin, Thomas 5: 70
Hoff, Marcian Edward 5: 71
Hoffmann, Friedrich 5: 72
Hoffmann, Roald 5: 73
Hofmann, Johann Wilhelm 5: 74
Hofmeister, Wilhelm 5: 75
Hofstadter, Douglas 5: 76

Just, Ernest Everett 5: 167

Kaluza, Theodor 5: 168
Kamen, Martin David 5: 169
Kamerlingh-Onnes, Heike 5: 170
Kamin, Leon 5: 171
Kammerer, Paul 5: 172
Kane, Sir Robert John 5: 173
Kant, Immanuel 5: 174
Kapitza, Pyotr 5: 175
Kapoor, Mitchell David 5: 176
Kapteyn, Jacobus Cornelius 5: 177
Karle, Isabella Helen 5: 178
Karle, Jerome 5: 179
Karrer, Paul 5: 180
Kastler, Alfred 5: 181
Katz, Bernard 5: 181
Keeler, James Edward 5: 182
Keenan, Philip Childs 5: 183
Keilin, David 5: 183
Keir, James 5: 184
Keith, Sir Arthur 5: 185
Kekulé von Stradonitz, Friedrich August 5: 186
Kellner, Karl 5: 189
Kelvin, William Thomson, Baron 5: 189
Kemeny, John George 5: 191
Kendall, Edward Calvin 5: 192
Kendall, Henry Way 5: 193
Kendrew, Sir John 5: 193
Kennelly, Arthur Edwin 5: 194
Kenyan anthropologist: 6: 79
Kepler, Johannes 5: 195
Kerr, John 5: 198
Kerst, Donald William 5: 198
Kettlewell, Henry 5: 199
Kety, Seymour Solomon 5: 200
Khorana, Har Gobind 5: 201
Kidd, John 5: 202
Kiddinu 5: 202
Kilby, Jack St. Clair 5: 203
Kildall, Gary 5: 204
Kimura, Doreen 5: 205
Kimura, Hisashi 5: 206
Kimura, Motoo 5: 207
Kinetic theory: 2: 2, 161; 5: 163; 7: 18; 10: 76
King, Charles Glen 5: 207
Kinsey, Alfred Charles 5: 208
Kipping, Frederic Stanley 5: 209
Kirchhoff, Gustav Robert 5: 210
Kirkwood, Daniel 5: 211
Kirwan, Richard 5: 212
Kistiakowsky, George Bogdan 5: 213
Kitasato, Baron Shibasaburo 5: 214
Kittel, Charles 5: 215
Kjeldahl, Johan Gustav Christoffer Thorsager 5: 216
Klaproth, Martin 5: 217
Klein, (Christian) Felix 5: 218
Klingenstierna, Samuel 5: 219
Klitzing, Klaus von 5: 220
Klug, Sir Aaron 6: 1
Knuth, Donald Ervin 6: 2
Koch, (Heinrich Hermann) Robert 6: 3
Kocher, Emil Theodor 6: 5
Köhler, Georges J. F. 6: 6
Kohlrausch, Friedrich 6: 7

Kohn, Walter 6: 8
Ko Hung 6: 9
Kolbe, Adolph 6: 10
Koller, Carl 6: 10
Kölliker, Rudolph Albert von 6: 11
Kolmogorov, Andrei 6: 12
Kopp, Hermann Franz Moritz 6: 13
Köppen, Wladimir Peter 6: 14
Kornberg, Arthur 6: 15
Korolev, Sergei Pavlovich 6: 16
Kossel, Albrecht 6: 17
Kosterlitz, Hans Walter 6: 18
Kouwenhoven, William 6: 19
Kovalevski, Aleksandr Onufrievich 6: 19
Kovalevsky, Sonya 6: 20
Kozyrev, Nikolay 6: 21
Kraft, Robert Paul 6: 22
Kramer, Paul Jackson 6: 22
Kratzer, Nicolas 6: 23
Kraus, Charles August 6: 24
Krebs, Edwin Gerhard 6: 24
Krebs, Sir Hans Adolf 6: 25
Krogh, Schack August Steenberg 6: 27
Kronecker, Leopold 6: 28
Kroto, Harold Walter 6: 29
Kuffler, Stephen William 6: 30
Kuhn, Richard 6: 31
Kuhn, Thomas Samuel 6: 32
Kühne, Wilhelm Friedrich 6: 33
Kuiper, Gerard Peter 6: 34
Kundt, August 6: 35
Kurchatov, Igor Vasilievich 6: 36
Kurti, Nicholas 6: 37
Kusch, Polykarp 6: 37

Lacaille, Nicolas Louis de 6: 39
Lack, David Lambert 6: 40
La Condamine, Charles Marie de 6: 41
Laënnec, René Théophile Hyacinthe 6: 42
Lagrange, Comte Joseph Louis 6: 43
Lakatos, Imre 6: 44
Lalande, Joseph de 6: 45
Lamarck, Jean Baptiste, Chevalier de 6: 46
Lamarckism: 2: 181; 5: 172; 6: 47; 10: 58
Lamb, Sir Horace 6: 47
Lamb, Hubert Horace 6: 48
Lamb, Willis Eugene, Jr. 6: 49
Lambert, Johann Heinrich 6: 50
Lamont, Johann von 6: 51
Lancisi, Giovanni Maria 6: 52
Land, Edwin Herbert 6: 52
Landau, Lev Davidovich 6: 53
Landolt, Hans Heinrich 6: 54
Landsteiner, Karl 6: 55
Langevin, Paul 6: 57
Langley, John Newport 6: 58
Langley, Samuel Pierpont 6: 59
Langmuir, Irving 6: 60
Lankester, Sir Edwin Ray 6: 61
Laplace, Marquis Pierre Simon de 6: 62
Lapworth, Arthur 6: 64
Lapworth, Charles 6: 64
Larmor, Sir Joseph 6: 65

Lartet, Edouard Armand Isidore Hippolyte 6: 66
Laser: 6: 202
Lassell, William 6: 67
Laurent, Auguste 6: 68
Laveran, Charles 6: 69
Lavoisier, Antoine Laurent 6: 70
Lavoisier, Marie Anne Pierrette 6: 71
Lawes, Sir John Bennet 6: 72
Lawless, Theodore 6: 73
Lawrence, Ernest Orlando 6: 74
Lax, Benjamin 6: 75
Lazear, Jesse Williams 6: 76
Leakey, Louis 6: 77
Leakey, Mary 6: 78
Leakey, Richard Erskine 6: 79
Leavitt, Henrietta Swan 6: 80
Lebedev, Pyotr 6: 82
Le Bel, Joseph Achille 6: 83
Lebesgue, Henri Léon 6: 84
Leblanc, Nicolas 6: 85
Le Chatelier, Henri Louis 6: 86
Leclanché, Georges 6: 87
Lecoq de Boisbaudran, Paul-Emile 6: 88
Lederberg, Joshua 6: 88
Lederman, Leon Max 6: 90
Lee, Tsung-Dao 6: 91
Lee, Yuan Tseh 6: 92
Leeuwenhoek, Anton van 6: 93
Leffall, LaSalle 6: 95
Le Gros Clark, Sir Wilfrid Edward 6: 95
Lehmann, Inge 6: 96
Lehn, Jean Marie Pierre 6: 97
Leibniz, Gottfried Wilhelm 6: 98
Leishman, Sir William 6: 100
Leloir, Luis Frederico 6: 101
Lemaître, Abbé Georges Edouard 6: 102
Lémery, Nicolas 6: 103
Lenard, Philipp Eduard Anton 6: 104
Lenat, Douglas 6: 106
Lennard-Jones, Sir John 6: 106
Lenoir, Jean Joseph Etienne 6: 107
Lenz, Heinrich 6: 108
Lepidopterist: 5: 199
Leucippus 6: 108
Leuckart, Karl 6: 109
Levene, Phoebus Aaron Theodor 6: 110
Le Verrier, Urbain Jean Joseph 6: 111
Levi-Montalcini, Rita 6: 112
Levinstein, Ivan 6: 114
Lewis, Edward B. 6: 115
Lewis, Gilbert Newton 6: 116
Lewis, Julian Herman 6: 117
Lewis, Timothy Richard 6: 118
L'Hôpital, Marquis Guillaume François Antoine de 6: 119
Lhwyd, Edward 6: 120
Li, Choh Hao 6: 120
Li, Shih-Chen 6: 121
Libavius, Andreas 6: 122
Libby, Willard Frank 6: 123
Lie, (Marius) Sophus 6: 124
Liebig, Justus von 6: 124
Lighthill, Sir Michael 6: 127
Lilienthal, Otto 6: 128

Metchnikoff, Elie **7**: 56
Meteorologists: **1**: 1, 164, 193, 194; **2**: 88, 210; **3**: 13, 14, 50, 162, 196, 216; **4**: 180; **6**: 14, 48, 160, 163; **7**: 209; **8**: 122, 143, 173; **9**: 56, 72; **10**: 86
Metius, Jacobus **7**: 57
Meton **7**: 57
Mexican chemist: **7**: 90
Meyer, Julius Lothar **7**: 58
Meyer, Karl **7**: 59
Meyer, Viktor **7**: 60
Meyerhof, Otto Fritz **7**: 61
Michaelis, Leonor **7**: 61
Michel, Hartmut **7**: 62
Michell, John **7**: 63
Michelson, Albert Abraham **7**: 64
Microscope: **6**: 145; **7**: 51; **10**: 193
Midgley, Thomas Jr. **7**: 66
Miescher, Johann Friedrich **7**: 67
Milankovich, Milutin **7**: 68
Military Scientists: **6**: 206; **9**: 163
Miller, Dayton Clarence **7**: 69
Miller, Hugh **7**: 70
Miller, Jacques Francis Albert Pierre **7**: 71
Miller, Stanley Lloyd **7**: 72
Millikan, Robert Andrews **7**: 73
Mills, Bernard Yarnton **7**: 74
Mills, William Hobson **7**: 75
Milne, Edward Arthur **7**: 76
Milne, John **7**: 77
Milstein, César **7**: 78
Mineralogists: **1**: 147; **2**: 207; **3**: 12, 48, 50; **4**: 60, 160; **5**: 1, 62, 212; **7**: 89; **8**: 127; **10**: 100
Mining Engineer: **1**: 127
Minkowski, Hermann **7**: 79
Minkowski, Rudolph Leo **7**: 80
Minot, George Richards **7**: 81
Minsky, Marvin Lee **7**: 81
Misner, Charles William **7**: 83
Mitchell, Maria **7**: 84
Mitchell, Peter Dennis **7**: 85
Mitscherlich, Eilhardt **7**: 86
Möbius, August Ferdinand **7**: 87
Mohl, Hugo von **7**: 87
Mohorovičić, Andrija **7**: 88
Mohs, Friedrich **7**: 89
Moissan, Ferdinand Frédéric Henri **7**: 89
Molina, Mario José **7**: 90
Mond, Ludwig **7**: 91
Mondino de Luzzi **7**: 93
Monge, Gaspard **7**: 94
Monod, Jacques Lucien **7**: 95
Monro, Alexander (Primus) **7**: 96
Monro, Alexander (Secundus) **7**: 97
Montagnier, Luc **7**: 98
Montgolfier, Etienne Jacques de **7**: 99
Montgolfier, Michel Joseph de **7**: 99
Moore, Stanford **7**: 100
Mordell, Louis Joel **7**: 101
Morgagni, Giovanni Batista **7**: 102
Morgan, Thomas Hunt **7**: 103

Morgan, William Wilson **7**: 104
Morley, Edward Williams **7**: 105
Morse, Samuel **7**: 106
Morton, William **7**: 107
Mosander, Carl Gustav **7**: 108
Moseley, Henry Gwyn Jeffreys **7**: 109
Mössbauer, Rudolph Ludwig **7**: 110
Mott, Sir Nevill Francis **7**: 111
Mottelson, Benjamin Roy **7**: 112
Moulton, Forest Ray **7**: 113
Mueller, Erwin Wilhelm **7**: 114
Muller, Alex **7**: 115
Müller, Franz Joseph, Baron von Reichenstein **7**: 116
Muller, Hermann Joseph **7**: 117
Müller, Johannes Peter **7**: 118
Müller, Otto Friedrich **7**: 120
Müller, Paul Hermann **7**: 120
Muller, Richard August **7**: 121
Mulliken, Robert Sanderson **7**: 122
Mullis, Kary Banks **7**: 123
Munk, Walter Heinrich **7**: 124
Murchison, Sir Roderick Impey **7**: 125
Murphy, William Parry **7**: 126
Murray, Sir John **7**: 127
Murray, Joseph Edward **7**: 127
Muscle contraction: **5**: 54, 90, 124; **9**: 159
Muspratt, James **7**: 129
Musschenbroek, Pieter van **7**: 130
Muybridge, Eadweard James **7**: 131

Naegeli, Karl Wilhelm von **7**: 133
Nagaoka, Hantaro **7**: 134
Nambu, Yoichipo **7**: 135
Nansen, Fridtjof **7**: 136
Napier, John **7**: 137
Nasmyth, James **7**: 138
Nathans, Daniel **7**: 139
Natta, Giulio **7**: 140
Naturalists: **1**: 26, 51, 77, 133, 146, 156; **2**: 6, 32, 72, 74, 133; **3**: 18; **4**: 13, 105; **7**: 142; **8**: 118, 188; **9**: 152; **10**: 66, 114
Naudin, Charles **7**: 141
Nebulae: **1**: 124; **5**: 108; **7**: 55; **10**: 159
Nebular hypothesis: **5**: 147, 174; **6**: 63; **10**: 95
Needham, Dorothy Mary Moyle **7**: 142
Needham, John Turberville **7**: 142
Needham, Joseph **7**: 143
Néel, Louis Eugène Félix **7**: 144
Ne'eman, Yuval **7**: 145
Nef, John Ulric **7**: 146
Neher, Erwin **7**: 147
Neisser, Albert Ludwig Siegmund **7**: 148
Nernst, Walther Hermann **7**: 148
Nerve action: **1**: 15; **3**: 97, 157; **4**: 81; **5**: 68, 182; **6**: 178
Nerve cells: **3**: 115; **7**: 119; **8**: 114, 132

Nervous system: **1**: 152; **4**: 10, 79, 136; **6**: 200; **9**: 60
Newcomb, Simon **7**: 150
Newcomen, Thomas **7**: 151
Newell, Allan **7**: 151
Newlands, John Alexander Reina **7**: 152
Newton, Alfred **7**: 153
Newton, Sir Isaac **7**: 154
New Zealand biochemist: **10**: 143
New Zealand physicist: **8**: 201
Nicholas of Cusa **7**: 160
Nicholson, Seth Barnes **7**: 161
Nicholson, William **7**: 162
Nicol, William **7**: 163
Nicolle, Charles Jules Henri **7**: 164
Niepce, Joseph-Nicéphore **7**: 165
Nieuwland, Julius Arthur **7**: 166
Nilson, Lars Fredrick **7**: 166
Nirenberg, Marshall Warren **7**: 167
Nitrogen fixation: **1**: 190; **4**: 177
Nobel, Alfred Bernhard **7**: 168
Nobili, Leopoldo **7**: 169
Noddack, Ida Eva Tacke **7**: 170
Noddack, Walter **7**: 170
Noguchi, (Seisako) Hideyo **7**: 171
Nollet, Abbé Jean Antoine **7**: 172
Nordenskiöld, Nils Adolf Eric **7**: 173
Norlund, Niels Erik **7**: 173
Norman, Robert **7**: 174
Norrish, Ronald **7**: 174
Northrop, John Howard **7**: 175
Norton, Thomas **7**: 176
Norwegian bacteriologist: **4**: 205
Norwegian biologist: **7**: 136
Norwegian chemists: **1**: 190; **4**: 132, 171, 218; **10**: 57
Norwegian engineer: **3**: 174
Norwegian explorer: **7**: 136
Norwegian industrialist: **3**: 174
Norwegian mathematicians: **1**: 6; **6**: 124; **9**: 76
Norwegian meteorologists: **1**: 193, 194
Norwegian physicist: **1**: 190
Noyce, Robert Norton **7**: 176
Noyes, William Albert **7**: 177
Nuclear fission: **4**: 49, 184; **7**: 35, 170; **9**: 173; **10**: 12
Nuclear magnetic resonance: **1**: 203; **6**: 209; **8**: 99
Nucleic acids: **2**: 31; **6**: 17; **7**: 67
Nucleotide bases: **3**: 210; **6**: 110; **9**: 205
Nucleus: **1**: 215; **4**: 125; **5**: 151; **7**: 112; **8**: 105
Nüsslein-Volhard, Christiane **7**: 178

Oakley, Kenneth Page **7**: 179
Oberth, Hermann Julius **7**: 180
Occhialini, Giuseppe Paolo Stanislao **7**: 181
Ocean currents: **3**: 140; **5**: 9, 113; **7**: 17
Oceanography: **2**: 200
Ochoa, Severo **7**: 182

Shizuki, Tadao **9**: 61
Shockley, William Bradford **9**: 62
Shull, Clifford Glenwood **9**: 63
Sidgwick, Nevil Vincent **9**: 64
Siebold, Karl Theodor Ernst von **9**: 65
Siegbahn, Kai Manne Börje **9**: 66
Siegbahn, Karl Manne Georg **9**: 67
Siemens, Ernst Werner von **9**: 68
Siemens, Sir William **9**: 69
Sierpiński, Waclaw **9**: 70
Silliman, Benjamin **9**: 70
Simon, Sir Francis Eugen **9**: 71
Simpson, Sir George Clark **9**: 72
Simpson, George Gaylord **9**: 73
Simpson, Sir James Young **9**: 74
Simpson, Thomas **9**: 75
Škoda, Josef **9**: 75
Skolem, Thoralf Albert **9**: 76
Skraup, Zdenko Hans **9**: 77
Slipher, Vesto Melvin **9**: 77
Smalley, Richard Errett **9**: 79
Smallpox: **5**: 150
Smellie, William **9**: 79
Smith, Hamilton Othanel **9**: 80
Smith, Henry John **9**: 81
Smith, Michael **9**: 82
Smith, Theobald **9**: 83
Smith, William **9**: 84
Smithson, James **9**: 85
Smoot, George Fitzgerald III **9**: 86
Smyth, Charles Piazzi **9**: 87
Snell, George Davis **9**: 88
Snell, Willebrord van Roijen **9**: 89
Snow, John **9**: 90
Snyder, Solomon Halbert **9**: 90
Sobrero, Ascanio **9**: 92
Sociologists: **7**: 50; **8**: 103
Socrates **9**: 93
Soddy, Frederick **9**: 94
Software Designer: **4**: 82
Sokoloff, Louis **9**: 95
Solar system: **1**: 27
Solvay, Ernest **9**: 96
Somerville, Mary **9**: 97
Sommerfeld, Arnold Johannes Wilhelm **9**: 99
Sondheimer, Franz **9**: 100
Sonneborn, Tracy Morton **9**: 101
Sorby, Henry Clifton **9**: 102
Sørensen, Søren Peter Lauritz **9**: 103
Sosigenes **9**: 103
South African anatomist: **2**: 58
South African biologist: **6**: 1
South African earth scientist: **3**: 108
South African paleontologist: **2**: 58
South African physician: **1**: 123
South African physicist: **2**: 188
Spallanzani, Lazzaro **9**: 104
Spanish alchemists: **1**: 69; **4**: 88
Spanish-American biologist: **1**: 86
Spanish chemist: **3**: 48
Spanish histologist: **8**: 108
Spanish mineralogists: **3**: 48, 50
Spanish-Muslim philosopher: **1**: 81

Spanish-Muslim physician: **1**: 81
Spanish physician: **9**: 49
Spectroscopy: **5**: 38; **7**: 111
Spectrum: **2**: 77; **4**: 35; **5**: 210; **7**: 158
Spedding, Frank Harold **9**: 105
Speed of light: **1**: 60; **3**: 133, 217; **4**: 18; **7**: 64; **8**: 167
Spemann, Hans **9**: 106
Spence, Peter **9**: 107
Spencer, Herbert **9**: 108
Spencer Jones, Sir Harold **9**: 109
Sperry, Elmer Ambrose **9**: 110
Sperry, Roger Wolcott **9**: 111
Spiegelman, Sol **9**: 112
Spitzer, Lyman Jr. **9**: 113
Spontaneous generation: **9**: 104; **10**: 17
Spörer, Gustav Friedrich Wilhelm **9**: 114
Stahl, Franklin William **9**: 114
Stahl, Georg Ernst **9**: 115
Stanley, Wendell Meredith **9**: 116
Stark, Johannes **9**: 117
Starling, Ernest Henry **9**: 118
Stas, Jean Servais **9**: 119
Staudinger, Hermann **9**: 120
Steady-state theory: **2**: 5; **4**: 129; **5**: 95
Steam engine: **2**: 211; **3**: 57; **5**: 25; **7**: 151, 212; **8**: 113; **10**: 82
Stebbins, George Ledyard **9**: 121
Steel: **1**: 181; **4**: 112, 179; **9**: 185
Steenstrup, Johann Japetus Smith **9**: 122
Stefan, Josef **9**: 123
Stein, William Howard **9**: 123
Steinberger, Jack **9**: 124
Steno, Nicolaus **9**: 125
Stephenson, George **9**: 126
Stereochemistry: **8**: 84; **10**: 28
Stern, Curt **9**: 127
Stern, Otto **9**: 128
Steroids: **5**: 192; **8**: 129; **10**: 150
Stevin, Simon **9**: 129
Stewart, Balfour **9**: 130
Stibitz, George Robert **9**: 131
Stirling, Robert **9**: 132
Stock, Alfred **9**: 133
Stokes, Adrian **9**: 134
Stokes, Sir George Gabriel **9**: 135
Stoney, George **9**: 136
Strabo **9**: 137
Strachey, Christopher **9**: 138
Strasburger, Eduard Adolf **9**: 138
Strassmann, Fritz **9**: 139
Strato of Lampsacus **9**: 140
String theory: **7**: 136; **9**: 34
Strohmeyer, Friedrich **9**: 140
Strömgren, Bengt Georg Daniel **9**: 141
Struve, Friedrich Georg Wilhelm von **9**: 142
Struve, Otto **9**: 143
Sturgeon, William **9**: 144
Sturtevant, Alfred Henry **9**: 145
Suess, Eduard **9**: 146
Sugden, Samuel **9**: 147
Sugita, Genpaku **9**: 148
Sumner, James Batcheller **9**: 148

Sunspots: **4**: 190; **7**: 13; **9**: 16
Superconductivity: **1**: 48, 119, 212; **2**: 113, 180; **5**: 170; **6**: 54; **9**: 26
Superfluid: **1**: 49, 212
Superstring theory: **9**: 34; **10**: 154
Surgery: **1**: 187; **3**: 125; **7**: 217; **8**: 35
Su Sung **9**: 149
Sutherland, Earl **9**: 150
Svedberg, Theodor **9**: 151
Swammerdam, Jan **9**: 152
Swan, Sir Joseph Wilson **9**: 153
Swedish anatomist: **8**: 134
Swedish astronomers: **1**: 54; **2**: 126; **6**: 132, 181
Swedish biochemists: **1**: 167; **3**: 168; **9**: 3, 181
Swedish botanists: **4**: 46; **6**: 135
Swedish chemists: **1**: 70, 165, 177; **2**: 40, 163, 207; **3**: 139; **4**: 60; **5**: 44, 66; **7**: 108, 166, 168; **9**: 15, 43, 151, 201
Swedish cytologist: **2**: 114
Swedish earth scientists: **3**: 140; **4**: 90
Swedish engineers: **3**: 8; **7**: 168
Swedish entomologist: **3**: 42
Swedish inventor: **7**: 168
Swedish mathematicians: **4**: 36; **5**: 219
Swedish metallurgist: **5**: 66
Swedish meteorologist: **1**: 164
Swedish mineralogists: **2**: 207; **4**: 60; **5**: 62
Swedish naturalist: **8**: 188
Swedish physician: **4**: 172
Swedish physicists: **1**: 27, 54; **3**: 123; **5**: 219; **7**: 34; **8**: 205; **9**: 66, 67; **10**: 129
Swedish physiologists: **10**: 50, 126
Swiss-American biologist: **1**: 16
Swiss anatomist: **5**: 61
Swiss astronomer: **10**: 158
Swiss bacteriologist: **10**: 185
Swiss biochemists: **7**: 67; **8**: 129
Swiss biologist: **1**: 61
Swiss botanists: **2**: 96; **4**: 41; **7**: 133
Swiss chemists: **3**: 158, 161; **5**: 120, 180; **6**: 219; **7**: 120; **8**: 45, 84, 204
Swiss earth scientists: **2**: 147; **3**: 50; **9**: 9
Swiss embryologist: **6**: 11
Swiss histologist: **6**: 11
Swiss mathematicians: **1**: 111, 171, 172, 173; **3**: 166
Swiss meteorologist: **3**: 50
Swiss naturalists: **2**: 6; **4**: 105
Swiss physicians: **4**: 105; **6**: 5
Swiss physicists: **4**: 169; **7**: 115; **8**: 7, 42, 45, 85, 164; **9**: 9
Swiss physiologists: **4**: 197; **5**: 42, 61
Swiss psychiatrist: **5**: 165
Swiss psychologist: **5**: 165
Swiss zoologist: **9**: 215
Sydenham, Thomas **9**: 154
Sylvester, James Joseph **9**: 155
Sylvius, Franciscus **9**: 156
Synge, Richard Laurence Millington **9**: 157